ON THE BEATEN PATH

ON THE BEATEN PATH

An Appalachian Pilgrimage

Robert Alden Rubin

THE LYONS PRESS

All inquiries should be addressed to: The Lyons Press, 123 West 18th Street, New York, New York 10011

Printed in the United States of America

Library of Congress Cataloging-in-Publication Data

Rubin, Robert Alden, 1958–
On the beaten path : an appalachian pilgrimage/Robert Alden Rubin.
p. cm.
ISBN 1-58574-023-3
1. Hiking—Appalachian Trail. 2. Appalachian Trail—Description and travel. I. Title.

GV199.42.A68 R82 1999
796.51'0974—dc21 99-056989

For Cathy

Levavi oculos

They make pretty free with a human being's idea of time, up here.

—Thomas Mann,
The Magic Mountain

Contents

Acknowledgments

THESE PAGES ARE THE product of two journeys, and neither would have been possible without help.

Thanks to Dave Deming, for taking the time to sit down and talk to me about the world of thruhiking when I was first considering writing about it—and joining it myself. The fast-fingered contributors to AT-L and ATML, especially Dan Bruce and Jim and Ginny Owen, helped me examine both my motivations and my preparations beforehand, and helped me keep my facts straight after the hike. The good folks at the Appalachian Trail Conference provided facts cheerfully. Bill Strachan bought the idea and sent me forth; we parted company somewhere in southwest Virginia, and I am only sorry we didn't have a chance to finish the hike, and the book, together. Betty Kram took the time to talk to a stranger about her son, which must have been difficult. Clint Kawanishi, Parthena Martin, Joe Lowman, Paul Lyons, and my father all read the manuscript when it was far too long, for which they deserve trail magic, not just my gratitude. Ingrid Pisetsky helped me figure some things out and keep moving forward. Liz Darhansoff believed in the journey and stuck with me, even after I was late reaching Oquossoc. Nick Lyons tracked me down when I was off the trail, got me moving again, and made finishing possible. Enrica Gadler helped me along the last few steps.

Between Springer and Kathadin, friends and family took me in, assisted me with gear and supplies, and helped me finish. Thanks to Bob and Cary Phillips, Homer and Therese Witcher, Dinty Moore, Charles and Diana Wells, Manning and Jane Rubin, Julia Randall, Mark Wallace, and Allison Bulsterbaum. Special thanks to the Richards for rescuing me on a cold, wet day. Mostly, though, I am indebted to all who walked north in 1997, particularly those who talked with me about what it meant to them. Special thanks to Stephanie Allen, Mike and Jennifer Baehre, Josh Baresh, Lisa Barter, John Collins, Bob Cornell, Diane Doyle, Mike Eppinger, Houston Feaster, John Foley, Mike Freed, Arthur Gaudet, Steve Guerreri, Dan Hayes, Ken Hee, Don Hendry, Walt Holly, Leslie Kitchens, Sara Kurtinitis, Franklin Lafond, Mike Livingston, Chris Miller, Larkspur Morton, Gib and Donna Mueller, Jennifer Neumann, Jerry Purcell, Kurt Reike, Jeremy Reiter, Brett Schusterbauer, Mike Snider, Mark Stover, Neil Taylor, Kevin Thome, Tanis Walker, Adam Wiggett, and Paul Williamson. You know who you are.

Prologue: Facing North

Oh, do not ask, "What is it?"
Let us go and make our visit.
—T. S. Eliot, "The Love Song of J. Alfred Prufrock"

ON THE MAP, The Appalachian Mountains roll like a river down the eastern third of the United States and fan out into a delta of foothills across northern Georgia and Alabama. At Springer Mountain in Georgia two main branches converge in one last massive standing wave before subsiding into the lowlands. To the south, between Springer and the glass cylinders and boxes of Atlanta that glisten on the horizon, isolated uplands rise from eddies of rolling farmland and suburbs. Away north stretch tumbling crests of pine and hardwood—the Blue Ridge that marked the end of settled lands and the beginning of the great western wilderness until the time of Andrew Jackson's presidency. Only tiny pockets of the old wilderness remain now, like pools at the beach when the tide retreats. And this tide is gone for good.

There are still plenty of trees, though—almost ten million acres of national forest and national park lands along the mountain ridges between Florida and Pennsylvania, and tens of thousands more in northern New England. Nor does that even take into account the millions of privately held acres, many of them owned by timber and paper companies that plant and tend and harvest them or let them lie fallow like farmers rotating crops. It's not virgin timber. These eastern forests have been logged time and again since the rivers were explored and the railroads came through; the few stands of old trees that linger on do so in steep corners and small forest preserves, more by chance than by any plan or program to save them. They are like islands, as are the mountains themselves, their very inconvenience cutting them off somewhat from the headlong change all around. Change comes, of course, but it comes late, just as winter lingers along the high ridges in Georgia for weeks after azaleas, dogwoods, and daffodils have run riot in the lowlands and dazzled travelers bound for the Masters golf tournament or for the garden tours in Savannah.

Along those ridges snakes a footpath, a recreational hiking trail that follows the eastern mountains all the way down the coast from Katahdin in Maine to Springer in Georgia. It is marked, or "blazed," with rectangles of white paint slapped on trees or rocks along the way. From end to end, as the crow flies, it stretches about a thousand miles. But crows don't fly the Appalachian Trail: hikers walk it, which translates to about 2,160 miles of zigzagging over ridges or peaks, teetering along the crests of great geologic folds, worming in and out of valleys, and switching back and forth through gaps and notches. It's crossed by many roads, but it remains a mere path itself: horses, bicycles, and all-terrain vehicles are not permitted, except on a few scattered miles where it intersects other paths. It rarely takes a straight line or follows the obvious route. Most of the millions who walk it see only a few miles at a time, and that is enough, for it is not an efficient way to do anything more than work up a sweat and rub blisters on your soles and heels. Indeed, its builders never thought of it as a means of long-distance travel at all. It's about the slowest, most inconvenient way imaginable of going two thousand miles. Yet every year there are a few thousand people who set out to do to the thing entire.

Most show up at a state park in north Georgia between the first of March and the first of May, arriving singly or in small groups and quickly disappearing into the woods. A few start at the other end, in Maine, in early summer, after the blackflies have stopped biting. Some hitch rides, some pay taxicabs to drive them from the airport or train station, some come with families they intend to leave, or bewildered and uneasy spouses. They come from across the continental United States, from Alaska and Hawaii, from Europe, Africa, and the Far East. Some of them are old, some young, a few somewhere in the uneasy middle.

No matter that the Himalayas or the Rockies rise higher; that much of the trail lies within a couple of hours' drive of cities like Atlanta, Washington, Baltimore, Pittsburgh, Philadelphia, New York, Boston, and the tens of millions who live in them; that the air isn't thin and the trail only rarely climbs into alpine zones; that the path is well marked and well worn. The whole point for the walkers who seek to follow the entirety of this beaten path is not getting to the top of the hill. It's going up there and not coming down again—not, at least, until they have found what they have lost, what they've gone looking for.

And make no mistake. Whatever they tell you, they are all looking for something.

ONE
PILGRIMS' WAY

Thanne longen folk to goon on pilgrimages,
And palmers for to seken straunge strondes
To ferne halwes, kowth in sondry londes.
—*Chaucer, "The General Prologue,"* The Canterbury Tales

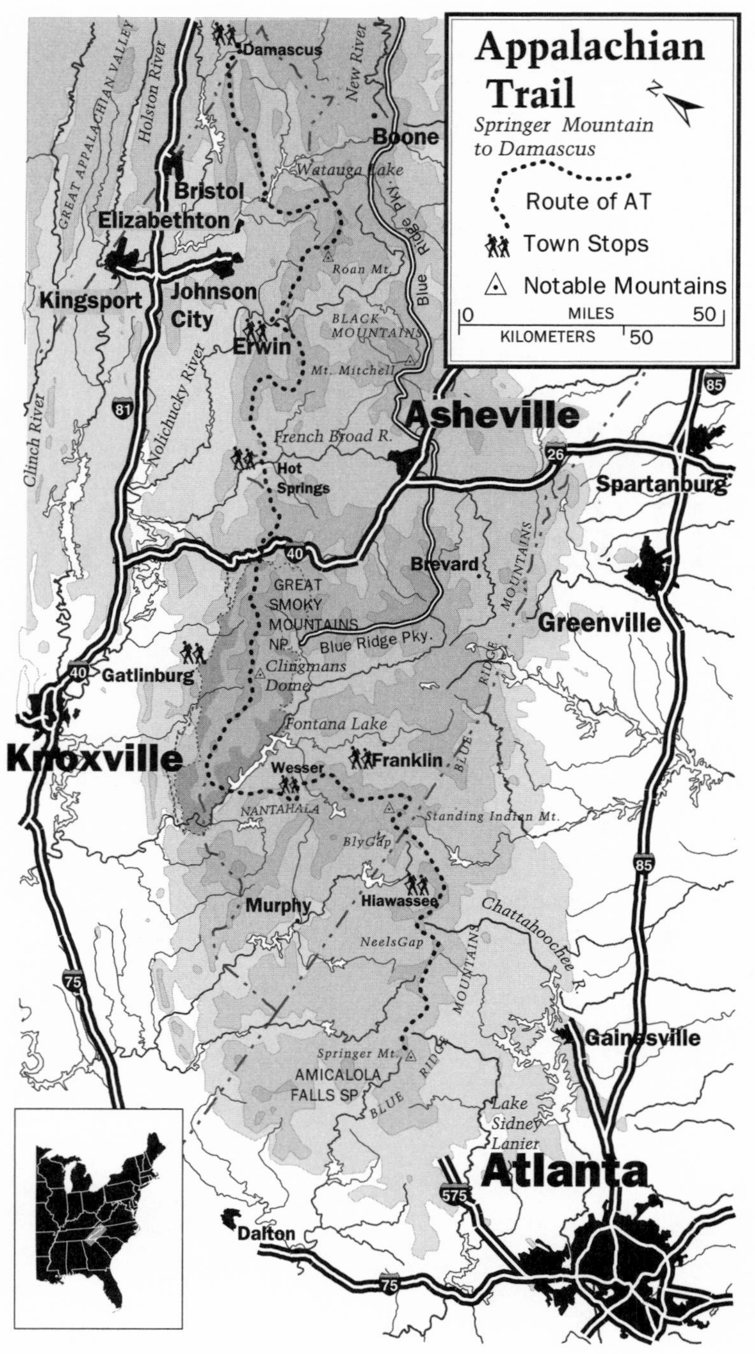
Appalachian Trail
Springer Mountain to Damascus
Route of AT
Town Stops
Notable Mountains
0 MILES 50
KILOMETERS 50
Damascus
New River
Boone
Watauga Lake
Blue Ridge Pky.
GREAT APPALACHIAN VALLEY
Holston River
Bristol
Elizabethton
Kingsport
Johnson City
Roan Mt.
BLACK MOUNTAINS
Erwin
Mt. Mitchell
Clinch River
Nolichucky River
Asheville
French Broad R.
Hot Springs
Spartanburg
Brevard
GREAT SMOKY MOUNTAINS NP
Blue Ridge Pky.
Greenville
Gatlinburg
Clingmans Dome
Fontana Lake
Knoxville
Wesser
Franklin
NANTAHALA
Standing Indian Mt.
BlyGap
Hiawassee
Murphy
Chattahoochee R.
NeelsGap
BLUE RIDGE MOUNTAINS
Gainesville
Springer Mt.
AMICALOLA FALLS SP
Lake Sidney Lanier
Atlanta
Dalton
81
40
26
85
75
575

1

ABOUT THE TIME MY JOB started to go bad a few years ago, I began collecting maps and considering places I would rather be. As the world closed in around me, as I learned to dread work I'd once loved and to hide my heart from friends, I would come home and reach for one of the maps stacked in the corners of my study. It never occurred to me to call a real estate agent and to look for a new house and a new job—I didn't want to *move* so much as to *go*.

When you intend to leave everything behind, climb the hill and not come down again, first you look for a way out. Next you look for a new name.

The pattern isn't new: a traveler leaves home disowned by friends and family, or chasing visions, or running from the law, or hunting fortune and adventure, and takes a new name for the road, for the new life, for the new story of himself that he will tell. Saul the Pharisee sees the light on the way to Damascus and becomes Paul the Apostle. The bride leaves home and family to take the bridegroom's name. Jim Gatz goes east and becomes Jay Gatsby. The Dust Bowl hobo adopts a "road name" and hops a slow-running freight. Marion Morrison turns west and becomes John Wayne. Maybe this traveler hopes to journey in secret, or to reinvent himself, or just to run away, but the old name weighs heavy. Going incognito means telling a new story, creating a new world, carrying a lighter burden.

By the time I found my way to the beaten path, as the old century was running out, "trail names" had been a convention in the subculture of Appalachian Trail hikers for decades. When you climbed the mountain, you left behind your old name and your old life to join a society of walkers like yourself, who had come for obscure reasons and who purposed to give themselves over wholly to the journey for a while. That's what the path promises. Over the years the route has been exactly mapped out and described, thousands of people have hiked it end to end, while parts have been walked by millions more. But however exact the trail map, room remains for imagination to fill in the blanks. It promises something beyond the printed greens and blues and yellows and reds, beyond lines dotted and solid and straight and jagged, beyond the mathematically precise distortions of the U.S. Geological Survey topographic quadrants, beyond the meridians and great circles, beyond the feel of crisp folded paper. It promises possibility.

Even the most impeccably printed, exactly drawn, perfectly scaled trail map is a virtual reality, a cartographer's attempt to reduce rocky paths and gurgling brooks to symbolic abstraction. We can let that genie back out of the bottle, if we so choose. What will happen, we wonder, if we put the surveyor's science and art to the test, stop surveying and just *go*? The landscape may be terra cognita to the rest of the world, well trodden and fully explored, but eventually we begin to hear the path whispering: *see for yourself, it's here somewhere, come find what you're looking for.*

Trail tradition has it that your fellow walkers will give you your name, a badge of initiation, a pledge pin for the fellowship of the winged foot. But that's mostly just a leftover from the trail's golden age, the 1970s and early 1980s, when walkers climbed that first mountain in north Georgia not expecting that they'd be entering an obscure outdoors counterculture with its own codes and conventions and expectations. That counterculture is well publicized now, described in books and promoted on Internet Web sites. Now walkers come deliberately seeking transformation, hoping against hope that they can somehow reinvent themselves; consequently they arrive both impatient for their new name and uneasy about letting someone else choose it. Soul Traveler, Globetrotter, Time to Fly, Lost Soul, Space Wrangler, Gyro-Vag, RockDancer: no one gives you a name like that, you give it to yourself, drawing not on the realities of the trail but on the imagined journey.

It didn't take me long to choose mine. Once, when the phenomenon of the Internet was still fairly new, I'd joined an online poetry group. After a while I'd grown tired of earnest discussions of verse and technique and the writing life, so I arranged with my Internet host for a second "user ID"—a user *id* might be more accurate—a new name to go along with my old one. This new persona was not an earnest discusser, but an edgy, opinionated arguer. Everything he "said," even casual conversation, was in rhymed epigrams; he was clever, satiric, and loved wordplay. While I would never blow up and "flame" a member of the group who started saying mean things to the beginning writers there, the Rhymin' Worm, as my shadow called himself, had no such compunctions. He stung the offender like a crude modern-day Alexander Pope:

> The Rhymin' Worm prefers online decorum
> But will defend the honor of this forum.
> When assholes like you shame honest beginners
> You make yourselves the more obnoxious sinners.
> We learn to love the Word by playing with it,
> And not by empty sneers and pompous bullshit.

The Worm's name came from an old book of "Pogo" cartoons, where a minor character by that name had appeared for a few weeks one year, driving Albert the Alligator to distraction with supple versifying, until at last it was discovered that the Rhymin' Worm was a fraud—he was plagiarizing his own daughter's school poems. My Rhymin' Worm was a fraud too, but he made that online discussion group a more interesting place for a few months.

I came to like the Rhymin' Worm better than I liked myself: he was more entertaining, more open, more clever, less eager to please, less self-conscious and anxious. Maybe I couldn't climb the mountain and never come down again, but perhaps the Rhymin' Worm could. So I brought him back.

The week before I left for Georgia, the Rhymin' Worm wrote the first lines of "The Ballad of the Rhymin' Worm." Instead of keeping a journal of his long walk north, he would write doggerel poetry—one stanza of ballad meter for every day of the hike—and record it in the register books of the shelters he passed along the way. It would describe what he saw, where he was, and what he felt like. It would be bad, obvious stuff, but the Worm didn't care. That night, as he packed his gear and prepared food parcels for half a year on the mountaintop, he composed the first lines, the refrain, of the "Ballad":

The Worm went south to Springer Mount,
    burning all his bridges,
his next six months a series of
    Appalachian ridges.

2

White Blaze—Day 1
Tuesday, April 1, 1997 • Springer Mountain terminus • Georgia
Blue Ridge Mountains • 0 miles hiked • 2,160 miles to go
Clear and windy • Low 28, high 50
Elevation 3,782 feet

APRIL FOOLS' DAY OF 1997: a cold, brilliant morning after a night of wind and overcast. The first hint of spring has come to the hollows of north Georgia's hills near Amicalola Falls State Park like a Seurat painting, a dotting of yellow-green leaf tips, red buds and white dogwood bracts overlaying dry winter hillsides of sinuous tree trunks and gray-brown leaves. Snow has been forecast to the north along the Appalachian Mountains as a nor'easter skates up the coast, strengthening, gathering moisture from the ocean and whirling it counterclockwise into arctic air pushing down from midcontinent. Back at the glassy modernist chalet called Amicalola Lodge, a state-run inn near the head of the falls, the morning's news buzzes with reports of a massive snowstorm pounding New England. It's a good day for sitting over scrambled eggs and hot coffee, gazing out through the window at the powder blue panorama of foothills, not for pushing past the heavy glass doors, stepping into the edge of the north wind, and climbing a hill with no intention of coming back down. But there stands the Rhymin' Worm.

Amicalola Falls is where that first ascent begins, the eight-mile approach to mile zero, the summit of Springer Mountain, where I'll find the first white blaze of the Appalachian Trail, where today's hike turns from outing to journey, pastime to pilgrimage.

There are other, shorter ways up, but hiking the approach trail is traditional, an initiation into the rituals of the walkers I've heard and read so much about. The first eight miles have a reputation for being tough, though by any objective standards they should be reasonably easy for a backpacker in decent condition: rolling terrain, well-groomed trails never more than moderately steep, climbs of only five hundred to a thousand feet at a time, shelters aplenty, and abundant water along the way.

Two miles from the lodge, though, I heave myself down, gasping, on a stump next to the path, swimming in sweat underneath a fleece vest and glossy blue Gore-Tex jacket. My backpack already drags at my shoulders. It features a sophisticated suspension system meant to direct the weight to the padded hip belt. Good in theory, but in order to work it requires hips to rest on, and mine are buried under rolls of fat. No matter how corset-tight I cinch the straps and how I readjust the suspension, the belt keeps slipping over my hips and down my butt, bringing all sixty-plus pounds to bear on back and shoulders.

Who is this intrepid Rhymin' Worm of ours? A big man, about six foot three and weighing in around two hundred and seventy-five pounds, the last seventy-five of which have accreted during the recent downhill slide toward middle age. At age thirty-eight, his is the bulk of an athlete gone to seed—trunklike thighs, a massive butt, a heavy roll around the waist, a double chin, a superstructure of broad shoulders and big bones undergirding a drapery of blubber—the effect orcalike. His hair has been buzzed short along the sides, with a little left on top. It is normally thick and unruly, dark brown with a few touches of white, but no signs of baldness. His whiskers are coming in salt-and-pepper gray, and he has not shaved for a couple of days already, as he plans to grow a beard for the trail. Now, after an hour of his first day in the woods, his face is all blotchy from the initial climb, pulse pounding in his ears. He wonders if he will collapse. A couple of years earlier the doctor said he should get more exercise and lose some weight. Well, okay, Doc. This oughta do it.

Next to me, where I've shrugged it off on a damp pile of winter leaves, rests a massive red-and-black expedition-style backpack, like the ones the rime-whiskered L. L. Bean Vikings wear while postholing along snowy ridgelines in the catalogs. It's basically a big red nylon sack sewn onto a frame of black webbing straps, foam pads and aluminum stays that make it bearable when full. And full it is—I've stuffed it with equipment for many contingencies, along with a week's food, a cook stove and pots, several changes of clothes, a sleeping bag, notebooks, two camp mattresses, a tent, and spares for everything from shoelaces to candles and batteries. It adds up.

Slowly now my pulse comes back down, and I strip away jacket and vest, lash them with a bungee cord to the pack, gulp water from one of the gray Lexan bottles holstered on the hip belt, breathe deep, and take a moment to look around. The first climb away from Amicalola is behind me. I've done it—gotten clean away. I'm no longer the husband kissing his wife good-bye, an embarrassing midlife spectacle to friends and family. I'm the Rhymin' Worm, solitary pilgrim. Now all I have to do is find others like me.

They must be here somewhere.

The wooded ridges of the Chattahoochee National Forest are eerily bare. No buds have begun swelling the branch tips yet. Only the tiny green spades of a few early trilliums and the parasol-like crowns of mayapples mushroom up through the forest duff. No birds sing. No squirrels rustle the crust of dry bleached-brown leaves, just stray eddies of the dry north wind that roars in the bare branches high on the ridgeline above. When Hurricane Opal whirled through north Georgia two years earlier, it felled thousands of trees. They litter the wooded slopes, and only those that fell across the path have been sawn through or removed by the volunteer trail maintainers. The rest lie like toppled columns at a Greek ruin, great gray corpses dappled by shadows. Sometimes they have taken three or four neighbors down with them, opening up the forest floor to the hard sunlight. Some are pines, tall and straight, others are massive spreading hardwoods, with great footprints of broken roots and soil that loom up over the path. There is no one here to point it out to. Surely other pilgrims will be at the summit. A last deep breath, and I hoist the pack.

The weight surprises me again, and I let it drop back a moment as I get a better grip on the straps, then grunt and pull it up to rest on my bent knee. From there I wriggle sideways into the straps, bending to take the full weight on my back while I suck in my gut, cinch the hip belt, and try to make the suspension function. I pick up the two telescopic aluminum "trekking poles" propped against a tree trunk, check my map, then clatter away uphill like a cross-country skier.

The last steep push up to the 3,782-foot crest of Springer Mountain comes late that afternoon, after about seven hours of walking, and I emerge from a screen of scrawny trees onto a rocky outcropping, where a boulder marks the summit. I stroll the last few yards, bend over and touch the first white blaze painted on the rock near the boulder, then drop the pack gratefully and sit down.

Springer Mountain is an otherwise unremarkable hump-with-a-view, miles from anywhere. When the trail was first completed in 1937, it didn't even stop there, but went rolling on a few miles south to Mount Oglethorpe. Mount Oglethorpe was surrounded by private land, though, and during the 1950s too many houses and stinking chicken farms sprang up around the old terminus. So the trail was shortened by a few miles and the terminus set at Springer, in the national forest, on a rock face that juts west out of the trees. There a bronze plaque has been bolted to the mica-bright stone, bearing the image of a hiker from the early 1930s, hatchet at his belt, rucksack on his back, long pants tucked into high boots, felt hat shading his eyes, ascending purposefully and stoically as the horizon of hills stretches out in the distance like ocean waves. It reads:

APPALACHIAN TRAIL
GEORGIA TO MAINE
A Footpath for
Those who seek
Fellowship with
the Wilderness

Fellowship—I look around to see if I've found it yet. Four others are seeking fellowship with the wilderness on the rocky outcropping. A gay couple in cardigans, neatly creased chinos and suede Timberland boots hold hands and watch the sun dip toward the western horizon. One is smoking a Dr. Graybow pipe. Two young day hikers in Gore-Tex and polyester fleece sit nearby, at the edge of the outcropping, inhaling deeply on some unfiltered cigarettes. None of them passed me on the way up the south side of the mountain—they have all come in from the north, where the trail crosses a U.S. Forest Service road less than a mile from the summit. We exchange pleasantries: Nice view, hey? Glad that snow held off. Everyone nods and beams and gazes thoughtfully at the western horizon.

No, no pilgrims today. For the others here it is an outing; they've come for the view, and it's as far as they're going this cold April afternoon before they return to the cars parked on the Forest Service road, and from there home. The Worm is the only one who will stay.

3

A FEW MONTHS BEFORE I STARTED up Springer, I found myself on foot crossing Lower Manhattan. I was a book editor at the time, and I'd just spent the morning at a sales conference in Chelsea, where I'd been crowded into a restaurant banquet room with several dozen reps who were not much interested in hearing me suggest ways to sell books. The weather was cold and overcast—winter was just starting to bite in Manhattan—and I needed to walk off the morning's frustration. I didn't want to think about it. I wanted to think about gear. I'd heard of a good camping and hiking store a couple of miles downtown, on Park Place, and decided to walk instead of taking the subway. Hurrying along the streets I felt inconspicuous, camouflaged in the uniform of sales presentations everywhere: a navy blue pin-striped suit, a long charcoal gray woolen coat, a silk tie, a wool scarf, black wingtip shoes, a briefcase.

Ahead of me on the sidewalk I noticed a kid wearing a shiny gold-and-black Gore-Tex mountaineering shell made by the North Face—top-of-the-line waterproof hiking gear that probably cost about $400, not including the matching $300 Gore-Tex pants. A hiker? Here? And then I saw another jacket like it on another kid across Nineteenth

Street, also from the North Face, its colors Day-Glo green and black. Passing me in the other direction two more urban hikers wore puffy North Face down jackets and Timberland boots. And suddenly as I turned onto Broadway and started downtown toward Union Square, a pricey urban fantasy of the Great Outdoors, of Gore-Tex and spandex and microfiber nylon and Nubuck leather, was about me wherever I looked—lounging in doorways, crossing streets, window-shopping, ready for storm and snow and hail, ready to brave the elements of the Lower East Side or Brooklyn, to overnight in extreme conditions at a rave or a house party.

That was fashion, I told myself: outdoor gear just looks cool, and they'd noticed in Manhattan. On the trail, at least, we put it to its intended purpose. Or are we just rationalizing?

"Beware of all enterprises that require new clothes," Thoreau wrote, "and not rather a new wearer of clothes." A lot he knew. Before I worked up the courage to quit my job and head south to begin this new enterprise, even before I admitted to myself the possibility of anything more than the occasional weekend overnight hikes I'd been taking, every salary bonus and every unexpected check, not to mention the periodic fast-cash withdrawal from the ATM near the camping store, began going toward gear. At first it was just the bare minimum needed for an overnight. Then the bare minimum needed for a comfortable overnight. Then the bare minimum needed for a longer walk. Then the bare minimum needed for a more efficient long walk. My stock of gear kept growing: backpack, sleeping bag, water filter, self-inflating mattress, tent, boots, rain jacket, gaiters, stove, water bottles, hiking socks, long johns, Swiss Army knife, emergency blanket, pack cover, hiking poles, and more that would have made our hairshirt philosopher wince.

But would you consider walking into a business presentation wearing jeans and a T-shirt? You'd better be pretty sure of yourself if you're going to pull it off. If you are—if, say, you're some hotshot dot-com entrepreneur who's there to show the suits what's what—maybe you can get away with going naked. Most of us can't. We're unsure of ourselves. We need that business suit to talk for us. We need the fashionable outfit at the party so we won't feel ugly or awkward. Before we go looking for fellowship with the wilderness—or fellowship *in* the wilderness—we tell ourselves that we need a thousand dollars' worth of hiking and camping gear to show the others that we belong out there, and to convince ourselves we're ready.

Like anything else these days, the marketers are happy to oblige. Fueling the exploits of thin-air junkies, peak baggers, and Mountain Dew–slamming outdoor dudes humping packs to the beat of that different drum machine are a dizzying array of specialty manufacturers selling elaborate and expensive high-technology clothing and equipment. Go to the nearest camping store, or to a newsstand for a copy of *Backpacker* or *Outside* or *Men's Journal*. There you will behold the gear fetish in all its glory. "Breathable" waterproof clothing, super-lightweight structural composites, "bomb-proof" fabrics, portable hydration packs, handheld GPS satellite navigation devices, altimeter watches, highly engineered "systems" for feet, fluids, food, and so on. Backpacking, by its very name, inextricably ties the act of walking to the task of carrying *stuff* while doing so, and the stuff just gets sexier and cooler each year.

What makes the fetish compelling is the way function and fashion tangle. The well-patched wool sweater that would have pleased Thoreau will keep you warm enough when it gets wet, but it will be bulkier, soggier and scratchier than its high-tech counterpart; you can walk farther and faster when your boots are lighter, drier, and more comfortable—assuming, of course, that you have no philosophical objection to walking farther and faster.

Always I coveted the top-of-the-line stuff: the lightest, the strongest, the most ergonomic. Always I settled for what I could afford: last year's model, this week's clearance item, the slightly bulkier and heavier sleeping bag that cost hundreds less. But it wasn't army-surplus cheap, either: five years earlier it would have been top-shelf stuff. With each new purchase it became easier and easier to imagine climbing the mountain and not coming down again. When I walked out the glass doors of Amicalola Lodge on that April Fools' Day, shakily confident that I had what I needed to see the thing through, I took with me almost fifty pounds of lightweight backpacking equipment, not counting food and water, having left another sixty pounds of redundant stuff at home.

If I failed, I told myself, starting with the wrong equipment wouldn't be the reason. No, getting hurt was more likely. Either that or lack of character.

4

White Blaze—Day 2
Wednesday, April 2, 1997 • Hawk Mountain Shelter • Georgia Blue Ridge Mountains • 8 miles hiked • 2,052 miles to go
Fair • Low 24, high 62
Elevation 3,200 feet

HAWK MOUNTAIN SHELTER is one of several hundred wilderness lean-tos that punctuate the Appalachian Trail, usually near a spring or a creek in an area screened from the wind. Most of the long-distance walkers gather around them at day's end, setting up their tents in nearby clearings or packing in with the crowd under the roof. Shelters can be anything from ramshackle arrangements of tar paper and knotty logs to elaborately designed multilevel woodland castles that would look at home in Myrtle Beach or Nags Head, except for the lack of doors, screens, and indoor plumbing, and except that they're open to the elements on one side. Some besooted stone hovels date back to Civilian Conservation Corps days, some plywood domes or timbered polyhedrons are the work of public-spirited Scout troops or architectural dreamers, but most shelters nowadays are built by volunteer trail crews according to standard designs.

Hawk Mountain's is large and relatively new, bolted and pegged together out of heavy pressure-treated beams and planks weathering yellow-gray, topped by an overhanging roof shingled mud-red, its sleeping platform raised above the ground on concrete footings. I turn from the white-blazed footpath and follow a side trail marked with blue paint blazes a few hundred yards off the crest of the hill, relieved that the first day of white blazes is over, and relieved that I'm not alone. After nearly two days hiking solo, suddenly here are others bound for Maine. An old man is tying plastic bags to tree branches. Two or three younger hikers lounge around a picnic table throwing dice. Someone has started a fire, and the smoke drifts into the shelter, half-choking several others who've already rolled out sleeping bags and claimed a spot under the roof. They're taking turns reading the shelter register, comparing gear, and commenting on the hikers they've met. Equipment reposes everywhere, piled in corners of the shelter, hung from small trees, or propped up against the walls and the picnic table: backpacks, tents, metal hiking poles, gnarled wooden walking sticks, water bags, cooking kits, boots, tarpaulins, sleeping bags, sweaters, plastic bags of food, nylon bags of food, coats, and humid socks seasoning in the smoky April air.

"Any room at the inn?" I say, and one of the others on the platform nods and edges over silently, giving me room to unshoulder my pack and collapse next to the wall. I sit blinking in the smoke, watching the others and chewing on a Snickers bar for a few minutes while the sweat turns cold on my lower back. We circulate cautiously, checking each other out, admiring gear, asking about trail names, explaining our own, joking, and making mental notes, trying to remember who is who. It's all we have to go on for now: what we carry, and who we say we are. Twilight and the chill of evening descend on the mountain, but no one is ready for dinner and sleep just yet—the moment is too electric, we are too aware, sore from a day or two of hiking, giddy with anticipation.

One trim little man with gray hair wanders around the campfire, fiddling with a cell phone. His wife is going to call him at seven, he explains. After a few minutes his phone chirps, cricketlike, and the other hikers glower at him across the campfire. The little man is oblivious—he brightens and answers.

"Yes, I hear you fine," he says, wandering to the edge of the firelight. "Yes. That's right, I'm at a shelter. No, the signal is strong here. Right. It should work just about anywhere. I walked seven miles. Yes, there are a lot of others here. It's cold, but there's a campfire."

He wanders away from shelter, still talking. It *is* cold, now that the sun has gone down and I'm not walking anymore, so I pull the jacket from my pack and zip it up under my chin. I have a wife too, though I have been trying not to think about her for two days now. I haven't brought our cell phone. A year earlier I'd bought one for Cathy to carry in her car when she commuted, and when I first announced I was quitting the job and taking to the trail, she suggested I take it with me. No! I huffed. A cell phone in the wilderness? Ridiculous. I'd be laughed off the mountain. It would be too heavy. It wouldn't work reliably. She didn't argue the point, and now I wish she had—wish she'd implored the departing penitent to carry his technological Saint Christopher charm. But no, we are incommunicado.

One of the hikers throwing dice on the picnic table asks me if I'm thruhiking and comments on my hiking poles: do they help much? He squints pleasantly at me. "Some," I say. "I've got bad ankles." I estimate he's in his thirties—a trim man with a week's growth of beard, close-cropped brown hair and a receding hairline he's casually disguised with a red bandanna. Later I'll learn that he's a chef who's sold his interest in a Pennsylvania deli to hike the trail.

"Whattya think about this?" He grins and picks up a wooden staff taller than he is, the heavy white trunk of an ash sapling. He's obviously spent a lot of time making it perfect, whittling and smoothing the body, carefully varnishing it to seal out water. He carries it butt side down, and to keep the end from splintering he's banded on a heavy rubber plumbing cap the size of a coffee cup.

"At least you don't have to worry about dogs hassling you," I say, admiring the workmanship. "Not with this monster."

"Hell no. Dogs won't be a problem. They better not," he laughs, gripping the staff like a club.

I introduce myself.

"D-Bear," he says, reaching out to shake hands. "Short for Dancing Bear." When I look puzzled, he smirks and pulls down his sock to show a tattoo of multicolored bears, a ring of them, dancing around his ankle. It's one of the icons of the Grateful Dead. Like me, he's named himself.

Next to me in the shelter a rangy guy in his thirties, with a toothy grin and nervous laugh, introduces himself by his real name.

"No trail name?" D-Bear says.

"Not yet," he says.

"We've got to get you one, then."

"You should call him Sherpa," one of the others says.

"Why Sherpa?" I ask.

"Try lifting his pack."

Sherpa's old aluminum-framed backpack is resting against the wall of the shelter. He has crammed it with woolen army-surplus sweaters, thick foam sleeping pads, an old quilted flannel sleeping bag, a vast green tarpaulin, and stores of canned food, knives, can openers, and utensils. All this is strapped together with thick belts, ropes, and bungee cords.

"Christ," one of the others says. "This must weight seventy pounds."

"Try eighty," Sherpa says, grimacing. He can't weigh much more than twice that himself.

"Oh, man, are you going to be hurting," D-Bear says.

"I'm already hurting," Sherpa laughs. "I can't *believe* how much I'm hurting. I can't *believe* I'm going to carry this to Maine. I can't *believe* how fucking cold it is here. I can't *believe* I'm not back home in Florida, where it's warm."

And suddenly none of us can believe it. Here we are in the woods with our traveling companions for the next six months—characters in a story that will unfold with each new turn in the trail. Some of us will make it all the way. Some of us will hurt ourselves, or be drawn away, or give up. Oh, it will be a grand adventure, all right.

Someone in a tent behind the shelter begins snoring. It's the old fellow who'd been setting up camp when I arrived. Apparently he'd heard it was a good idea to hang your food cache from trees so marauding animals wouldn't invade it, and had stuffed what he'd brought into plastic trash bags that he hung at eye level from some branches. No one said a thing, but I'd seen a couple of the others fight back smiles: the books all recommend hanging your food ten feet off the ground, out of easy reach. But maybe the bears out here are really short. No one has taken it upon themselves to embarrass him by pointing out the problem.

The woods darken around Hawk Mountain. We troop down the hill to the creek, where we pump water through our portable filters into bottles and cook pots, or purify it with iodine tablets; camp stoves sputter and flare to life; noodles boil, cocoa brews.

"Hey!" somebody says. "Over here! Look!"

Four or five of us move out of the firelight and among the skeletal trees of late winter, away from the smoke and guttering camp stoves in front of the shelter. Our breath goes up in clouds. A couple of hikers have strapped on camping headlamps, and they lead us into a partial clearing behind the shelter, the beams of light strobing through the trees. Once the lights are extinguished, through the bare branches to the northeast we can see Comet Hale-Bopp, brightening with the stars as the last deep blue of twilight leaves the sky. No one says a thing. I can hear the roll of dice on the picnic table and some low murmuring conversation back by the shelter. We watch in silence as the night deepens and the ghostly tails fork out behind Hale-Bopp's coma, growing more distinct with every minute.

No one needs to say a thing. We have done it. We have left the world behind. For a little while at least.

5

ARE YOU THRUHIKING? D-Bear had asked. Do you belong to the secret society too, or are you just another weekender out for some fresh air and scenic views from a mountaintop? You're only in the club if you walk the walk, if you've finished a long trail, or you're trying to finish one. Maybe you hiked the Pacific Crest Trail out West, along the Sierras from Mexico to Canada; or up the spine of the Rockies on the unfinished Continental Divide Trail; or Vermont's Long Trail, oldest of them all, along the crest of the Green Mountains to Canada. That's the private handshake—rich or poor or old doesn't matter, just so long as you're going from one end to another, climbing the mountain and not coming down for a while.

Only on the Appalachian Trail has this become institutionalized, with rules and rituals all the nonconformists follow. Consider the word itself: *thruhike*, both verb and noun. One hikes through to the end, sees the hike through, does not stop along the way. Someone engaged in this is through-hiking, is a through-hiker (or, more correctly, a *thruhiker*, the abbreviation intensifying the sense of continuity). The official term for someone who has completed the entire trail is "2,000-miler," and the trail's governing body, the Appalachian Trail Conference, does not formally acknowledge any difference between those who've done it over many years, a week or two at a time, and those who, as we were doing, attempt it in a single continuous hike.

Hikers coined the term *thruhiker* themselves, and insist on it rather than the other common appellations—*long-distance hiker, end-to-ender, 2000-miler*—because it carries with it not only the sense of the journey, but of the lifestyle.

And make no mistake, thruhiking *is* a lifestyle, not just a technical distinction. Out on the trail hikers come in all shapes and styles—fast and slow, express trains and idlers. The distinction arises once they get to camp, or to town, at the end of the day. That's when thruhikers congregate with other thruhikers, separate themselves subtly from weekenders and recreational hikers, put away the solitude of the trail for the companionship of the camp, the shared pilgrimage, the sense of being cut off from the rest of the world. If you come to Georgia in the spring and walk north, you've little choice but to immerse yourself in this society.

And why not? April seems a good time for penance and fresh starts. It's when Chaucer wrote about Canterbury pilgrims, who from every shire's end sought the road from Winchester known as the Pilgrims' Way: *When April's sweet showers pierce root-deep the dry March chill, when small birds improvise their songs and sleep wide-eyed through the night, then people long to go on pilgrimage, and pilgrims seek strange shores in scattered lands.*

On the Appalachian Trail you'll run into a kind of pilgrim that Chaucer might recognize, though it is not the holy blissful martyr they seek, but something harder to define. When a trail from New England to the South was first proposed in 1920 by a Yankee dreamer named Benton MacKaye who'd grown up reading Thoreau and Ralph Waldo Emerson and Walt Whitman, few people would have foreseen a time when each year thousands would saunter from one end to the other. MacKaye certainly didn't, but oddly enough his proposal anticipated the reasons why, as the millennium neared, pilgrims came by the thousands to north Georgia. Technology disturbed him—or at least the way it was being used: not, as its apologists insisted, to make work more efficient, so Americans would have more free time, but rather to get them to produce *more work* in the same amount of time, to tie them even more closely to their jobs. MacKaye's dreamy vision of a ridgeline society captured the imagination of some hard-headed realists who, during the 1920s and 1930s, went about the business of creating the infrastructure, linking together a system of trails and building primitive shelters along them. At first it was just an unofficial footpath, routed and rerouted over the years, maintained by pipe-smoking, khaki-wearing volunteers. The federal government, which had always more or less encouraged it, officially embraced the idea in the 1960s, and put money behind it in the 1970s and 1980s, so that now the Appalachian National Scenic Trail runs almost wholly along government-owned land or federally protected easements.

The first pilgrim to thruhike to Maine from Georgia belonged to the generation that fought World War II, a young ex-soldier named Earl Shaffer who came to the trail in 1948 trying to escape his depression and the recollection of war's horrors. Though the trail had been essentially complete since the mid-1930s, no one had ever tried to do the whole thing in one continuous hike. Only a few of those who knew about it had hiked more than a small percentage of its two thousand miles in a given year. Shaffer asked no one's permission, got no one's approval, but just showed up at Mount Oglethorpe one day in the spring and started walking, periodically stopping to resupply at trailside towns as he went north. After he finished, no one believed he'd made it the whole way, but news of his hike soon inspired one or two others to try it in subsequent years, and they in turn inspired several more.

Even so, thruhikes remained rare until a new generation embraced backpacking in the 1970s. By 1972, nearly a quarter century after Shaffer's first thruhike, fewer than three dozen people had completed the trail in a single shot. But national publicity that year led to the first mass pilgrimage, with over eighty people reporting complete hikes in

1973. And after that it never really let up. Statistics from the Appalachian Trail Conference, which supervises the trail, recognized about 1,800 would-be thruhikers in 1996, the year before I left, 319 of whom claimed to have finished. I'd heard predictions that as many as 3,000 would be starting within a month or two of the day I left.

Like the first thruhikers, Christian pilgrims to the Holy Land made up the rules as they went along. They weren't numerous at first, and typically went off with a letter in hand from the local bishop asking other churches, officials, and monasteries along the way to offer help. But once large numbers of medieval Christians adopted the practice, regular routes sprang up and traditions developed. Pilgrims often adopted a conventional garb—cowl, belt, broad-brimmed hat, staff, sack, and gourd. And, as their numbers grew and the idea of penitential pilgrimages became institutionalized, cottage industries and "pilgrim resorts" sprang up along the route, offering all sorts of amenities and selling religious relics to the gullible. Some of these hospices and resorts, in the passes and ports on the way to medieval shrines, grew into famous cities and towns: Tours, Canterbury, Great Saint Bernard Pass, Marseilles, Santiago de Compostela, Cologne, Aix-la-Chapelle.

The Appalachian Trail has its pilgrim resorts too, and the first of these is at Neels Gap, Georgia, where U.S. Route 19 crests the Blue Ridge. The trail comes down from Blood Mountain, crosses the highway, then leads beneath a wood-and-stone breezeway connecting the two halves of Walasi-Yi Center. The Civilian Conservation Corps built Walasi-Yi and nearby Blood Mountain Shelter during the Great Depression, originally as a seasonal inn connected to nearby Vogel State Park. Though renovated periodically, lack of a dependable well and troublesome septic systems always plagued the inn and led to its closing in favor of an artists colony during the late 1970s. A former thruhiker and her husband took over the concession in the early 1980s and built it into a superb hiking store called Mountain Crossings, along with a twelve-bunk basement hostel for thruhikers. After five days on the trail, during which neophyte hikers discover how much they can hurt, it might as well be a cathedral.

6

White Blaze—Day 6
Sunday, April 6, 1977 • U.S. 19, Neels Gap • Georgia
Blue Ridge Mountains • 40 miles hiked • 2,120 miles to go
Partly cloudy • Low 50, high 70
Elevation 3,000 feet

OUTSIDE THE BASEMENT bunkroom, I hear the gurgle of gutters and susurration of steady rain, cars splashing by on the highway. Inside, a tribe is gathering. For now, I am part of it. The patriarch, "Loon," paces back and forth along the worn indoor-outdoor carpet, cackling and waving a spiral notebook, the hostel register. He has discovered my rhyme about yesterday's hike over Blood Mountain.

"You wrote this?" he says.

"That was me." I'm stretched across a hard wooden bunk on my disordered sleeping bag, sore-footed, pleased to be inside, pleased someone has noticed. Whenever I've explained why I'm "Rhymin' Worm," I've gotten blank stares.

Loon is a stumpy, red-cheeked fellow, with white hair, finely etched laugh lines, and a bristling white beard. He wears running shoes and a French Foreign Legion–style hat, with a flap of fabric that drapes over his neck for sun protection. More important to those of us in the Walasi-Yi bunkroom, he's a 2,000-miler: he completed his thruhike years earlier, and now is trying it again, evangelizing the trail as he goes. He has spent much of a rainy Saturday evening and Sunday morning helping us see the light.

"Ha!" he barks. When no one minds him at first he whistles and imitates a loon call, until everyone looks. "See what Rhymin' put in the register!" he says, and poses in front of the sink, the spiral notebook in front of him like a play script, to recite my stanza: "'Blood Mountain Shelter was a pit / despite the panoramas. / Bigfoot in his gorilla mask / was posing for the cameras.' Ha!"

Bigfoot snorts from over at the table where he's eating breakfast, a sleepy grin spreading over his great moonlike face. He is a big-boned dark-haired kid right out of college, about six foot seven, who has partnered up with two other young hikers, Icebox and Raintree. We met the day before, when I was eating lunch at the old CCC shelter on the 4,000-foot summit of Blood Mountain. It was a chill, dingy, spider-infested rock-walled hovel, with only the superb view to recommend it. They had overtaken me there, and I'd watched Bigfoot capering atop a rock outcropping, wearing a rubber gorilla mask, while the others egged him on and some day-hiking Boy Scouts gawked at him.

"Yes, that's the secret!" Loon says. "A gorilla mask. A rhyme in the register. That's what it takes to make it to Maine. That's the *real* trail magic—the unexpected. It's what will get you there.

"And do you know what will keep you from finishing?" He looks around, his eyes bright. "*Too* far . . . *too* fast . . . *too* heavy . . . *too* soon! Remember that. It means sore knees, sore ankles, no fun, and you're off the trail."

He cackles and scans the room brightly to see who's paying attention. Too much food! Lose the weight or you won't make it to Maine. You won't even make it to Damascus. Get rid of the cans. Get rid of the bottles. Don't pack for a week when it's only three days to the next town to buy groceries! Why carry a month's worth of stove fuel when it's only a week to your next resupply stop? He holds up his small pack: thirty-two pounds! Repeat after me: *Too* far . . . *too* fast . . . *too* heavy . . . *too* soon!

The eight members of Loon's Tribe sprawl around the bunkroom, packs open, surrounded by supply packages we've sent ourselves in care of the Walasi-Yi store. Loon is our wise elder; here too are the thirty-somethings, like me and D-Bear, trying to convince ourselves that graying hair and receding hairlines don't tell the whole story; and the young warriors like Bigfoot, in their twenties, the youngest just out of high school. A happy few, a band of brothers: weight is the enemy. Those who carry too much, like Sherpa at Hawk Mountain, have already fallen behind. What can we get rid of?

I place a cardboard box next to me on the bunk, addressed to myself in care of a rural post office where I plan to stop in two weeks. Into it I put a brass candle lantern (which I'd planned to use for nighttime reading instead of my headlamp), an extra pair of long underwear (surely one is enough), an extra pair of hiking socks (leaving me three), a pair of Gore-Tex socks, an emergency "vapor barrier" liner for my sleeping bag (it won't get *that* cold, will it?), a tube of Barge cement for boot repair (my boots are still pretty new), maps that I won't need for weeks, an extra journal, a belt, extra straps for my pack, extra batteries, envelopes. . . . Pretty soon the box is full of extras, and getting heavy.

Next to the table is a Rubbermaid tub into which the others are dumping leftover food—a "hiker box," free for the taking to any needy walker. I add to it three extra days' rations of dried macaroni and cheese dinners, a can of sardines, an extra roll of Ritz crackers. Bigfoot needs a food bag, so I give him my spare: a waterproof green nylon "stuff sack" I'd brought for miscellaneous gear,

"Gonna send the mask home, Bigfoot?" D-Bear says. A few minutes earlier everyone was trying it on.

"I don't know," Bigfoot says, chuckling. "Like Loon says, it's pretty crucial."

Yesterday was Bigfoot's birthday, and last night several of the staff members from the store had showed up carrying a cupcake with a lighted birthday candle on it. Everybody joined in singing "Happy Birthday," with Bigfoot standing there grinning hugely. "This," he'd said, "is the greatest birthday ever." Now, as we're repacking and trading gear, one of the same guys from the store shows up, all business. Everyone has to be out of the hostel by eight, he says. The pilgrim resort is closed.

Half an hour later, the others are gone, except for Loon, who picks carefully through the hiker box, stocking up on rice and pasta the others have cast off. Ha! I think. That's why we got the speech. It was a con to get free food.

Outside it starts raining harder.

Climbing out of Neels Gap means climbing into a chill fog and drizzle blanketing the hills. Bigfoot, Loon, and several others linger in the store, or on the porch of Walasi-Yi, reluctant to start the rainy walk. But there's no sense putting it off, I figure, so I bundle up in my fleece vest and Gore-Tex shell to stay warm and dry. Within half an hour I have to stop to strip off the fleece, soaked by sweat as completely as if I hadn't been wearing a waterproof jacket at all. A mile or two farther, I fall for the first time.

Don't believe anyone who tells you they hiked the whole Appalachian Trail and never fell. Everybody falls. It's the basis of all slapstick, the universe's comment on human vanity, the great equalizer that strips away prestige and power and turns us all back into babies trying to hold ourselves upright. We wear exotic boots with computer-designed tread patterns, we support ourselves with everything from knotty sticks to hundred-dollar German hiking poles, and still we tumble.

Everything happens in slow motion when you fall. You've just crested a small rise, over some rocks maybe, and the trail descends steeply down a bank of clay covered by leaf mold. Before the subconscious warning can register you've already planted your foot, heel first, and a patch of leaves has lost its adhesion to the wet stratum of clay. The fifty pounds on your back drags at you, keeps you from compensating properly, you lurch madly, arms akimbo, lose traction again, and gravity takes over. Down you sit with a bump. Your hiking poles, planted firmly in the ground and attached to your wrists with webbing loops, lever your arms up over your head like crucified Christ as you slide a foot or two farther. Not bad as falls go—nothing broken, no one to laugh at you in the silent, dripping forest, only the fog of your own breath and the feel of wet leaves soaking through your nylon hiking shorts.

I've already fallen a second time when I hear someone behind me on the trail and turn to squint through the fog enveloping Wolf Laurel Top. It's Bigfoot. He fades in like some strange apparition in the gray woods. Tall, silent, his head covered by a strange nunlike black hood attached to the rain cover of his backpack, he paces along using bright white downhill ski poles as walking sticks. We continue along for another minute or two as he closes the gap between us with his great, heronlike strides. I figure he's trying to catch the others, who've left me behind, so we exchange pleasantries and I move to the side. He disappears into the fog ahead. I round a corner and start down into a little hollow. Suddenly there he is again, on his butt in a mudhole this time, slowly reassembling himself and shaking the slop from his hands. I can see the skid mark where he's lost his footing, and ask if he's okay.

"Yeah," he grumbles, and then turns over and starts to lever himself up. His foot slips again and he goes back down on one knee in the mud. "Man!" he says, and throws a handful of leaf mold into the woods. "What a fucking miserable day!"

I offer him a candy bar and we sit there in the rain and fog for a couple of minutes, chewing. We have both been hurrying, pushing forward as if we could outrun the bad weather, and it feels good to stop. About half the tribe has pushed out early, aiming to stay at a shelter some ten miles farther north. But Bigfoot's feet hurt, and he admits that his two young partners have been getting on his nerves a little, always daring each other to walk farther and faster, always playing the one-up game. How far am I going? Maybe Whitley Gap Shelter, three miles farther and a mile off the trail. It will mean hiking only six miles today, but in the rain the idea becomes more appealing, and I'm just not in shape to hike much farther. Bigfoot likes the idea of getting out of the rain. We set out again, Bigfoot subdued and brooding behind me. At Tesnatee Gap, two miles farther north, I stop to eat a lunch of peanut butter crackers, and he hikes on.

After an acquaintance of only a day and a night, I like Bigfoot. He is the heart of Loon's Tribe, a great gangling fellow with a big-boned forehead, sleepy hollow-socketed eyes, and a joyful rumble of a laugh; he must have been the uncoordinated kid that others picked on in junior high school, who always felt awkward. Now all that is done with, though: he's out of college and off in the woods, where suddenly he has the room he needs to stretch out, where he is strong and graceful. He fits out here. The other young men in the bunkroom last night regarded the trail as a kind of obstacle course to be mastered. Bigfoot is looking for something else, and I only hope he's not in too much of a hurry to find it, because I know I won't be able keep up.

Eight miles a day is about my limit for now—farther than that and I'll exhaust or hurt myself. My wife and I have agreed to meet for our anniversary, in Damascus, Virginia, three hundred miles north. But that's more than month away. Surely I can hike myself into shape by then. Loon's wisdom about not going too far, too fast jives with the complaints of a body that's been desk-bound and donut-fed too long. I struggle on out of Tesnatee Gap, up a steep, snaking trail for half a mile to where a sign and blue blazes on the trees mark the side trail to Whitley Gap Shelter. Sure enough, in the mud I can make out the imprint of Bigfoot's size 15 Sundowner boots leading up the side trail. It will be a short day for him too.

When I reach the shelter in the deepening chill of afternoon, two local high school kids are setting up a cheap dome tent, and they glare at us. Trash lies scattered around inside the shelter, blackened beer cans fill the fire pit in front of it, and the register is full of ballpoint scrawls and vulgarities. Graffiti decorates the walls, including a drawing of a giant rat and the word BEWARE! Clearly this place is not as isolated as I'd thought, and the underage drinkers of White County, Georgia, know it well. It's not worth the two-mile detour. Bigfoot's pack rests up against the back wall of the shelter, and I can hear him off at the nearby spring, filtering water. By the time I've spread out my gear, walked to the spring to fill my own water bottles, and broken out my cook stove to fix dinner, Bigfoot has wrapped himself up in his sleeping bag in the shelter and is slurping some ramen noodles he's boiled on his stove. He's feeling better.

We look at each other, then out of the junky shelter, where a hint of late afternoon sun prisms into the dim hollow through dispersing mist. One of the high schoolers self-consciously breaks out a pack of cigarettes. Our next move doesn't require much discussion.

Ten minutes later we are pounding up Wildcat Ridge, back the way we've come, headed for the ridgeline. On top we find a grassy area sheltered by rhododendron and stunted hardwoods, a perfect tentsite, with the remains of a camper's fire ring and some logs to sit on. And now for the first time all day a view presents itself: a last bank of ragged gray-footed clouds drifts over, revealing the setting sun, and turns rose and orange against the deep blue of early evening. To the east great castles of cumulonimbus loom, glowing in the light of sunset, as they are pushed seaward by a cold northwest wind sweeping in over the hills. Soon the mountains surround us like dusky blue ocean swells against the bright horizon, and darkness fills up the valleys. We stake our tents down on the rocky soil. Maybe it isn't such a lousy day after all.

Loon shows up a few minutes later, in running shoes and a light pack, the tribe's shaman allowing the young warriors to rush out, blazing the way, and following craftily behind them. No needless slogging through a downpour for him: he knows better, and has waited at Neels Gap for things to clear off.

We listen to him hum and talk to himself as he sets up camp and cooks dinner near our tents. He's short on water and borrows some from us. We watch as the last light goes, as the stars come out, undiminished by moonlight or townlight, and as Comet Hale-Bopp fans again amazingly across half the sky.

It's the sort of sunset and comet-rise that makes heroic outdoor adventurers get all soft and fuzzy and philosophical. They talk late into the night, watching the stars. Bigfoot has a geology degree, but no wish to put it to use prospecting for oil, where the jobs are. Since his older brother traveled a lot before settling down, Mom has been understanding—she sees the thruhike as a chance to think about things. The Rhymin' Worm has a bad case of job burnout, and he confesses that he's hurt his wife by going off like this. What comes after the trail? He doesn't know. Why choose? Loon asks. He's been back every year since his own divorce, for a few weeks at least. This beaten path is always here when you need it.

7

NEELS GAP, LOW GAP, Whitley Gap, Tesnatee Gap, Unicoi Gap, Addis Gap, Dicks Creek Gap, Bly Gap—these obscure chinks in the Blue Ridge of Georgia don't show up on road maps, only on the detailed topographic and trail maps that hikers carry. When you're in your car, following a road as it twists through the mountains, you don't need to know the name of each hill it skirts and each ridge it parallels. Each one has a name, though, usually known only to locals, to hunters, and to those who venture off the road. You learn them when you're walking, when it takes as long to climb that hill or descend to that gap as it might take a car to cross an entire county. Soon the names become as memorable and distinct as scenic stops on a driving tour. Each mile on the trail has its streams and balds and cliffs whose names tell stories about the settling and taming and exploration of these hills. Each highway crossing or gravel Forest Service road becomes a link back to the world of cars and motels and grocery stores. Taken together, they become your means of judging the day's progress, the markers walkers have in common, like chapters in the unfolding tale of your walk.

After only eleven days, I had become immersed in that story's rhythms:

Dawn: wake up with the sun, pull on hiking shorts for the stumble to the woods or to a privy; return to boil water for coffee and talk about the coming day with other sleepy campers; pack up the disordered clothes and equipment around the sleeping bag; check maps and guidebooks to confirm the route; secret away some snacks for later; fill the water bottles for the day's walk.

Morning: climb to the first ridgeline, out of the hollow or gap, away from camp, from the road, from other hikers; move north with the sun flickering to the right through the bare trees of early spring; strip off hat and jacket as sweat begins flowing and as the aching back and sore feet loosen up; listen for birds calling in the trees or tiny rust-red grasshoppers rustling the leaf mold along the trail's edge; as midmorning nears, feel the first tugs of hunger and begin looking for a place to sit, a view to enjoy, a chance to eat a Snickers bar and figure out how much of the map remains before the next shelter and a full-blown lunch break.

Midday: turn down the blue-blazed trail to the shelter (who else will be there?) and drop the pack by the picnic table; spend a few minutes flipping through the register (how long ago were Bigfoot and D-Bear here? Did they leave a message?) and maybe write a dumb rhyme about yesterday's walk; spread peanut butter over Ritz crackers, unwrap a piece of cheddar cheese, bite an apple, eat another Snickers bar.

Afternoon: brood over an old conversation, a commitment broken, a promise betrayed, the sadness in Cathy's voice over the phone at Neels Gap; sense the anxiety draining away as the day's steepest climb drives out all other thoughts, the beat of feet and heart syncopated like drums with the rhythm of breath, glimpses of ridges teasing through the trees above (which will the trail ascend?); exchange pleasantries with some young thruhikers, who charge past and disappear up ahead; see the day's walk opening like a map, yesterday's regrets folded out of sight with the hills already crossed; feel the exhaustion of the day's journey gradually work back into legs, feet, and lungs as the sun sinks in the west.

Evening: find a campsite or a shelter, drop the pack, and collapse; take off hot boots and put on cool rubber Teva camp sandals; stumble down to the nearby spring and filter water for cooking, for dishes, for the morning's breakfast and the next day's hike; sit back as one by one other hikers arrive, introduce themselves, and busy themselves in their own routines; laugh and joke over dinner with these friends of the day, maybe never to be encountered again; consider the coming weather, pitch a tent or roll out the sleeping pads and sleeping bag next to the others in the shelter; hang the food bag to keep mice and skunks from raiding it, and slip into the silk cocoon as light leaves the sky.

Now, vary that theme, day upon day, each variation building on or echoing or in counterpoint to the one before, each different in its crescendos and diminuendos, its rests and retards, its prestos, allegros, and largos. It has a shape and flow of its own, this theme, and though you can confine it with plans and schedules, you can never predict just how it will play out.

Pretty soon I had walked off the Georgia map and into North Carolina.

8

White Blaze—Day 12
Saturday, April 12, 1997 • Muskrat Creek Shelter • North Carolina
Blue Ridge Mountains • 79 miles hiked • 2,082 miles to go
Fog and rain • Low 41, high 56
Elevation 4,600 feet

NORTH OF BLY GAP, at the Georgia-Carolina border, the trail rears up on its hind legs and kicks me in the teeth. Coming up the ridge from

Georgia has been easy enough, and at the gap there's a well-trampled area for camping, a dependable spring, and protection from north winds. Immediately after the gap, though, the trail turns hard right and ascends Sharp Top and Courthouse Bald, a couple of rocky, rhododendron-bristled fells on the flanks of massive 5,499-foot Standing Indian Mountain—the first really formidable mountain northbound thruhikers encounter. There are steeper and longer ascents on the trail, especially along the Tennessee border and in New England, but the climb out of Bly Gap is as tough as any, particularly if you're not ready for it.

I've tented in the gap near five other thruhikers rather than tackle the climb late in the day, and wind roars all evening as a front moves in, a deep-throated rush in the bare branches of the gap that sets the trees to groaning and creaking in complaint around me. It starts raining hard about three o'clock in the morning and I huddle in the beetle-shaped dome of my tent, sometimes trying to write a letter to Cathy, sometimes sleeping fitfully. Before dawn I wake to find that water is seeping through where the tent's waterproof "rain fly" zips shut, dribbling down the inside wall, and pooling near the door. I mop it up with a pack towel, but most of the floor is damp by then, including the foot of my sleeping bag and some of the clothes I've scattered in the night. It's a cold, relentless winter rain, and by the time the sky brightens and I finally resolve to climb out of my bag I realize I have to either hike in the rain or hole up all day in a damp tent.

Muskrat Creek Shelter, three miles away, looks like the best compromise. I'll eat a few handfuls of trail mix, pack up inside the tent, and wait until I get to the shelter for a hot meal. Surely I can hold out for three miles.

It takes me three hours. I have grown used to the Georgia trail, which is mostly engineered to zigzag up mountains in a series of switchbacks. Here it goes straight up the ridge. Suddenly each step up is an ordeal, my boots and hiking sticks slip and snag on the rocky trail, cold rain rattles down around me, and my breath gasps out in great clouds.

With my pack full of food from a recent resupply stop, and wet clothes and a wet tent making it even heavier, I find myself drenched with sweat inside the Gore-Tex jacket. Two of the hikers I've left back at Bly Gap, young women who'd come into camp late in the evening, catch me near the base of Courthouse Bald; I must look pathetic because they ask if I'm okay, but once I assure them I'm fine they charge past me like I'm landscape. I feel like it, too, and all I can think of is getting into dry clothes and making some hot coffee.

The temperature drops all morning, and when I finally stumble into Muskrat Creek Shelter, which is tucked in a high dell on the shoulder of Standing Indian, and stop walking, I feel chilled. My shirt is soaked, and when I unzip my rain shell the wind cuts right through to my skin.

"You made it!" It's one of the two young women from Bly Gap who passed me on the trail. They're both having something hot to drink and conversing with two men I haven't met before. The men look like they've settled in for the duration, though it's not even noon. The women introduce themselves as Meg and Sara—no trail names yet—and explain they're just taking a break before moving on; the two men introduce themselves as Singing Bear and Señor Wiggly, both 2,000-milers from previous seasons, out to revisit their thruhikes. I introduce myself to a hot cup of coffee and some hot oatmeal as soon as I can get my stove going. Then I discreetly retreat into the back of the shelter to strip off my wet clothes and pull on all the layers of dry clothes I can manage: a long-sleeved polypropylene undershirt, a nylon shirt, a synthetic fleece vest, a Gore-Tex shell, polypropylene long johns, and long nylon pants.

Thruhikers in the 1990s don't wear cotton because it gets waterlogged easily and can hasten hypothermia. Before I started I'd carefully assembled a selection of high-tech hiking clothes meant to keep me warm even when I was wet. None of them help now. I can see the shapes of clouds rushing through the trees as a chill wind sweeps down the hollow where the shelter stands; I get colder and colder as I try to join the conversation. The cold seeps into my joints, my hands ache with it, my skin feels numb. I start to shiver. It occurs to me that maybe I am getting hypothermic, even with all my polypropylene and Gore-Tex and nylon and Polartec and the temperature well above freezing, so I unroll my sleeping pads and still-damp sleeping bag, crawl in, and draw it tight around me.

When you're thruhiking, a heavy winter coat becomes too bulky to pack and too hot to hike in, so you layer on just enough nylon and fleece to turn away the windchill while walking and let the furnace of your own metabolism warm you up. If you get really cold when you stop, your sleeping bag becomes your coat—a kind of cocoon in which to metamorphose after the day's walk, and from which on foul days you emerge only to cook, eat, fetch water, or pee in the woods. Wrapped in my bag, gradually feeling warmer, I drowse in and out of consciousness as morning turns to afternoon and hikers come and go from the shelter. Singing Bear and Señor Wiggly smoke cigarettes and tell trail stories, Meg and Sara leave, a couple of younger hikers stop in for lunch and push on. Then Loon arrives.

Loon's Tribe has fragmented and left him behind, as it has me. Too far, too fast, too soon—we cannot keep up with the young men, or we'll hurt ourselves trying. We were both at Dicks Creek Gap on Thursday, having taken a day off the trail at a popular hostel called the Blueberry Patch, an organic farm run by a former thruhiker and his wife, near the small town of Hiawassee, Georgia. The tribe had made it into the Blueberry Patch more or less together, but we hadn't all made it out.

At just under seventy miles north of Springer Mountain and about eight from the state line, Dicks Creek Gap is where mechanics start overcoming macho: if your boots have been rubbing your heels into hamburger, if your knee feels like it's being stabbed every time you step down off a rock, if you have to sit down on a log every half hour because your pack weighs too much, after seventy miles of it you begin facing facts. Hurting pilgrims show up at the Blueberry Patch regularly, and the proprietors, Gary and Lennie Poteet, know just where to send them. They sent two of us into Hiawassee to have a doctor look at some blisters that had become infected, and the news was not good: the infection had spread up one hiker's foot and into his joints. The other hiker's girlfriend had just dumped him over the phone at Walasi-Yi, and that, combined with his badly blistered feet, had killed the adventure. Another hiker's backpack was disintegrating under an absurdly heavy load that included things like a portable electric mixer, and he needed a ride back to Neels Gap to buy a new pack. A retirement-age couple had already gone to the hospital with knee problems; two young newlyweds, thruhiking on a whim, had been stopped by an abscessed tooth that required a root canal. And me? I had lasted nine days. Nothing hurt too badly. Nothing had broken. But if I didn't take a day off the trail soon, a malfunction in the mechanism seemed inevitable. So after spending the night at the hostel, I booked a motel room in town with two of the walking wounded. D-Bear, Icebox, Bigfoot, and Raintree hiked on, a leaner version of the big tribe from Neels Gap. I'd just have to catch them, I told myself.

Now, at Muskrat Creek, as I fight off hypothermia, I realize that I have no intention of catching anybody, that I won't emerge from my cocoon until it is time for dinner. A new group of thruhikers is catching up to me. I'd seen some of them at Dicks Creek Gap, lined up for the ride in to the Blueberry Patch as I was dropped off. Now they start showing up here, filling the small shelter in their eagerness to get out of the raw weather. A young thruhiking couple, flushed and red-cheeked by the cold ascent from Bly Gap, arrives in matching L. L. Bean outfits. A small gnarled man with a quizzical look on his face comes in looking even more exhausted and near-hypothermic than I did, having hiked the whole ten miles in the rain. He sits shivering under the overhanging roof of the shelter, too tired, wet, and dazed to break out a stove or sleeping bag; Loon sees he's in trouble and boils a cup of ramen noodles for him. The gnarled man eats it gratefully, drinks some hot chocolate, and comes back to us.

I've changed my mind about Loon. It isn't a con. Clearly the wise thruhiking gnome is the part of him he lets free when he comes to the woods, not all of who he is. At Neels Gap he'd been testing us, trying to figure out who would shut him out and who would take him in. Maybe he *was* looking to pick up some free food then, but his advice about lightening our loads had been heartfelt: he traveled light himself, and it had become apparent over the next couple of days that he took a genuine joy in the company of young, idealistic thruhikers just finding their trail legs. On Wildcat Ridge I'd learned that Loon held a Ph.D. in forest management and had finished the trail himself as part of a cooperative group thruhike led by the notorious ten-time thruhiker Warren Doyle. Since then he'd come back to the trail a number of times, sometimes with the idea of hiking to Maine again, sometimes just with the idea of hiking awhile. He'd rushed past me to reach Dicks Creek Gap and then spent nearly three days there doing extra work at the Blueberry Patch as the proprietors tried to cope with the crush of thruhikers and run their organic farm on the donations they received.

People do fall in love with the Appalachian Trail and its world. The couple running the Blueberry Patch considered it their ministry. Loon? In the world beyond the Appalachian Trail he'd been chairman of a university department and had worked as an expert environmental consultant in Russia, but year after year he came back here, where no one cared, where he could leave that other part of his life behind and become "Loon." Now he was here with two other 2,000-milers, who'd also been drawn back: Señor Wiggly's hike the year before had come during a divorce, but here on trail he could chain-smoke and revel in the memory of that year's pilgrimage, relive his own journey from innocence to experience through the other first-time hikers, and maybe have a beer or two with them when he got to town. And Singing Bear?

Well, he'd completed his hike, years before, carrying a guitar on his back the whole way. Now he was back, with the guitar, walking more slowly this time, paying the trail world back for kindness received. Each night a new crowd of hikers would overtake him, and each night he would play for them and sing.

He sings for us. Fingers stiff and cold on the frets, he strums and fingerpicks and croons, filling the shelter with a deep, smoky warble of a voice as rain drips from the surrounding trees and the overhang of the shelter. Curled away from the wind and mist, buried deep in my sleeping bag, safe, warm, full of dinner, and comfortable once again, it is as if this body of mine that was so cold and unresponsive climbing the hill that morning is no longer here, as if a part of me that I've thought dead finds itself freed for a moment, alive once again in the communion of singer and audience in that high hollow on the ridge.

9

NO ONE *QUITS* A THRUHIKE. They go *off the trail.* "Yeah, I'm off the trail for now," they say. "Just until I can get some more money together. Just until my feet stop hurting. Just until I get finished with this job that's calling me back. One of these days."

The thruhikers who remain talk about it like it's a kind of death. "Did you hear about Fish?" someone says. "I hear he's off the trail now."

"No!" someone replies. "Too bad. Foot problems, I guess."

"Yeah, he was taking time off in Hiawassee."

"A good guy. His girlfriend broke up with him over the phone at Neels Gap. Took it hard."

What's not said: Poor bastard. He's out of the club. He didn't have the fire down below. But we do. We're still walking. No way it will ever happen to *us*.

It does, though. Most of the people who go off the trail during a Georgia-to-Maine thruhike do so before they reach Damascus, Virginia, 450 miles from the beginning. The first week in Georgia gets the ones who were completely unprepared, the pure dreamers who came out never having carried a pack up a hill before, the TV watchers with ill-fitting boots, the college dropouts who have heard of this thruhiking thing and just want to check out the scene, the sixty-five-year-olds who've waited just a little too long to get into shape, the midlifers who discover that they really do miss good coffee every morning and a comfortable mattress at night. Between Dicks Creek Gap and Fontana Dam, at the foot of the Great Smoky Mountains National Park, joints and ankles and backs are what send people off the trail—chronic pain that becomes too much to bear, ligaments that tear under the strain of carrying heavy loads down steep hills, arches that start to fall, ankles that twist on rocks and log steps, blisters that become infected, knees that blow out.

Once past the Smokies, the highest mountains of the entire two-thousand-mile journey, it's generally boredom or money or unfinished business with family and loved ones that sends hikers home. Bill Bryson's *A Walk in the Woods* told of his failed 1996 Appalachian Trail thruhike, which only made it as far as the Smokies before degenerating into a miscellany of day hikes and short backpacking sections between there and Maine, totaling about a third of the trail. Bryson simply got bored and discouraged. He had come out imagining a walk on the wild side, and instead had found a well-trodden path and a pack of stinking dropouts for whom he had no empathy. There are plenty of reasons to quit.

I wasn't quite ready. When I'd announced two months earlier that I would leave my job as an editor, everybody at work had been most polite and solicitous.

"Are you sure?" they asked. "What will we do without you?"

They'd given me a going-away party at the Dead Mule, a local watering hole, toasted me and my adventure, presented me with a gift certificate to a gear store, and bid me a gracious adieu. But it had been high time to go: I'd overstayed my welcome there by a couple of years, and the problems were piling up.

"I want some time to think," I'd told people before I left, as all the minute-by-minute demands of my work and my concluding obligations pressed down on me. That's what you imagine.

But you're so busy putting in the miles during a thruhike you rarely get a chance to sit on a rock and put your life in order. The shelter-to-shelter ridgeline world is a kind of limbo, somewhere between heaven and hell, but in this world of the fringe you're too busy to think yourself into damnation. You turn things over in your mind while you walk, but not with any sort of analytical precision. A thought, like a sock in the dryer, goes around and around, mixing with other tumbling thoughts, appearing, disappearing, hidden except for a flash of color, reappearing upside down and inside out, but finally not going anywhere. Your conscious mind is so busy staying on the path, avoiding roots and loose rocks, looking for bears or deer, or worrying about how hot or cold you are that your obsessions get mixed in with everything else. All the crisp edges get worn smooth and fuzzy by the tumbling. It's hard to dwell on a problem because you have to pay so much attention to staying just upright, to staying on the trail. You just walk. And walk.

10

White Blaze—Day 15
Tuesday, April 15, 1997 • Wallace Gap • North Carolina
Nantahala Mountains • 104 miles hiked • 2,056 miles to go
Clear and cold • Low 22, high 56
Elevation 3,738 feet

THRUHIKERS ARE CHEAPSKATES—some by necessity, some by choice. No one gets a salary for taking a six-month walk in the mountains, though a few find ways to defray the cost through sponsorships, writing, or photography. Some have lost jobs or, like me, have quit them. A few are rich. But most wait until after ending a career or, like Bigfoot, start before beginning one. A typical thruhiker spends around $2,500 for the trip, not counting what it costs to buy gear. Some manage to do it for less, and it's easy to spend more. Averaged over six months that works out to a bit over $400 a month for groceries, supplies, stops in town, and the occasional beer or pizza. Four hundred dollars a month doesn't buy much these days, but, then, you can sleep in the woods for free.

Multiply $2,500 by the estimated three thousand would-be thruhikers who hit the trail in 1997, though, and you get $7.5 million worth of stinking, muddy-booted spending power setting out to walk the ridge crests. And where there's a supply of money, there's usually someone to help it get spread around. As the trail has evolved from an obscure path in the woods championed by a few odd fresh-air enthusiasts into a federally sanctioned but largely unregulated national scenic trail attracting millions of recreational hikers, and as thruhiking has evolved from novelty to rite of passage, a sort of fringe economy has grown up around the pilgrim resorts—a cash-up-front world where at the end of the day the IRS doesn't get the full story and there are no money-back guarantees. Here all mattresses are stained and all box springs sag, Spam and potted meat fill cupboard shelves, shower stalls smell of mildew, doors don't lock, windows admit drafts, groceries come in small portions at high prices, insulation hangs loose from Sheetrock, and all cars smoke blue. This is the Planet of Naked Bulbs, Mix-Your-Whites-and-Colors Land. Damn the inspections, full speed ahead.

Most low-rent accommodations and cheap eats have been scouted out by enterprising thruhikers over the years, and in the 1980s someone first gathered them into the *Philosophers Guide* to the trail, which got passed from hiker to hiker. Today's pilgrim can choose from several professionally published and annually revised guidebooks that list the best places to buy groceries and hiking supplies, the hours of banks and ZIP codes of trailside post offices, accommodations where hikers can clean themselves and their laundry, and places at which to eat, drink, and be merry while in town. They depend on the reports of hikers to stay up-to-date, and so tend to include the cheap motels and exclude the elegant bed-and-breakfasts.

If you're a thruhiker, you wouldn't have it any other way—down from the hills, towel off the day's sweat, put on the least offensive shirt, stick out a thumb, and hitch a ride into town (in most areas a backpack serves as your ticket—people who don't normally pick up hitchhikers will give lifts to backpackers). After a week of sleeping in open shelters and tenting on ridges, you're ready for a hot shower, a trip to the coin laundry, fresh supplies, and hot food other than boiled rice or pasta and rehydrated sauce. But on your own terms: cheap, no Yuppie packaging, no frills, no dress code. Grunge is good. A bed-and-breakfast? No thanks. A motel will do, a really cheap motel is better, and a hostel in someone's garage is best.

That's why hikers stay at Rainbow Springs Campground. It's situated near where the trail comes down from the Nantahala Mountains at Wallace Gap. Walk a mile down the road from the gap along the banks of the upper reaches of the Nantahala River and you find yourself in the realm of a husband and wife team that caters to hundred-thousand-dollar motor homes and impoverished backpackers alike. They live above the cluttered campground store that sells everything from groceries to stove fuel to hiking socks, and they hold court from behind its counter during the day. You can get just about anything you need there, but maybe not anything you want: selection is small, prices are high, and if you don't want what they've got, well, honey, you're free to catch a ride in to the grocery store at Franklin, half an hour away.

One of the hikers who arrives with me at Rainbow Springs I call "Java Joe," a big important guy ready for some creature comforts after a couple of weeks on the trail. The rest of us go to the communal hiker bunkhouse, but he rents one of the private cabins. The next morning he's complaining at the desk.

"There's no toilet paper! Here I'm paying thirty dollars a night for a drafty cabin with mice in it, the least I expect is some toilet paper in my bathroom!"

The woman looks at him coolly. "If you thruhikers didn't run off with it all the time, maybe we'd put more out."

Three others share the hiker bunkhouse with me that night, each paying $12 for a no-frills plywood bunk and ratty mattress in a cabin with electric light, a refrigerator, a woodstove, and no plumbing. By the time I reach the bunkhouse they've managed to dispose of a few beers, and the woodstove is quickly consuming the meager supply of wood that the proprietors have laid in. A thruhiker named Grizzz is recounting how, as he came down from Standing Indian Mountain, he'd run across some local residents digging bagfuls of ramps in the woods.

"What are ramps?" he'd asked. "I never heard of anything like that up north."

They'd taught him how to identify ramps, a kind of wild leek, and had given him one to try. He hadn't eaten it right away. Who could blame a Boston Irishman for being suspicious about a strange dirty bulb handed him by a ramp collector in the North Carolina mountains? He'd taken it with him to Rainbow Springs for a second opinion.

"Tell me about ramps," he'd said to the woman behind the counter. "This guy gave me one."

"A ramp?" she'd asked.

"Yeah," he said, holding out the small scallionlike plant for her inspection.

"Just one? What's you gonna do with one ramp?"

That night, as the woodstove roars and the cold deepens outside, he shares the ramp around the bunkhouse, inviting us to taste it, delighted by the absurdity of it all, and the story is repeated and hilariously embellished. Later I will come across an entry in a shelter register announcing that henceforth Grizzz is no more. He's rechristened himself "One Ramp."

At Rainbow Springs I plan to take it slow: resupply at the camp store, put my clothes in the wash, and finally call my former employer. When I'd picked up my mail at the Blueberry Patch, five days earlier, I'd gotten a note to call work, but never found the time to do so until now. It will be a short day—I'll hike out about noon, maybe go seven miles or so to the next shelter. Coming into Rainbow Springs, I hiked thirteen miles, my longest day yet, and after the long, pounding downhill to the gap, my knees had hurt badly; maybe I was pushing too far, too fast, too soon.

A night's sleep has helped. I feel pretty good. I'm only slightly behind schedule, and I'm feeling gradually more fit, more ready to tackle the high country ahead of me. The walking is getting better and better. Here on the trail I'm the Rhymin' Worm, thruhiker, not Exhibit A in a cautionary tale about job burnout. The Rhymin' Worm doesn't much want to call the office, but maybe it won't be so bad. He still remembers the 800 number and calls up, expecting to tell them all about the first two weeks of walking. It's only three weeks since he quit, after all.

He makes the call and things begin with a dutiful pleasantry or two, as he's passed from phone to phone, but then comes the dressing down as his sins are enumerated: Promises not kept. Piles of unread manuscripts and unanswered letters. Lies told. Incomplete files. Indignant writers. All of this has been dumped in the boss's lap now that he's gone. Does he realize how this makes the company look? How it makes him look? Does he realize what harm it will do his reputation?

It goes on for about ten minutes, me taking it, lamely searching for explanations, trying to apologize, to recall where things are, to explain, to excuse what I can't excuse or justify. Then it's over, the phone is back on the hook, and I'm standing alone in a stony parking lot next to a phone booth, outside a mom-and-pop store along a back road in Macon County, North Carolina, the April sun breaking over mountains tinged with the green of spring.

I can't excuse it. I can't excuse any of it. I've run out of excuses. That's why I'm here.

I hear the buzzer of the dryer go off. My clothes are ready. I wander over and stuff the steaming laundry into a mesh bag and jam it deep in my backpack. A pickup truck driven by some dayhikers stops by the store for supplies, and the driver offers me a ride back to the trail. Fifteen minutes later I'm climbing away from the road again, back toward the ridge, back to the limbo that I enter more and more fully with each passing day.

11

I have not said much yet about my wife, Cathy. To tell the truth, I had been trying not to think about how all of this affected her. For a hundred miles now I'd been not thinking of her, as hard as I could. After all, it was my insanity, not hers. Back when she signed on for the marriage, she wasn't expecting her husband to crash professionally before he turned forty, quit a good-paying job, and leave her to go wandering with a bunch of ragged hikers for God only knew how long. Though maybe she could have seen it coming.

"Wouldn't it be fun," I'd suggested as we were planning a honeymoon in England, ten years earlier, "to walk part of the old Canterbury pilgrims' trail together?"

Yes, it sounded quaint. We would be rooming at a quaint bed-and-breakfast in a quaint old village in quaint old England. A walk in the country, with a cathedral at the end? That would be lovely. So I bought the official Ordnance Survey maps for Kent and found the Pilgrim's Way, a "public footpath" that approximated the old pilgrims' route. It followed the crest of a long line of downs above the Great Stour valley. The last ten miles into Canterbury looked like a reasonable dayhike for a twenty-something couple, newly wed, healthy, optimistic, with all the future ahead.

We had never walked far together other than afternoon strolls through the botanical gardens back home, or we would have known: ten miles is ten miles—a long way when you're not ready for it. And we weren't. In fact, I hadn't been hiking since I was a teenager, and she'd never walked more than a few miles at a time. But something about the idea of the walk to Canterbury drew me anyway, and she figured I knew what I was doing.

We started at Chilham Castle, a ruined tower behind an eighteenth-century country mansion. The day was overcast, with occasional drizzle. Cathy was all for lingering on the premises, enjoying the dry coziness of the gift shop, taking the tour of the grounds and gardens, where peacocks strutted and flowers bloomed; I insisted we get moving. Stop bullying me, she wanted to say. Stop holding me back, I wanted to say. Instead, we both got silently mad: she teared up and I fumed. Oh, honey! Our first fight as newlyweds! Click. Put it in the wedding album.

When we finally did begin, following occasional trail markers along hedgerows, down lanes, and up damp forest paths flanked by bluebells and daffodils, it took us several miles to apologize our way past the anger and start paying attention to the lovely, mist-veiled landscape we were walking through. We had dressed inappropriately, in heavy canvas trench coats and woolen sweaters that soon had us simultaneously soggy and overheated. After an hour or two we started getting hungry and thirsty, but we'd neglected to bring food or water—this was quaint old England, after all, and there were pubs along the way. But it was afternoon, the pubs had closed, and the quaint English country houses had locked gates. We even got lost once, when we still had five miles to go, starting out across an open field only to find our way blocked by a flock of horned sheep, the ram glowering in our direction.

Eventually we reached the outskirts of Canterbury, too waterlogged and footsore to complete the pilgrimage with due reverence. Instead we rode the last two miles in to the old town center on a municipal bus. By then it was early evening, and outside the cathedral most shops on the square were beginning to shut down. As we got there, the tour buses were pulling out, and a few visitors still milled around by the west entrance. I'd expected spires and vaulted arches, somehow, not this great dragonlike crucifix of craggy buttressed stone. From a carillon somewhere in the square bells began sounding. Someone was ringing changes. The sound came cascading and echoing across the cathedral grounds, sequence after sequence of precise dissonant mathematical variation and repetition. Cathy and I stood there exhausted and uncertain for a few minutes as the voices of the bells cried at us.

Funny how you repeat yourself. I'd dragged her along on this pilgrim's trail too, even though she was home in our living room with our old black dog, in our brick ranch house in a well-manicured circa 1965 subdivision. Over the last two or three years she'd watched helplessly as my job gradually came apart and I grew quieter and angrier, flailing around for a new direction. At first, as I discovered the Appalachian Trail and started going off for camping trips and weekends with a hiking club, the idea sounded like a constructive way to let off steam. No, I don't think so, she'd said when I invited her on those weekends—too many unpleasant memories from her days as a cold, miserable, self-conscious, and maladroit Girl Scout. Though she'd grown up to be a strong, competent woman, she'd had quite enough camping, thank you. But here she was anyway, dragged along as logistical support staff, chief information officer, and sole wage earner.

I'd hit her with my announcement about two months before I gave notice at work. What could she say? Should she leave? Would I be coming back? Not really knowing the answer, she'd driven me down to Georgia at the end of March, and we'd spent a weekend together at that glassy lodge at Amicalola Falls. I could sense her trying to keep calm, to be supportive and upbeat as she tried to convince herself that I knew what I was doing, that it would all work out somehow, that I meant it when I said I'd be coming back, that she'd forgive me enough to take me. She hurt bitterly, but I just couldn't bear to think about that anymore. I'd hurt a lot of people lately, myself worst of all. What I needed now were the few things left that didn't hurt: the woods and the mountains opening out before me, the unfolding story of moving through them toward an end.

That last chilly morning we walked down the trail from the lodge toward the falls, where the approach trail to Springer crossed the path. When we reached the crossing, I took my backpack off and put aside my hiking poles. We hugged unsatisfactorily through our jackets, and kissed, and talked about everything except exactly what we were feeling. We'd meet for our anniversary in Damascus, if I made it that far. Perhaps before then, if she could get away from work. She took some pictures of me clowning by the sign for the approach trail. Then we ran out of things to say, and there was nothing for me to do but put the pack on and start. About a hundred yards up the trail I looked back, and I could still see her watching me, alone at the crossroads in a blue woolen pea jacket, holding a purse and a camera bag, her shoulders hunched against the cold. We waved and both turned away. Looking back again I saw her start to pick her way back up the path to the lodge. In another hundred yards I turned back one last time, and all I saw were trees.

12

White Blaze—Day 17
Thursday, April 17, 1997 • Cold Spring Shelter • North Carolina
Nantahala Range • 123 miles hiked • 2,037 miles to go
Snow • Low 30, high 51
Elevation 4,920 feet

WAKING UP TO SNOW ALWAYS MAKES ME FEEL like I'm ten years old again and they've called off school. Everything gets quiet, the world appears freshly painted, rough edges are smoothed away and hard parts softened.

From my sleeping bag in the back of the shelter, peering past the hanging nylon food bags and damp socks, I can see the snowy trail continuing on up toward Copper Ridge Bald, the footprints of an early-rising hiker already marking it. Slate-colored juncos, the bold little gray snowbirds that nest along the trail in the mountains and fly out from next to your feet as you walk past, are hunting for crumbs near the ring of soot-blackened stones and coals still smoldering from last night's campfire. Less than an inch of snow has fallen. It isn't enough to make walking difficult, just a dusting of the high ridges to remind us that winter isn't done with the mountains quite yet.

Copper Ridge Bald is only one of several high, open summits along the Nantahalas, a line of mountains that slants northwest for about fifty miles, linking the two primary Appalachian ridges, the Blue Ridge and the Smokies. The trail follows the eastern mountains, the Blue Ridge proper, up from Georgia to Standing Indian Mountain before bending northwest along the Nantahalas toward the higher and more remote Smokies, which overlook the Tennessee Valley on the western side of the Appalachians. In between lies high country and river bottoms only now beginning to fill in with vacation homes and golf resorts.

I am sharing the shelter with five hikers who've been moving at roughly my pace, but whom I don't much like. They don't much like me, either, though no one wants to appear antisocial, so we remain outwardly cheerful and friendly. A kind of frantic camaraderie characterizes these first weeks on the trail. Everyone is nervous about what lies ahead, unsure of themselves, and we've been bonding desperately, forming "trail families" like Loon's Tribe. Family members cross paths during the day, camp together at day's end, hitchhike into town together for supplies, share motel rooms and hostels, and tease and exhort one another to keep going. But these families are constantly fragmenting and reforming, and many solo hikers, and pairs, are wandering around unattached, looking for a family to join. This leads to alliances of convenience like the one I'm in now that may endure anywhere from a day or two to several weeks, until someone hurries ahead or drops off the pace.

What remains of Loon's Tribe has come through here three days earlier, and now I've given up hope of ever catching up to them. Loon himself has gotten off the trail to take care of some business in the small mountain town of Franklin. Bigfoot, D-Bear, Icebox, and Raintree are pushing north fast, and in shelter registers Bigfoot begins leaving whimsical commentaries about the trail and the trip, signing them with a loose, goofy drawing of a footprint and cartoonish lettering. "A North Carolina Switchback," he labels one, drawing a vertical line straight up the page. They're having a great time.

We, on the other hand, mostly just endure one another in the evenings and go our separate ways each morning, wondering if we'll finally lose the others. Our group revolves around a moneyed young couple that I call the Princess and the Pea. I met them the day I holed up at Muskrat Creek Shelter, when Singing Bear played for us. They're pleasant enough, but hold themselves apart from other hikers: it isn't a pilgrimage for them, it's a kind of slumming in the trail's youth culture. Java Joe, the big self-important guy from Rainbow Springs, is here too, as is Kodiak, a rugged six-foot-seven kid in grunge flannels who's running out of money and trying to sponge off the rest of us. I'm brooding and somewhat withdrawn after the disastrous phone call at Rainbow Springs, so I'm not good company. The only really sympathetic person in the bunch is Termite, the gnarled little man who nearly succumbed to hypothermia back at Muskrat Creek. The Princess and the Pea have adopted him, and each night they share their cache of hot cocoa. He delights in building campfires for them—it turns out that he's a volunteer fireman back home. I wonder if any of these five will make it to Maine.

Not Kodiak. He's just back from a long, wild weekend at a motel in Franklin, where he and some friends have blown all his money on food, beer, and pot. He's hiking again now, well supplied with pot but with only enough food to get him to the road crossing at Wesser, a day farther north. It's just starting to dawn on him that he's off the trail. Dude, it sucks.

Maybe Java Joe, though I doubt it. He's a big strong guy, a little older than me and carrying too much weight; he's profoundly dissatisfied with everything and everybody out here except maybe the Princess and the Pea, with whom he's been tagging along. He doesn't really like hiking alone.

The Princess and the Pea have the resources to make it. This hike is ostensibly to raise funds for a charity back home; the farther north they get, the more money they raise. They're young, strong, and well equipped, and they're from New England, so they'll be hiking home. The Pea might do it, I think: he's got the Freeport Nordic fashion statement down pat, with his close-cropped hair, granny glasses, and first-rate gear. He's clearly enjoying himself. He relishes getting a little grubby, shaving only now and then, and rolling his own cigarettes. But if the Princess drops off, he will too. And I can't see the Princess finishing. She's small and strong, but she hasn't embraced the sweat and stink of the trail. Most thruhiking women enjoy not having to worry about shaving legs or underarms. She's having none of that—she hates feeling chilled and grimy, and she applies makeup in the morning before she starts walking. So far she's enduring, hiking fast but always complaining about how cold and uncomfortable she is. When other hikers talk to her, she eyes them as if they're after something. You don't have a conversation with her; she interviews you.

The one who's motivated to make it is the one who says he's leaving—Termite. He didn't expect to be here, but he'd needed time away from a prickly marriage and a maddening job; when an old friend announced plans to thruhike, Termite agreed to tag along for a month. His friend hurt himself the first day out and was off the trail before Neels Gap, but Termite kept going, fascinated by the world he'd found, the challenge of continuing, the company of the Princess and the Pea, and the changing cast of characters surrounding him. But he says he'll be going back to programming computers in two weeks. We'll see.

No, I'm not likely to find a sympathetic hiking partner in this crowd. But I'm stuck with them for a while, at least until I get to the town of Wesser, in a day. I'll take some time off there, and Cathy will meet me—we hadn't expected to see each other before our anniversary, in May.

I've been worrying about this, which is part of the reason I've kept up with the pace set by the Princess and the Pea—to rendezvous by the prearranged time. Though we haven't been completely incommunicado, three weeks of hiking means I've now been away from her longer than at any time during our ten-year marriage. And I'm just getting started. I've phoned home once a week, during supply stops at Neels Gap, Hiawassee, and Rainbow Springs. Just when I've begun to enter this timeless fringe world, suddenly I'm on a schedule.

I hike out early, half-wishing I could stay wrapped up in my sleeping bag, with the silent snow all around. By afternoon, though, all the snow has melted away. As I reach Wesser Bald, I can see the high wall of the Smokies thirty miles to the northwest, still wreathed in white and glinting in the sun. Below me lies the five-mile, 3,000-foot descent into Nantahala Gorge, Wesser, a taste of civilization, and a familiar face.

Once upon a pre-*Deliverance* time some "sports hippies" who'd had it with the campus scene discovered the white-water rivers of western North Carolina and decided to try making a living guiding flatlanders down them on rafts, canoes, and kayaks. Decades later, what were once informal expeditions in vans and old school buses to the put-ins along the riverbanks have turned into thriving recreational enterprises. Just drive along U.S. 19 near the Nantahala River and you'll see outfitter after outfitter beckoning vacationers to get wet and wild. You still make the trip to the river in buses with rafts or kayaks strapped on top, but now the parking lots are full of gleaming Grand Cherokees and Range

Rovers instead of old VWs. And where the railroad depot for the hamlet of Wesser used to be, there's the Nantahala Outdoor Center.

I wait for Cathy in front of NOC's well-equipped outfitting store and watch through its glass display windows as Ralph Lauren–clad adventurers wander the aisles in rapturous communion with the gear fetish. Nearby, hikers dodge traffic on U.S. 19, following the white blazes that lead across the highway and right through NOC's rough-hewn campus. It's an extensive complex: dormitories, showers, social centers, a travel office, stores, snack bars, laundry facilities, two restaurants, and, down the middle of it all, running under a footbridge, the dam-regulated white waters of the Nantahala River. As you eat in the restaurant you can watch raft expeditions float into camp from upstream or kayakers practice on slalom gates just outside the picture windows. The voice of the river fills the gorge.

Cathy arrives around noon, and as I walk over to where she's parked the Mazda I can see her talking and pointing me out to our old dog, who's riding in the back seat.

"Look!" I see her say behind the glass. "Who's that? It's your pa, Tig!"

The old dog, a black Lab mix gone white around the muzzle, looks around excitedly, but her eyes are weak and she doesn't see me until I stand next to the car. Ten years ago, we'd adopted Tig as a puppy, two months after getting back from our honeymoon. We figured she was born the day of our marriage ceremony. We have no kids, so old Tig is the whole family, and we spoil her. Cathy closes the car door and walks forward to embrace me, with the dog snuffling and straining through the half-open window, joyous to reunite the pack.

"Hey there," Cathy says, "look at you!" We embrace again. "You, sir, need a shower," she says after a minute.

And just like that, for twenty-four hours I'm not the Rhymin' Worm anymore. I'm just another vacationer. A few snapshots in front of the footbridge with the dog. A shower, underarm deodorant, a crisp flannel shirt and a pair of jeans, wallet in pocket, Nikes instead of hiking boots—it doesn't take much. Soon I'm behind the wheel of a car like any other sightseer in the mountains, with wife and dog and camera, touring the points of scenic interest: Wesser, the Nantahala River, Fontana Village, Fontana Lake and Dam, the Tellico-Robbinsville Skyway, Santeetlah Lake, Slickrock Wilderness, the Joyce Kilmer Memorial Forest. We drive farther in a day than I've walked in three weeks, then eat a tasteless broiled fish dinner at the local high school booster hangout. We end up spending the night together in a small mom-and-pop motel that accepts pets. On the table of the kitchenette are some letters and some papers to sign regarding my power of attorney, and taxes, and a home equity line of credit we've applied for. All night the old dog wheezes gratefully on the floor next to the too small bed with its sagging box springs.

13

ONLY SIX MONTHS, I'd told Cathy. Half a year isn't really so long. If you live to be seventy-five, you'll spend twenty-five of those years just sleeping. We'd each spent months away from home when we went off to college, and Cathy spent her junior year abroad. Six months? Our parents just shrugged: chump change. Try getting drafted into the army and posted to Europe or some godforsaken base waiting to be shipped off to war. Try having your company transfer you across the country or the ocean. You don't get the option of turning down *that* transfer. Want to keep the paycheck? Take the assignment. Why, back when we started out you were just happy if you could keep the family in applesauce and diapers and TV dinners.

Thus spake the Generation of Absent Fathers in its gray flannel suits and 1957 Chevys. And when I think back on it, my father was always going off and coming back: two weeks here, a month there, a summer teaching in Boston while we stayed home with Mom, a conference in Chicago, a hurried trip abroad. Before I was born, before Long-Distance Relationships even became a syndrome, he and my mother spent months or semesters apart, chasing jobs and degrees. But he always came home, and it never occurred to me that I had lost anything. I would wait at the train station for the locomotive pulling his train to appear down the tracks, or watch him walk down to the tarmac from a propjet's ramp and across to the airport gate, where my brother and I would tear through his travel bag to discover the presents he'd secreted away. Six months isn't so long.

Then as I'd moved out of my twenties and into my thirties, six months became almost no time at all. Ten years after Cathy and I married it still sometimes felt like we were newlyweds trying to learn each other's idiosyncrasies. Only the dog had aged, her muzzle graying, fatty tumors appearing on her flanks, her eyes clouding. Lately a work week would blink by almost before I woke up—five days of struggling out of bed in the morning, sorting through bad manuscripts, churning out copy, making excuses, racing deadlines, asking favors, sucking up. The weekend would slip by too, and no book or movie or Internet chat session could slow it down.

Only when I came out here to the trail had things moved more like the way I remembered them. Since I'd begun walking, almost four weeks earlier, each day had passed deliberately, unfolding slowly, and in detail, like a stop-action film of a flower blooming. These weeks had stretched longer than the previous six months, as if without a calendar governing it a different sort of time reasserted itself.

How do you explain that? I kept trying to tell Cathy, and each time after a few minutes I would catch myself breathless, my voice up in my throat as I went on and on about the rhythm of the walk, and who would make it to Maine, and who wouldn't, and who I'd met, and what I'd seen, until I became suddenly aware of how quiet she had become over on her side of the car. I might as well have been explaining

Saussurean linguistics. She had come out here to meet me, half-expecting, I think, that by now I would have seen that this had all been some horrible mistake, and that any minute now I would wake up and shake my head, come back with her to work, to our home, and start shoveling away the truckload of gravel I'd dropped on her with the lame excuse that it was only for six months. And for a moment, behind the wheel of the Mazda with the old dog curled up in the back seat, it almost seemed possible to me, too.

But the next morning when I woke up I was in that little motel room with a kitchenette. Where else would I go? So we drove back to the restaurant at Nantahala Outdoor Center for breakfast and ate at a table next to the picture window that looked out over the river. A kayaker in helmet and wetsuit slalomed back and forth through the whitewater as the rain came down. I felt a cold coming on. Seated at the next table were Termite, and Java Joe, and the Princess and the Pea, and One Ramp, and Sherpa and some of the other thruhikers who'd holed up at the Wesser bunkhouses waiting for the rain to clear off. They'd grinned strangely at me, seeing me differently all of a sudden—not the Rhymin' Worm they'd known, but someone else. You coming back? their expressions said. Yes, I guessed so.

After breakfast Cathy and I shopped at the gear store for souvenirs that she could take back to our niece and nephew. She left after lunch, the old dog peering at me from the back window of the Mazda, confused again. And it wasn't until Cathy was gone that I realized we'd been so busy being normal we hadn't had time to settle anything except what was on the tax forms.

14

White Blaze—Day 26
Saturday, April 26, 1997 • Clingmans Dome • North Carolina
Great Smoky Mountains • 163 miles hiked • 1,997 miles to go
Rain • Low 35, high 55
Elevation 6,643 feet

SOMEONE SHOULD DO a statistical analysis of the relationship between the number of people on the top of a given mountain and its height. I already have a name for this phenomenon: the Rule of Diminishing Vistas. According to the rule, a small, lovely little mountain remains deserted and inaccessible. If it's a little bigger and promises a view, a trail will have been blazed to its summit for the occasional hiker to find; if it's a significant mountain and the views are good, there are multiple trails and a steady parade of hikers and backpackers ascending to enjoy them from parking lots at the nearest roadside; if it's the tallest mountain in the state, there's a road leading to the top so that many thousands of people can search for alpine solitude from the comfort of bucket seats.

Clingmans Dome, the second-highest U.S. mountain east of the Rockies, marks not only the high point of the entire 2,160-mile Appalachian Trail, but also the center of the Great Smoky Mountains National Park. As I near it, telltale signs of the Rule of Diminishing Vistas become evident: picnicking couples in sneakers with no sort of pack at all; a muddy, eroded ditch of a footpath on the steep sections; side trails to every vista or rock outcropping. At the summit the trail converges with an asphalt walkway crowded with sightseers. They troop up from a nearby parking lot to the massive spiral concrete ramp of Clingmans' handicap-accessible observation tower.

The park forms a vast ragged ellipse, the boundaries of which take in what was once the highest and most desolate part of the Appalachians.

It comprises almost half a million acres along a backbone of high ridges between the Little Tennessee River to the south and the Pigeon River to the north. Desolate no longer. Each year more people visit the Smokies than any other national park, more even than the great western preserves such as Yellowstone, Grand Canyon, and Yosemite. As the most significant national wilderness reserve east of the Mississippi, the Smokies attract RVs, minivans, and Scout troops like a bug light draws mosquitoes on a Georgia evening. In April, though, with the exception of Clingmans Dome, thruhikers have the high country pretty much to themselves.

Hiking from end to end will take about a week, and we start up from Fontana Lake and the Little Tennessee River Basin. The ascent leads up from a lakeshore alive with the snowy bracts of blooming dogwood, the pink of redbuds, and a profusion of bright green poison ivy and honeysuckle vine scattered beneath loblolly pines; into the winter forest of oaks, poplars, white pines, tupelos, and sweet gums of the middle elevations; then through thickets of rhododendron and mountain laurel high on the mountainside; and at last to the boreal fir, hemlock, and spruce above 5,000 feet. The trail through the Smokies climbs north up Shuckstack Mountain then turns nearly due east along the ridge toward Clingmans Dome, thirty miles distant. From there it's a hitch to Gatlinburg, Tennessee, for supplies, then another three days of ridgetops to the park's northern boundary.

For the first time I begin to sense just how many people are out here walking to Maine this spring. I'm keeping pace with several trail families now, all on approximately the same schedule, imposed on us by the park's permit restrictions, which obligate us to stay at a handful of strictly designated camping areas near existing trail shelters. Each night I camp with between twenty and thirty others at the shelters, and there is no way to free myself from the wave of thruhikers. Speed up and I'll catch the wave ahead, whose comments I've been reading in the shelter registers. Slow down and another wave will catch me.

Everyone is pushing hard just to get through the park, as if the trail's highest point is a hurdle between us and the end. It has snowed up here as recently as a week ago, and no one wants to contend with April snowstorms of the sort that stranded thruhikers in 1996. Back on my first day in the park I'd stopped to climb a fire tower on Shuckstack Mountain; from there I could see Fontana Lake, and the Nantahala Range that I'd been following, with the Blue Ridge on the far southern horizon and the ridgeline of the Smokies marching ahead of me east toward Clingmans in the distance. Returning to the trail from the lookout, I met half a dozen thruhikers coming up the trail from Fontana. They passed me—heads down, pushing hard. Among them was One Ramp, hurrying to keep up with some college-age kids.

"Hell of a good view from the tower," I said.

"Oh yeah?" he said, looking doubtfully at the steep side trail up to the structure. "I got the rest of the summer to look at views." And the wave rolled on by.

Now, not only am I camping with a crowd, for the first time I have a hiking partner. His name is Earl, and though I don't know him well we're members of the same weekend trail club. When I announced that I intended to thruhike, he asked to meet me at Fontana Lake and do the park traverse with me. He's a slight, sharp-featured man of about fifty, with an easy North Carolina lilt to his voice and dark staring owl-like eyes; like most weekend backpackers, he's carrying too much weight, but he's nevertheless exhilarated to be out here with thruhikers, like the car hobbyist who gets to run a couple of laps wide open at Indianapolis Motor Speedway.

It's strange having Earl along. Just as I've started to grow used to hiking alone, now there's someone shadowing me, ten yards back every time I turn around. Though I'm still one of the slower thruhikers, my four weeks of conditioning starts to tell, and Earl sometimes falls behind as we ascend—his pack weight drags at him and an old chronic foot problem flares up. He has come all this way to hike with me, though, so he doesn't quit or complain, and I pause periodically to let him catch up. What takes the most getting used to, though, is the way he talks constantly while we're hiking—a running commentary about backpacking trips he's taken with the church youth group he leads, hiking buddies he'd had, and the thruhikers out here with us. Over the years he's managed to hike most of the trail between Springer and Harpers Ferry, West Virginia, a section at a time. When he quit a dead-end job with a big plumbing company earlier this winter, he mentioned the subject of thruhiking to his wife, but she brought him down hard. "No sir," she said. "Not this year." Their daughter was back in school after a bout with a life-threatening illness, and there were doctor's bills to pay. It was not the time. If he took off for six months, she wouldn't be there when he got back. He grins at me and shakes his head as he tells the story.

"Buddy, I wish I was going to Maine with you," he says.

Gradually, as the week goes by, a darkness creeps into the periphery of Earl's conversation. Something happened years ago, some terrible loss he doesn't explain—there was a year spent in California as a young man, trying to make it in acting school, and something that brought him back South, where he's built the life he has now. He'll be the same genial NASCAR-loving ol' boy I've known, who goes to church every Sunday and is just happy to be afoot in the backcountry with his good buddy, then in the middle of a funny story about camping with the youth group he'll casually drop a racial slur into the conversation—*the niggers have spoilt it*—and I'll look around to see his glittering owl eyes staring up at me over that easy grin.

Each day we arrive in the early evening at trail shelters full to overflowing with thruhikers and a few dazed weekenders ill at ease among the crowd: at Mollies Ridge Shelter Earl counts fourteen tents; even more blossom around Derrick Knob Shelter the following night, like a multicolored mushroom patch. Foraging bears can be a problem in the Smokies, so the stone-walled shelters are closed off with chain-link fencing, but with this many hikers the only thing to do is hang food inside the enclosure and hope no bear will visit your unprotected tent if it doesn't have food in it. Hikers scour the woods for fallen limbs for the fireplaces in the old Depression-era CCC shelters. Earl and I walk along forested ridges that vary from second-growth woods and rhododendron thickets to lightly wooded clearings, where carpets of white-fringed phacelia, bluets, and foamflower spread under the trees, to grassy meadows along the crests. As we move above 6,000 feet to the height of the massif, a ghostly boneyard of diseased evergreens stressed by acid rain and insects, the trail turns sloppy and the weather goes ice gray.

15

HOT SPRINGS, N.C., MAY 3

Dear C—

I got the maildrop and the letter—thanks! Arrived here Saturday morning, and, of course, the bank was closed. So I have the option of hanging around, spending money on my credit card or the ATM, or pushing on and trying to cash the check in the next town—Erwin, Tennessee. I think that's what I'll do.

Hot Springs is a pretty little mountain town—no stores except for groceries, souvenirs, hardware, and hiking supplies—with not much going on (with the exception of today, which is their "Hiker Appreciation Day," and involves a lot of local festivities), but there are some nice B&Bs, and a few good restaurants. Maybe we should visit here someday. My water filter cartridge was about to quit on me, so I bought a new one ($30) along with two new pairs of hiking socks (about $10 each)—all this on the credit card, since I was down to my last $22 in cash/travelers checks. I found an ATM, withdrew $40 (plus $1.25 fee), which should be plenty until I can get to Erwin.

I'm sitting here writing this from the front porch of a hiker's hostel. In fact, it's an oldish frame house that has been redone in aluminum siding, with starlings coming and going from under the eaves. There's a porch swing, some old rusted metal chairs, a coffee can of cigarette butts, an abandoned apple, and the shade cast by a couple of maple trees, which are just coming into leaf for the summer. Inside, on the wooden floors, a half dozen foam mattresses have been tossed into various corners, and we hikers have each claimed a spot, next to which we pile our junk. We've each paid $11, which gives us a real bathroom for showers, kitchen privileges, access to a washer/dryer for laundry, and a clock radio that's twanging out country tunes in the background as I write. I'll probably buy a cheap meal in town tonight and hike out in the morning.

A robin is pulling worms out of the front yard a few feet from me. It rained this morning (all night, really) and I hiked in from a shelter about three miles from town. I was sorely in need of the stop—filthy from three days' hiking, carrying laundry that reeked from six days of hiking from Gatlinburg (socks particularly bad—I have to reuse the dirty ones four or five times—gonna have to start washing them in streams between town stops, despite the environmental consequences), out of food (except for three coffee packs, one can tuna, one mac 'n cheese, and two oatmeals), and beat from pushing myself to get here (two sixteen-mile days, plus three miles today).

Why go through it all? Why get filthy and dirty and sweat-encrusted? I'm not sure I know the answer yet. There's some kind of elemental connection to the cycles of the day: getting up when it gets light, walking while the sun's out, finding a place to bed down before it gets dark, and eating dinner as the sun goes down. There's also a feeling of self-sufficiency with your whole world packed into your pack. And there's the sense of being in control of who you are and where you're going, rather than of being controlled by the clock, the paycheck, the demands of a job. Granted, much of this sense of control is illusory—there are very few actual bums out on the trail.

I'd go so far as to say that the A.T. thruhike is an elaborate escape fantasy—except that there do seem to be a lot of people here for whom it really is becoming a spiritual journey, for whom it becomes a chance to find out who they really are. The ones for whom it's pure fantasy have started dropping out now. The novelty is gone. They've proved (or failed to prove) that they can handle the physical part of it. By the time they get to the Smokies, they've toughed out 170-plus miles, been snowed on, rained on, frozen, baked, slimed, mucked, and deprived. They've squatted in the woods, farted at close quarters with others, eaten lousy food, gone without bathing for long stretches, climbed the trail's highest mountains, handled some of its stiffest ascents, and braved the worst of its crowds. Are they having fun yet? No. They've shown that they're physically capable, but they've also discovered that either they don't have the heart to finish, or they don't have a reason to.

One guy you met at Wesser, the one I call Java Joe, dropped off the trail when we finished the Smokies Wednesday, claiming that he was going home for his mother-in-law's funeral. All well and good, but he won't be back. It was very interesting to watch his hike progress. He was the kind of guy who knew everything, who'd done everything—I saw part of myself in him, the part that never finishes things. He bragged of how much money he'd made, dropped names of high-tech companies he'd dealt with, plants he'd worked at. At one point he learned that the people who run a motel near Fontana Dam had bought it for $105,000. "Ha," he said. "I've made more money than that in a day." He'd even been to Maine on several occasions, and had climbed Mount Katahdin twice. As we were coming down out of the Smokies, he bragged of this, comparing the trail conditions there (very poor) with Katahdin. Why make the hike if you've already seen the end? I'm sure that's what went through his mind. But you could see it happen as his hike progressed: he ran out of stories that would impress people. He had recently remarried and was giving some bullshit story about how this trip was his wife's idea. In reality, he was going stir-crazy back home after only a year, and came out here. What was left to him, as he ran out of stories, was the reality of walking, day after day after day—walking toward something that didn't answer his questions, that didn't fill the hole inside that all the bullshit was meant to hide.

Earl's gone now too. We got to his car on the north end of the park, and he was going to drive Termite, who you also met, to the Asheville bus station: like Earl, Termite had to get back home. Anyway, Java Joe got a ride too, and made a big deal about coming back to the trail after the funeral. If I see Java Joe again, I'll brush my teeth with my dirty socks. It was not what he bargained for.

So, is it what I bargained for? I don't know yet. When I saw you in Wesser, I'd have said maybe not. But hiking through the Smokies was good for me. I started to feel better, for one thing. The cold is gone now. But I also felt myself getting stronger, hiking better, feeling more at ease and less desperate out here.

Well, enough of this. A thruhiker named Barkeater and some others are asking me to go with them to the Hot Springs

Café. I'll call you tonight. And see you in Damascus in two weeks.

Love, R.

16

White Blaze—Day 33
Saturday, May 3, 1997 • Hot Springs • North Carolina
Bald Mountains • 269 miles hiked • 1,890 miles to go
Overcast • Low 53, high 71
Elevation 1,326 feet

ABOUT THIS TIME something changes in my hike. When Earl leaves, after the Smokies, I can't wait to strike out alone again. Two days later, descending switchback after switchback into Hot Springs, I hear the voice of the French Broad River getting louder and nearer. I've gotten used to silence along the ridgeline. The trail turns away from the edge of the gorge, into the quiet of a hollow, only to return farther down, switching again. Somewhere below a car accelerates. I smell wood smoke. A penned-up dog barks near town—just to hear its head go off, not at anything in particular. I emerge from tangled undergrowth onto a narrow town street. Once in town, with its barking dogs, its restaurants, its decorations for the weekend hiker festival, the rhythm of walking becomes irrelevant: I am back where the day is measured by a clock and governed by a light switch, and at the hostel I find myself dutifully calculating the days I will need to reach Damascus for my tenth wedding anniversary with Cathy, and a long weekend off the trail. Our plans have changed. After I write my letter we talk on the phone: a friend of hers will meet me in Damascus and drive me home to her. Later, I spend a few hours re-checking my route, my maildrops, my resupply stops.

Loon's Tribe is lingering in Hot Springs, having arrived several days before. I hadn't expected to catch them.

"Worm!" Bigfoot booms from across the tiled expanse of the local rescue squad's community room, where the Methodist church women are serving up a pancake breakfast for hikers. We pantomime greetings to each other, and that big goofy grin spreads across his long face. He lounges at a folding table with D-Bear, Icebox, and Raintree, as the gray-haired ladies in white aprons titter and fill plate after plate for them.

They are hiking out after breakfast. Or three of them are. Having pushed hard to get here, after an icy and muddy passage of the Smokies, they've lived large for a few days. Some strains are now starting to show in the family, though. Icebox and Raintree aren't really on speaking terms anymore. Bigfoot has been working for food and lodging at a bed-and-breakfast and plans to stay another day to meet his cousin, then try to catch up. Loon is off the trail for good—he drove by the day before to explain that he's developed a blood clot in his leg and can't hike. Too far, too fast, too soon. Only D-Bear is ebullient and knowing as ever. He's shaved his head completely, and abandoned the bandanna. He does his best to sell me on a local white water rafting expedition that he and Icebox have just taken.

The old high-country spa town of Hot Springs is the trail's version of bohemia, like the nearby city of Asheville, and it attracts counterculturalists, gays, sports hippies, good ol' boys, Buddhists, Jesuits, fundamentalist and mainline Protestants, dropouts, and entrepreneurs. All of these threads intertwine with the trail, which runs right down the main street. Bed-and-breakfasts and '90s-eclectic restaurants reside near communal homes and hiker hostels, rafting outfitters and RV campgrounds coexist with neatly proper churches, the diner and the hardware store are just down the hill from the Center for Appalachian Trail Studies, where "Wingfoot" Bruce publishes his annual *Thru-hiker's Handbook*. Hikers have crowded in for the town's first annual hiker festival, but it's been sedate. The highlight of the weekend occurs before the community dance, when a group of locals dress up in Wild West leathers and reenact the Shootout at the O.K. Corral in front of the old train depot. No one bothers to explain what it has to do with hikers, or with Hot Springs.

But it doesn't matter. Now we're itching to leave, anyway. What's really on our minds is the raucous festival that this one emulates—Trail Days in Damascus, Virginia, two weeks and over 180 miles away. We've all been talking about it since Georgia, and now we've come to the last push to get there. Ninety miles a week is doable, now that we're in better shape, but still pretty ambitious. Loon's Tribe heads out early Saturday morning, but I need a day's rest, so I let them go without me.

North of Hot Springs, the trail runs high along the Bald Mountain range of the western Appalachians at the Tennessee border, dropping briefly to cross the Nolichucky River near the town of Erwin, then returning to the high ridgelines and across the Roan Mountain massif. At Elk Park, it descends from the North Carolina highlands for good and crosses the northeastern corner of Tennessee along Iron Mountain, finally reaching the Virginia border just south of Damascus. Between Georgia and Maine it passes through many areas that are wilder, or populated more sparsely, but nowhere does it feel more isolated from contemporary America.

I struggle out of town about noon on Sunday with a heavy pack, deciding to skip a free hikers lunch sponsored by two of the town's churches. The trail zigzags its way up the cleft of the French Broad River, and as it nears the side of the gorge I hear the river's music below me, running high and fast from the spring rains, roaring over rocks. Then the path switches back into a wooded hollow, and the silence of the woods grows around me until the birdcalls and the wind in the trees sound loud. Then back out to the brink again, and the river below, a little more distant, its voice changing from brass to woodwinds. And then, at last, the ridge crest, a pause to drink and snack on a candy bar, and the final climb away from the gorge, leaving the flutelike whispers of the river behind, returning to the quieter harp notes of wind along the ridgeline.

Winter had been in full retreat when I started on the first of April, but climbing into the high country of north Georgia and southwestern North Carolina had taken me behind its lines. I'd spent most nights curled in my sleeping bag as temperatures dipped near freezing or below, and during the day had hiked through clear, crisp winter air, where the views from the leafless ridges opened out to the horizon. I'd listened to weather systems roar through the bare trees at night as cold air pushed down from midcontinent. I'd seen snow, walked through chill rains, waited out sleet and hail in the Smokies, and awakened several times to find my water bottles frozen nearly solid before I learned the trick of putting them into the bag with me at night. Now, even along the high ridges, the signs of spring are unmistakable.

First come the wildflowers—trillium and bloodroot, dwarf iris, squawroot and bird's-foot violet poking from the gray-brown forest duff to catch the early spring sun in the scant weeks before the summer canopy shuts out the light. No sooner have they peeked out than swarms of tiny grasshoppers leave them tattered and forlorn looking, and as I walk the hoppers scatter like popcorn from a hot skillet. Soon green tinges the whole understory of the forest: the hairy vines wrapping themselves around tree trunks manifest themselves as poison ivy, ramps and plantains sprout, clusters of bluets spread around mossy rocks, and on bare ridges the dried grasses green again.

The woods, which have sounded so empty, fill with birdsong and the shrill alarms of chipmunks. One particular bird, the red-eyed vireo, plays hide-and-seek for miles: *Here I am, listen to me, oh there I go, say can you see?* No sooner have I left it behind than it is ahead of me again. *Here, here again. Here I am now, listen to me.* What seems at first to be a distant lawn mower motor starts up, *thump thumpthump thump thumpthump thumpthumpthumpthumpthump* . . . not a motor at all but a ruffed grouse somewhere just out of sight, drumming its mating display next to a hollow log. Tiny olive-colored warblers of the deep woods, varieties that never venture to a windowsill suet block, flit around the tree trunks. A pileated woodpecker hammers methodically at the naked top of a dead spruce, then arrows away as I near. As I leave Hot Springs, spring is exploding all around me.

17

IN MALORY'S *MORTE D'ARTHUR*, the quest for the Holy Grail rewards only the purest of knights. Thruhikers talk a lot about purity too, and I sometimes wondered if slackpackers would achieve the grail. *Slackpacking* is a technique of thruhiking that allows you rack up the miles without actually humping a full pack. Usually it means taking your backpack to a road crossing and persuading (or pooling resources to pay) a driver into picking it up and ferrying it down the road to another road crossing or pilgrim resort you expect to reach by day's end. Hiking with only a light daypack, you can go faster and farther.

Thruhiker jargon defines several other variations worth noting: If you're a *purist*, you look down your nose at slackpacking. Pure thruhikers carry their packs the whole way, past every blaze. If you're pure about passing every white blaze, you're considered a *white blazer* (though some slackpackers are also white blazers, they're just not purists). *Blue blazers*, on the other hand, sometimes take blue-blazed side trails and shortcuts to avoid dull sections or *PUDs* (pointless ups and downs, where a climb leads to no view). The term has been extended to include *roadwalks*, which means getting off the trail to walk along a nearby road or lane. Most thruhikers, though they rarely admit it, do some blue-blazing. Roadwalkers used to be called *yellow blazers* (because they follow the yellow "blazes" of highway center lines), but now yellow blazers are hikers who stop merely walking along roads and start putting out their thumbs for rides. Yellow blazers are cunning about concealing their impurity, but you can usually tell that someone has been yellow-blazing when he shows up ahead of you unexpectedly, after you thought you'd left him behind. To *flip-flop* means to begin your hike going in one direction and finish going another. For instance, a flip-flopper might start in Georgia, hike nine hundred miles north to Harpers Ferry, West Virginia, take the bus up to Maine, and complete the trail by hiking south to Harpers Ferry. Yet some claim that even such a hike, past every white blaze, is not pure enough.

Not everyone hikes north to Maine. Every year about one of ten aspiring thruhikers decides to try it south to Georgia. This means starting and finishing later—long winters and fierce spring bugs make it hard to start in Maine before late June—and it also means sacrificing the sense of a larger pilgrim community; it's a more solitary experience, and *southbounders* tend to carry with them a quiet sense of their own badassness: "I did it southbound, man, without all that social shit—without those hostels and trail angels to fall back on." Others flip-flop. Determining to complete a long trail, ultimately, means setting your own rules. How far, how fast do you want to walk? What's most important: the going or the getting there? Everything else just becomes arbitrary. As the miles start to pile up, though, as completing the trail becomes more than an abstract act of penance and devotion, the impulse to change the rules become stronger and stronger.

The generally agreed-on rules for those attempting a "pure" thruhike are simple: do it within a twelve-month period and walk every foot of the marked trail. Of course, some take purity even further, adding their own restrictions and elaboration to their act of pedestrian contrition. My rule was that every day I'd begin where I'd ended the previous day, and walk from there, always north, never skipping ahead and hiking south. I'd also vowed, as part of my white-blaze penance, not to carry a radio or any book except a small Gideon New Testament and Psalter. I wanted to pay attention to where I was, and what I saw and heard. I had stayed pure for my first month, but now the temptations to stray were growing.

The Princess and the Pea had begun slackpacking. It wasn't hard to figure out why. For the last few weeks, when I'd camped with them, the Princess had complained more and more often about the grime of the trail and the work of carrying a full pack all day; she kept talking about getting to town, where she could clean off and indulge herself. One night, when we were in the Smokies, she and the Pea had arrived late at the shelter and grabbed the last available spaces as a storm rattled in, ending up next to a huge, talkative, grizzled man wrapped in his sleeping bag. He must have weighed over three hundred pounds, although he couldn't have been six feet tall. Rain had soaked his down sleeping bag the night before, and he was trying to dry it out with body heat. Thunder cracked and boomed close overhead. A few minutes later the rattle on the shelter's metal roof turned sharper, and suddenly hailstones began snapping down outside, bouncing off rocks and collecting in piles where they rolled off the roof. Lightning struck again, close by, and the air shook. Another hiker sprinted in, barely visible through the downpour, and burst past the open chain-link door. "My God," he said. "What a hellbucket of a storm!" The Princess smirked at him from her dry corner of the sleeping platform as he staked out a corner of muddy floor.

The rain began subsiding at dusk and we cooked dinner under the shelter. Then everyone began preparing for bed. The Princess had been interviewing the hiker on the floor, and now she turned to the big genial man settling in inches from her.

"Greetings," he grunted. "Snore Bear's the name."

"Excuse me?" she said.

"Snore Bear—my trail name."

Her eyes grew wide and she went silent for a minute as she took this in. "Oh my God," she said under her breath, and turned, panic-stricken, to the Pea. "Oh my Gaw-wd," she repeated to him. "He says his name is *Snoring* Bear." And all that night, as the rain pattered on the metal roof, the shelter's interior resounded with the huge shuddering rales and gasps of Snore Bear, whose chronic sleep apnea had prompted his doctor to suggest he try thruhiking to lose weight before an operation. The next morning the Princess had staggered away from the shelter, haggard and puffy-eyed. "When I get to Hot Springs," she hissed to the Pea, "I'm going to buy a really nice dress."

Slackpacking was one of the prime attractions of the Nolichucky Gorge Campground, a commercial site on the river east of Erwin, Tennessee. Several young guys hung around, offering (for a modest donation) to take hikers up the trail, sans pack, for a fast, painless high-mileage walk back. One of these was Jéfé, an injured thruhiker recuperating at the campground and making some pocket money on the side by shuttling hikers. He'd found me in the woods three days earlier and tried to talk me into it. *Look, man, you get to stay at the campground, in the bunkhouse, a really cool place, order pizza, party, and then you hike big miles with no pack to weigh you down. What's the downside?* Get thee behind me, Satan. I decided I'd carry the pack a while longer.

Others had given in, and today about six of them—including the Princess and the Pea—had paid Jéfé and another slackpack driver, Kampfire, to drive them back to where he'd taken them off the trail, at Sam's Gap. They would cover in a day what had taken me two days. The slackpackers left the campground before dawn, and that afternoon, as the pure of spirit sat around under the porch roof, recuperating, we started making bets about who would be the last one back. Even without packs, it was a hell of a long hike from Sam's Gap—over twenty miles. Thunderstorms rolled in that afternoon, and we started speculating about a couple of the slackpackers, who'd gone out without any sort of warm clothes and would be crossing the high open top of 5,200-foot Big Bald. But, one by one, they showed up, exhilarated and exhausted by the long, fast walk that a month earlier they wouldn't have dared to try. The last two in were two young women hiking together with a stray dog that they'd adopted back at Fontana Lake. "I win! Pay up!" someone in the bunkhouse said when they arrived, shivering and soaked, about half an hour before sunset.

One of the young women heard this and completely lost it.

"You guys were betting on us? *Betting on us*? Whether we'd make it or not? That's unbelievably insensitive! You bastards, what if we hadn't made it? *You bastards!* Who'd have won then?"

They were off the trail a week later. The pure of spirit pricked on northward.

18

White Blaze—Day 44
Wednesday, May 14, 1997 • Laurel Gorge • Tennessee
Unaka Mountains • 400 miles hiked • 1,760 miles to go
Partly cloudy, humid • Low 29, high 67
Elevation 2,543 feet

THE CAR FEELS LIKE A CAGE. Three other thruhikers are fellow inmates, but I'm the only one who appears to mind it.

Ever since Hot Springs I've been pushing, pushing, pushing to get to Damascus on time, to meet Cathy, to make Trail Days. And I keep falling behind schedule. After covering eighty miles in five days, I stumble into the campground at the Nolichucky River with throbbing feet and leg cramps that shoot up my calves and thighs once the sweat starts to cool, and I end up taking an unplanned day off the trail to resupply and let my feet recover. Then I cover sixty-five miles over the subsequent four days and give in to temptation, letting a fellow hiker's mother convince me to drop my pack in her station wagon so she can truck it to a hostel while I scamper unburdened over twenty-one miles of Tennessee foothills. When I collapse exhausted in the hostel's common room, I'm still two days behind Bigfoot and Loon's Tribe, still forty-five miles short of Damascus, with two days to get there, and my thirty-eight-year-old legs knot up again from dehydration. The Rhymin' Worm: slackpacker. No grail this week.

What makes things worse is that this section between Hot Springs and Damascus has taken me through some of the most spectacular scenery of the hike so far. The trail stays up above 4,000 feet across the Bald Mountains and Unaka Mountains, and over 5,000 through the Roan Highlands; at Roan High Knob it climbs above 6,000 feet again, and many of the surrounding mountains are open grassy summits that offer spectacular views of the Tennessee Valley to the west and the Blue Ridge to the east. But what I'm mostly doing is grousing about the rough and badly eroded trail, and fretting about the way it slows me down. How can you enjoy the scenery, how can you make decent time, I grumble, when you have to watch your feet with every step?

All that bad karma is lost on Bob Peoples, the slightly deaf hostel keeper, who takes us to town on a food and supply run, cheerfully pointing out various scenic highlights of Hampton and Elizabethton, Tennessee, along the way. Peoples has retired from a job in military intelligence to indulge his deep affection for the trail, and for thruhikers, by convincing his wife, Pat, to humor him in his dream of buying property near where the path descends from the hills to cross Dennis Cove Road. They've renovated an old tobacco barn and cabin and turned it into Kincorra, a new pilgrim resort if ever there was one. It hasn't even appeared in the guidebooks, yet word of mouth has already marked it as a don't-miss stop during its first year of operation: pay what you can, help out when you can, do your laundry if you need to, shower off, make a phone call; we're all in this together.

Except I'm not. I'm hunched in the crowded car, steam coming out of my ears and a small black cloud hovering inches from my head, blocking out the sun. As Peoples trundles us around Elizabethton on an endless four-hour errand from doctor's office to bookstore to discount store to hamburger restaurant to supermarket to produce stand, suddenly everything is beyond my control. I have no food left, so I can't just pack my pack and walk away as I'd done at Rainbow Springs. I have to smile and wait until others are taken care of. I have to sit in a doctor's office for an hour while my fellow middle-aged pilgrims Jiggs and Kilgore Trout learn from the doctor that, yes, their legs are sore and, yes, they should rest them if they want to keep hiking. I have to watch a day I'd planned to spend racing to Damascus waste away while I dawdle in grocery stores. I have to browse through a used-book store filled with pages upon pages of excess weight that I can't justify carrying in my backpack, even if my penitential vows didn't forbid it in favor of the Book of Nature. Fuck the Book of Nature. I feel like a grumpy, ungrateful, antisocial son of a bitch. I can't wait to get on the trail again.

Like me, Kilgore Trout and Jiggs have slackpacked here; they plan to recuperate at the hostel, resting sore knees and ankles. Also like me, they're somewhere in the maze of midlife, though both of them are closer to fifty, and maybe under other circumstances I would have recognized in Kilgore Trout the kindred spirit I've been looking for out here.

We've known each other about a week, having been on roughly the same pace since Hot Springs. He's a gnomish man with a curly gray-brown beard, high round Santa Claus cheeks, and sad eyes. I'd stopped at Little Laurel Shelter for a water break and found him there, resting an ankle he'd twisted two weeks earlier, in the Nantahalas, and that was still slowing him down. He pointed out the nearby spring to me, and warned me that it looked a little questionable.

"A little *Giardia* is a dangerous thing," I'd said, unlimbering my water filter and starting to fill my water bottles. "Drink deep or taste not Little Laurel spring." It was the sort of lame allusion I'd sometimes made out here, and that no one ever noticed. But Kilgore Trout had chuckled. "You must be the Rhymin' Worm I've heard about," he'd said.

His own trail name came from a novel, which I hadn't even picked up on until he mentioned it. Most thruhikers aren't novel readers, their literary tastes usually running to Louis L'Amour or *Lord of the Rings*; where trail names were concerned, I'd come across many a "Strider" or "Frodo" or "Gandalf," but not a lot of allusions to Vonnegut.

Now Peoples and Kilgore Trout are browsing through the secondhand bookstore in Elizabethton, and I'm still fuming. Shit. Shit. Shit. I'll never make it to Damascus at this rate. I've debauched my purity for nothing. There's a copy of *The Portable Walt Whitman* in the poetry section, and I'm ready to read something besides psalms. I've done enough penance, I think as I buy it. Screw the extra weight.

By the time I've gotten over my silent temper tantrum and we've returned to the hostel, more hikers have shown up: one is a red-haired guy who had been with me and Loon's Tribe back at the hostel in Georgia; one is an aggressive, flirtatious young woman who's been hiking fast and long, and is now slackpacking while her sore legs recover; two other young women are slackpacking with her, also trying to deal with leg injuries suffered during the push north from Hot Springs; all are pushing to reach Damascus for Trail Days. Another middle-aged hiker is there too, a studious-looking bearded fellow with round spectacles who introduces himself as RockDancer; I'd seen him slackpacking south toward the Nolichucky River the day I left. Some twelve of us altogether are here. The rage burns away as we concoct a communal spaghetti dinner in the hostel's cramped kitchen, and I spend twenty minutes chopping and tossing a monumental green salad.

The next morning Kilgore Trout and RockDancer arrange to rent a car, and as I get ready to hike out they drive off for a day trip to Mount Mitchell, in North Carolina. Peoples ferries the others from the hostel up the trail for another day of slackpacking. Tomorrow he'll shuttle them up to Damascus.

Trail Days! I'm going to miss it now. It's time to go home. I've promised Cathy. We're due at the beach for our tenth anniversary. I make a few phone calls to change travel arrangements, make sure the arranged-for ride can pick me up, then set out for a last short day of hiking. The trails are deserted—all the pilgrims have gone to Damascus. I drift through Laurel Gorge, spend an hour lying on a slab of rock next to a waterfall, climb Pond Mountain in the midday heat of mountain springtime, and dawdle by Watauga Lake, where the water is still too chill for swimming. Near sunset I meet my ride at a picnic ground along this long glassy lake, the great wall of the Iron Mountains stretching beyond it on northeastward toward Virginia, and the rest of the trail. I do not want to leave.

By midnight I am two hundred miles away, with Cathy, in my bed at home.

19

BEFORE I BEGAN MY LONG WALK, I lived in a subdivision near a high-tech industrial park, where first-time home owners could afford outdated homes and reconciled themselves to all the ticky-tacky because it was so convenient. Two blocks away stood the neighborhood school, and during good weather I'd often have to stop my car for the morning cavalry review of kids on bicycles.

In ones and twos the small brightly colored bikes rolled past, a procession of wobbly helmeted heads and small book bags—the daredevils, the dawdlers, the plodders—rolling down the street to school each morning before the first bell sounded. Then one day as I waited for them to pass I found myself wanting to cry. I had a vision, like Jason Robards in *A Thousand Clowns*, of a street full of charcoal-suited briefcase carriers. These weren't kids on bikes, they were commuters. That's what we were teaching them. A kid's bike should be for winging ad lib through the neighborhood like a swift, not homing mindlessly in on a dovecote like a pigeon. I drove past these miniature salarymen and women only to encounter their fathers and mothers as my car pulled out of the subdivision and onto the feeder road to the freeway, each of us walled off behind our tinted windows, listening to National Public Radio or the Morning Zoo or Books on Tape for the half hour we took to get to work. Until then we were only in one another's way—obstacles between here and there, between the people we'd been at home and the people we would become at the office.

I understand "road rage" better now. No matter how expensive our cars, the commute turns them into little anterooms in which life ticks away while we wait for admission. Who wouldn't rage? When that's your world, there's no joy in the going, no matter how luxurious the appointments.

The woods themselves are no sure remedy to this habit of mind, of course. From time to time in Georgia and North Carolina I'd encountered troops of Boy Scouts hiking in the opposite direction, and inevitably the Scouts in front asked me how much farther they had to go to reach the shelter or campsite I'd just left. Are we *there* yet? says the kid in the back seat of the car. No, not yet, son. Sit there and wait, keep still the wild thing that paces behind the door of the cage: maybe you can let it out when you get *there*. That is the way of it.

We live in an accelerated culture, a world of jump cuts rather than long takes, montage rather than mise en scène. But walking, without machines to make the distance go away, after a while it becomes harder to hurry up and wait, harder to sit stewing while the clock runs out. Hold on to the rage for acceleration and you'll probably either quit because you become frustrated by your inability to get *there* yet or you'll hurt yourself by trying to turn your body into a machine.

That's what had happened. After I'd left Hot Springs, I'd allowed the calendar to take hold, and let rage and frustration at delay sweep through me like a hot wind. What was I hurrying for? Only to leave this place I'd worked so hard and given up so much to reach. Only to let Cathy take me down from the mountaintop to a world where I didn't belong anymore. And for what? To celebrate the passage of ten years: ten years that had come and gone more swiftly than these last forty-five days on the road to Damascus.

20

White Blaze—Day 49
Monday, May 19, 1997 • Watauga Lake • Tennessee
Iron Mountains • 412 miles hiked • 1,748 miles to go
Showers • Low 50, high 74
Elevation 1,950 feet

CATHY AND I TAKE LONG walks along Sunset Beach, the sand under my bare feet feeling strange after a month and a half in hiking boots. My feet are numb—I can feel the texture of the sand, and the cool ocean water when it washes over my toes, but it is as if I have an inch of cotton between my soles and the nerves of my feet.

"That can't be right, can it?" Cathy asks. She is wearing sunglasses and a sleek one-piece bathing suit of blue-green chevron patterns, with a loose cotton shirt to keep the sun off her shoulders. Her hair is dark and drops in curls to her shoulders. We walk arm in arm toward a distant fishing pier, where the squeals of children come down the wind from crowds wading in the surf.

"I don't know," I say. "They don't really hurt. They're just numb."

"You shouldn't be walking," she says.

"This isn't walking," I say, and I run ahead, drawing her name in the sand with my feet, and then a wave washes over it. We stop and look out toward the vast flat horizon, so different from the horizon of a hill, and I point to a spot just beyond the breakers where a pod of bottle-nosed dolphins roll lazily along, paralleling the beach.

It feels so easy to be back together. We have been so silently furious at each other, she at me for going away, me at her for pulling me back. But right now she is beautiful and I love her, and I can just pretend it hasn't happened—the last year of arguing and sulking, and the time in the kitchen I got furious and threw a raw mushroom at her and watched horrified as it hit so hard it disintegrated, raising a welt on her shoulder.

It's as if the late nights dreaming of walking—of climbing the mountain and not coming down—have never happened, as if we are on our honeymoon again, ten years earlier, walking along the Pilgrims' Way. We might just go back to the beach cottage, where several other couples lounge around on the sandy porch. We might make pleasant conversation, drive to dinner down the road in Calabash, and walk along the beach again after sunset. Then we might go home, back to our lives, and our jobs, as if none of it has happened.

The next day we drive to Myrtle Beach. A Harley-Davidson rally is in progress, and chrome-brilliant Hogs jam the Strip: thousands upon thousands of them cruising up and down, pipes singing. Middle-aged men in black leather and steel-toed boots straddle $30,000 machines, long hair drifting behind their balding suntanned heads, their wives or girlfriends holding on behind, arms around them.

"Should I have bought a Harley for my midlife crisis?" I say. Cathy doesn't answer.

"You'd look great as a biker babe," I say.

"Could you please not talk about that?" she says.

We stop at a mall and spend a couple of hours watching *Austin Powers: International Man of Mystery*, a Mike Myers movie that she has picked, knowing I like dumb jokes and Monty Python–like silliness. It's okay. My favorite scene is when Myers farts in the hot tub, excusing himself by rhyming "rude" and "food." That evening we stop at an all-you-can-eat seafood buffet, which I expect to demolish with my hiker appetite but which, strangely enough, I don't have much of a taste for.

"Happy anniversary," I say that evening. And she starts crying.

The next morning we finish our last stroll down the beach and return to the Mazda for the drive home, back to the ranch house where the old dog will be waiting for us. Tomorrow morning she'll take me back to Watauga Lake, and the two and a half days of walking until I finally reach Damascus. It isn't like it's the other side of the world: just four hours from home, and for the next three weeks I'll actually be getting closer to home each day, as the trail bends eastward. We agree to meet at her parents' house in Virginia for Memorial Day weekend, just a week from now. By that time only four more months of hiking will remain. Four more months.

Driving back, we play the stereo a lot.

TWO

BLUE RIDGES

I cannot go so fast as I would, by reason of this Burden that is on my back.
—*John Bunyan*, The Pilgrim's Progress

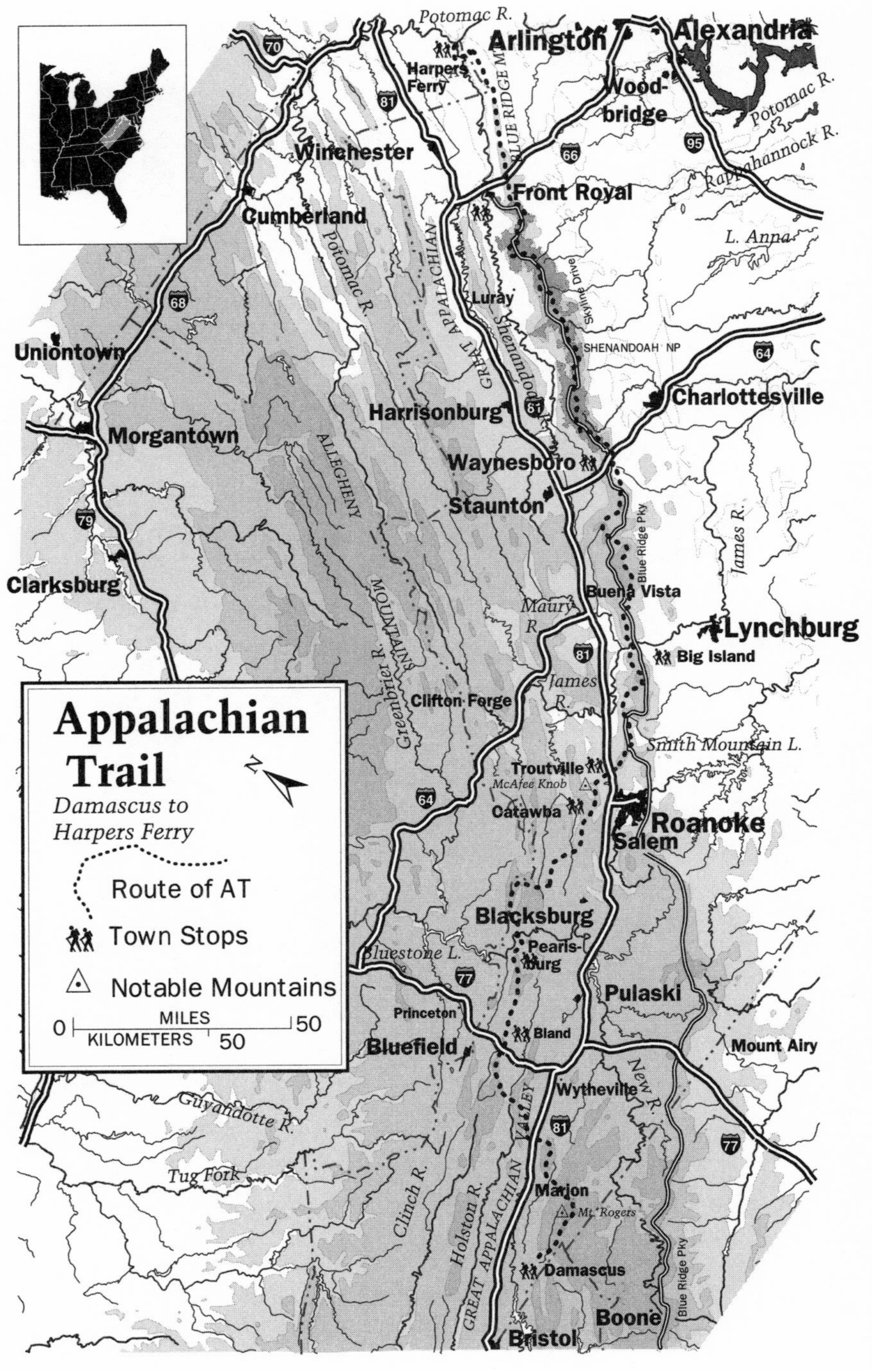
Appalachian Trail
Damascus to Harpers Ferry
Route of AT
Town Stops
Notable Mountains
0 MILES 50
KILOMETERS 50
Harpers Ferry
Arlington
Alexandria
Woodbridge
Winchester
Cumberland
Front Royal
Luray
Uniontown
Morgantown
Harrisonburg
Charlottesville
Waynesboro
Staunton
Clarksburg
Buena Vista
Lynchburg
Big Island
Clifton Forge
Troutville
McAfee Knob
Catawba
Roanoke
Salem
Blacksburg
Pearisburg
Pulaski
Princeton
Bland
Bluefield
Mount Airy
Wytheville
Marion
Mt. Rogers
Damascus
Boone
Bristol
SHENANDOAH NP
Skyline Drive
Blue Ridge Pky
BLUE RIDGE MTS.
GREAT APPALACHIAN VALLEY
ALLEGHENY MOUNTAINS
Potomac R.
Rappahannock R.
L. Anna
James R.
Maury R.
Smith Mountain L.
Greenbrier R.
Bluestone L.
New R.
Guyandotte R.
Tug Fork
Clinch R.
Holston R.
Shenandoah R.
70
81
66
95
68
64
79
77

21

DAMASCUS DURING TRAIL Days becomes a kind of pilgrim Woodstock, complete with talent show, and musicians, and drumming and singing and shouting that continue unceasing until morning, and sweaty hikers parading down Main Street, and panting trail dogs straining at the end of makeshift leashes, and plywood booths advertising mountain crafts, and soundtracked slide shows from 2,000-milers, and racks of fluorescent nylon gear at manufacturers' tents, and pizza, and covert drinking and pot smoking, and suspicious local cops cruising around. Thruhikers go off the trail there each year by the hundreds.

For weeks they've anticipated Trail Days and its particolored meadow of tents mushrooming up beneath the cliffs at the river bend. In the aftermath of the weeklong celebration, though, lies just another exhausting day of hiking, the first steps of a five-hundred-mile grind through Virginia—nearly a quarter of the trail to endure before the gateway to the mid-Atlantic uplands at Harpers Ferry, West Virginia, which itself isn't even halfway. With the passing of Trail Days, so too passes the giddy moment of thruhike incipient, the rolling trailtown-to-trailtown spree of late winter and early spring that has characterized the first month and a half. Maybe that's why leaving Damascus isn't easy. Many of those who arrive for Trail Days never manage to hike out, or do so only to abandon the hike over the next few weeks, depressed and uncertain about what happens next.

And then there's that damned map at the hostel.

It isn't one of the topographic maps meant for hiking. No, the Park Service gives it away free in brochures, and licenses a glossy poster version that hiking stores and organizations like the Appalachian Trail Conference resell for a few dollars—a diagonal slice from a Mercator projection on a strip of paper about four feet tall by nine inches wide. Through this narrow window the trail streams like Chinese ideograms down a background of oddly skewed state boundaries, national parks and forests, big hills, small towns, nearby cities, roads running by, and rivers running through. One cannot escape the context: rather than the manageable little pieces a hiker's used to tackling a week at a time, here unfolds the complete thing. Eventually some sadist got the brilliant idea of posting a copy on the wall at the hostel.

An average-sized male thruhiker's hand will not quite cover the eight-inch portion of the map that represents the 450 miles of trail between Springer and Damascus. Those eight inches have already meant six weeks of walking—out of April into May, over the 6000-foot summits of Clingmans Dome and Roan Mountain, through the nights when you wondered if you could endure the woods and weather, if you would get enough to eat or get sick from drinking the water, if the bears would plunder your food, if you would scream from loneliness, if you would cuss the other hikers jammed with you into mouse-lousy shelters, if the ligaments in your knees would tear, or, most haunting of all, if your will would collapse.

But you've done it. You've made it to Damascus. And just as you start to let the good feelings wash over you, whoop it up with the other Gore-Tex pilgrims and tell yourself that not many people ever walk 450 consecutive miles with a beast on their back, you encounter the damned map in the hostel and measure your progress with the span of your hand, and let your eyes follow the trail's calligraphy up the page, up and up, across an impossibly elongated Virginia and into West Virginia, Maryland, and Pennsylvania, then New Jersey and New York, then at last Connecticut, Massachusetts, Vermont, New Hampshire, and Maine. You've barely even started. You aren't even a quarter of the way done.

"The Place," where the map resides, stands half a block away from the greening maple trees and brick storefronts of Main Street, a sagging clapboard house that the adjacent Methodist church has fitted out for hikers with several rooms of plain wooden bunks. During the weekend of Trail Days and the several weeks bracketing it, their shouts and reek fill the rooms, and the old wooden steps inside shudder from stamping boots. Outside, the lawn sprouts tents, and hiking sticks form a knotty palisade around the front porch; inside, the showers and tubs are foul from the constant depuration of trail grime. The "hiker boxes" near the stairwell overflow with leftover Ziploc bags of rice and oatmeal, half-empty boot-waterproofing bottles, discarded or damaged gear, and dubious-looking dehydrated vegetables, all free for the taking.

Inevitably, some kind of stomach bug spreads through the pilgrim hordes, and the Place becomes a sort of pest house—upstairs several hikers lie nauseated and miserable on the plywood bunks near the bathroom. All the windows gape open to disperse the miasma and no one complains, even as evening temperatures drop into the upper forties.

When I finally came through, there among the post–Trail Days convalescents sat an old acquaintance, from that night impossibly long ago when I first found myself among thruhikers back in Georgia: Sherpa, he of the eighty-pound pack. His trail name was now Sherpa-911, which he'd earned when he quite literally saved the skin of an older hiker whose white hair caught fire one night as she bent over a camp stove. I'd last seen him at Fontana Dam, where he'd planned to take a few days off to rest sore feet. Ever since then he'd been gritting his way north, despite shooting pain in his ankles and knees, but the time off hadn't helped much, even though he'd reduced his pack weight by half. He'd pushed on through the Smokies, miserable and hurting with each step, missing the camp comforts he'd stripped away but finding walking no easier. From Hot Springs he'd yellow-blazed to the big party at Damascus, only to spend Trail Days and three days afterward retching and shivering on a bunk in the Place. Damascus was as far north as he would get. When he finally felt well enough to hike again, he planned to walk back south to Hot Springs, completing the section he'd yellow-blazed past.

"That's going to be it for me," he said, the toothy grin flickering even more nervously now. "I'll have hiked all the white blazes from Springer to Damascus. That's a lot. But it's just no fun when you hurt all the time. I can't see myself doing this for five more months. It just isn't worth it"—this last said almost to himself.

The end of Trail Days also meant the end of many partnerships formed during that first desperate month or two: since everyone had 450 miles on their boots now and the mere idea of climbing solo into the mountains no longer made throats tighten and hearts somersault, thruhikers had begun abandoning partnerships of convenience and striking out alone, or forming new tribes with fellow walkers whose interests, attitudes, and pace were more compatible. The Princess and the Pea hooked up with four other pleasure seekers and a car, and set out to slackpack their way north to Harpers Ferry as the "Virginia Six-Pack." Loon's Tribe disbanded for good: Icebox and Raintree left town days apart. Dancing Bear, the chef and culinary school graduate, grilled a spectacular feast for friends at the Place during Trail Days, then hung around afterward hoping to partner up with a girl he'd met in the Smokies; about the time I arrived he learned that she'd joined the Six-Pack, and he reluctantly hiked out alone. Bigfoot found a new band of free spirits during Trail Days, and walked north with them.

For all of them it's a new beginning, one more time. And just as I've missed Trail Days, and missed them, I've somehow missed that, too.

22

White Blaze—Day 58
Wednesday, May 28, 1997 • Raccoon Branch Shelter • Virginia
Iron Mountains • 501 miles hiked • 1,659 miles to go
Intermittent showers • Low 49, high 56
Elevation 3,570 feet

SINCE DAMASCUS I've been roughly on the same schedule as the Clan of the Hair Bear, as I call them—a trail family of rowdy young guys living large under the benevolent mentorship of a chunky 2,000-miler whose trail name comes from his mass of frizzy hair. If you're big and hairy or stocky or grizzled-looking, inevitably you give yourself—or are given by your fellow hikers—a "bear" name. A gay hiker I know thinks this is hilarious, because there's a "bear and cub" part of gay culture that celebrates hairy men. On the Appalachian Trail, though, no one really makes the association and it's all pretty innocent. Gruff, tough, wild, furry, hedonistic, and good-hearted: what's not to like about a bear? By the time I walk north out of Damascus I've run across the following variations, either in person or in the trail registers: Griz (signed with a drawing of a bear claw), Grizzz (later One Ramp), Kodiak (who dropped off at Wesser), Grizzly, Grizzly Bear, Bear (just plain Bear), Hair Bear, Snore Bear, Singing Bear (he of the guitar), Paka Bear, Papa Bear, Nine Bears (whose name actually changes every time he sees another real bear), Pooh Bear (a woman, I think), and Dancing Bear. There are probably more, but I lose count. My score so far: Hiker Bears 14, Wild Bears 0.

A day out of Damascus, Hair Bear lets me share in a string of trout the Clan has grilled over a campfire; he's wheedled them from a fisherman fly-casting along one of the stocked streams in the Mount Rogers National Recreation Area. When I go off the trail to see Cathy over Memorial Day weekend, I figure his group will leave me far behind, but as I come down from the high country three days later, I find them again in Raccoon Branch Shelter. They've all caught the Damascus stomach bug, and have spent a miserable couple of rainy days trying to outlast it.

I spend the night with them, sleeping next to Rubber Biscuit, a quarrelsome, bespectacled young thruhiker from Washington who looks like a Lubavitcher in Gore-Tex. He's accompanied by his dog, an absurd mix of basset hound and Australian shepherd that only its master appreciates. At mealtimes, it circulates from one thruhiker to another trying to steal food, or staring at them fixedly with one blue and one brown eye until they've eaten everything. It will follow you into the woods and nose around, sniffing you when you're taking a squat.

Having a dog along on the trail presents a big logistical challenge, but plenty of hikers try it. Why, with so many kindred spirits and fellow pilgrims out here, would someone want to spend trail time and town time looking after a dog? Perhaps because it's like looking after the part of yourself that never learned to be quiet and wait, the wild thing inside that your parents had to train to sit still and keep caged up so it wouldn't get out. *Are we there yet?* it asks. Sometimes I wish I'd brought along our old dog, even though I know she couldn't stand the wear and tear of the trail—though she would willingly have died trying.

And I wish Cathy was here. More and more, especially since Damascus, I have been noticing couples on the trail. Husbands and wives. Newlyweds. Boyfriends and girlfriends. On-trail romances between new acquaintances. Silver anniversarians embarking on their great post-retirement adventure.

Maybe that's what had made Memorial Day weekend so awkward: a week earlier Cathy and I had been a couple too, walking along Sunset Beach, cruising down Highway 17 laughing at the parade of Harleys, eating fried shrimp and watching stupid movies at the mall. It had been so easy to slip back into that life, to switch on the cruise control of the Mazda, turn up the stereo. No sooner had I torn myself away from it, though, returning to the grime and sweat of the trail, than her parents picked me up for Memorial Day just south of Mount Rogers and drove me to the town of Lexington, where Cathy joined us at a bluegrass concert. Once again I was "vacationing," sitting at an amphitheater next to my wife, watching the Seldom Scene clown their way through two sets with banjo, guitar, bass, mandolin, and dobro. Afterward the two of us spent a Sunday together at her parents' house. And then, as if my vacation was over, her parents drove me to the trailhead at Elk Garden on Monday, in a rainstorm. We waited there in the car for half an hour to see if it would slacken. What did they really think of this fellow who had walked off, quit his job, left their daughter behind? I couldn't tell. We'd sat in the car making small talk, as the windows fogged up and rain pelted down on the steaming car hood, showing no sign of abating. Finally I'd gotten out, buttoned up my Gore-Tex jacket, tightened the rain cover on my pack, and splashed away up an open hillside toward the woods, the horizon of the hill shrouded in fog and clouds, wind whipping cold rain in my eyes.

Five miles farther up an open shoulder of Mount Rogers, rain gave way to chill fog and wind. Mount Rogers is Virginia's highest mountain, and one of the trail's most beautiful sections. I'd been there when I could see a hundred miles back to Roan Mountain, across acres of open grasslands south of the mountain, where feral ponies grazed amid the rock outcroppings of Wilburn Ridge that jutted up like stony New Mexico buttes. Wild blueberries grew abundantly on wind-stunted bushes in the late summer. Now the only things visible were vague lineaments of clouds hurrying across the mountain's rocky, treeless south shoulder, surrounding me in shifting curtains of gray, and blowing in through the open front of the two-floor shelter at Thomas Knob. Half a dozen hikers huddled there uncomfortably, and from somewhere in the fog came a weird hollow insectlike buzz. Half-visible in the grayness behind the shelter, a white kid decked out in tie-dye shirt, dreadlocks, and an attitude was playing a didgeridoo.

At Raccoon Branch, a day after leaving Mount Rogers, I awake to find sunlight slanting through the trees, the mixed hardwood forest bright and springlike despite a slight overcast. The woods around me are lush with new growth and wet from the previous day's rain. Around me I hear the Clan of Hair Bear stirring, joking, beginning their morning's preparation. They are so happy to be out here together, despite the recent bad weather, and the stomach flu, and the memory of Damascus so recently behind them.

It is my choice to be out here too, after all. I chose to come out here, to escape, to hide out, to make the penitential pilgrimage. Surely that makes it unfair for me to envy the hikers whose whole world is this trail and who have no one scheduled to meet them at the next road crossing, no one whom they can neither leave behind nor take along with them. Surely it's unfair to Cathy to wish she and I were out here waking next to each other in the shelter every morning. But I do. And surely it's unfair to want to walk away uncaring and lose myself on this journey, like a child running away, until the world begs me to come home. But I do.

At least I am out of that chill fog up in the high country, and anyway it's time for breakfast. I ease out of my sleeping bag, stand up to grab my cooking kit, and nearly fall down as pain shoots up my left leg from ankle to knee.

"Probably shin splints or a stress fracture," one of the other hikers says after watching me holding a hiking pole and hopping around on one leg, grimacing, for a few minutes. If the former, I can walk through it. If the latter, it could end my hike. I try hobbling on both feet and after a while it feels a little better. Must be shin splints, I tell myself.

I eat a couple of Pop-Tarts and brew coffee on my camp stove. The other thruhikers are all up and around by this time, the dog freelancing from one breakfaster to another. There's no privy, and with my sore leg I don't feel like bushwhacking to a more private spot where I can squat and dig my "cat hole." I'm ready to start hiking, to leave them behind, so I pack up my gear and limp out of camp. The dog follows me for a hundred yards or so, until it is summoned back. I'll just find a spot along the trail when nature calls, I think, or I'll hold out until the next shelter, another three miles farther.

I last about two.

Your metabolism changes during a thruhike. Part of it is intake: you drink gallons of water each day to keep from becoming dehydrated; you crave fatty and sugary foods, like cheese and butter and candy bars. You crave fresh vegetables. You crave ice cream. Really, you crave just about anything packed with calories, except maybe the dehydrated rice and noodle dishes you eat night after night and which, before long, taste more like paste than pasta. After a few weeks your appetite kicks into high gear and you find yourself inhaling whole pizzas and devastating salad bars when you get to town.

"Wingfoot" Bruce, who intersperses the practical information of his *Thru-hiker's Handbook* with facts and trivia, estimates that a typical thruhiker burns 4,000 calories a day. And if you do it day after day, you burn more than you can take in. So you lose weight. I'd begun at Springer Mountain weighing about 275, and by the time I reached Damascus I'd lost a good twenty-five pounds: my pants fit loosely, my belly didn't hang over my belt anymore, and I could eat the way I had back in college, when getting fat was impossible. As the pounds dropped and my muscles grew used to constant work, without hiking harder I found myself hiking longer. I was just as tired at the end of the day, but I'd gone farther. And still the pounds fled.

But there's another side to a thruhiker's out-of-control metabolism. You don't burn everything away. The first couple of days on the trail it had been a novelty to pee in the woods—I felt like a mischievous boy pleased with his ability to water a tree when no one was looking. But soon my cast-iron bladder, which had seen me untroubled through twelve-hour road trips and interminable business meetings, let it be known that out here in the woods most of the time nobody *was* looking; consequently there wasn't any reason for all that iron resolution. Here all the world's a potty, the men and women merely pissers. Five, ten, fifteen times a day. And it wasn't only me. One young woman I met, who would end up leaving the trail halfway through to begin rabbinical study, wrote in her final trail register entry that it was one of the physical changes that most surprised her: she'd never thought she'd find herself stopping by woods on a snowy evening a dozen or more times a day.

Your plumbing also becomes ferociously regular on the trail. Oatmeal and raisins in the morning, peanut butter and dried fruit and candy bars all day, noodles and cheese and maybe a little canned chicken in the evening: watch out. It's as if the body, walking for hours and hours, governed by the primitive rhythms of sun and moon rather than electric light and alarm clock, goes back to a metabolic conservatism that reflects, to quote the philosopher Rush Limbaugh, "the way things ought to be."

And then, one morning, you break the routine, and before you can unstrap the pack and undo the buttons, will proves insufficient.

When you shit yourself, it's as if all the years since potty training never happened, as if suddenly a third of a century's cultivated restraint and sophistication, graduate and college degrees, years of high school, junior high, elementary school, adolescence, puberty, mastery of schoolyard bullies and kindergarten fears, as if suddenly all that has been stripped away, leaving you small, helpless, and humiliated there amid your own stink. This is the creature we want most to keep caged, the one that truly terrifies us, the animal.

After a minute I strip off my befouled running shorts and walk around ludicrously in just my boots and a shirt on the narrow sidehill trail where I've trapped myself, steep hill on one side, steep drop-off on the other. Man in the state of nature. Fortunately, civilization is only as far away as my backpack. I find several packets of moist towelettes and use them to clean what I can off the pants. I still have my "town" pants and a pair of briefs to wear until I can wash the running shorts.

Then I hear someone coming up the trail: one of Hair Bear's clan. I look around and hurriedly pull the briefs on over my boots. My soiled shorts and the crumpled towelettes and foil wrappers lie at the edge of the treadway as he approaches; my pack is scattered and open. He pauses and takes it all in, and nods sagely.

"*Giardia?*" he says.

"Don't think so." *Just go,* I think, and he does, on up the hill and around the bend. At least he has the grace not to laugh in my face.

I seal the shorts up in a Ziploc bag for washing at the next shelter, reload the pack, look around at the silent empty forest reproaching me, take a deep breath, and start uphill. Never never never again; how incredibly stupid; what was I thinking?

About ten minutes later I hear someone else ahead, where the trail levels out and rounds an outcropping just before crossing the ridgeline. Who now?

An old tree has come down and lies half across the trail about twenty-five yards away. A bear grubs at it. It looks up and sees me. I freeze. Its coat is a lush impenetrable black, like a hole in the forest reflecting no light. For a second neither of us moves, then without making a sound the creature bobs, pivots liquidly, and lopes off into the undergrowth down the ridge, silently at first and then crashing through some dry leaves. It stops about fifty yards away, behind some trees, turns, and stares back calmly at me. It looks about the size of a large dog, not round or roly-poly but lithe and silent and considering. We eye each other for a minute, and then it turns once more and crashes off into a rhododendron thicket and out of sight down the ridge. It takes me a couple of minutes before I realize how my heart is beating.

Score one for the wild things.

23

AFTER FIVE HUNDRED MILES, the trail becomes a kind of beloved adversary, ready to surprise you one moment by twisting through Zen gardens of lichen-bearded rocks and break your leg the next by leading you down precarious moss-slick ledges. You must constantly consider the next step. Do otherwise and you risk turning an ankle, or slipping on a wet log and tearing cartilage or ligaments as boots skate out from beneath balance. The ground underfoot becomes like a character in the story of your hike—its personality changing from ridge to ridge, valley to valley, from the spongy duff of pine barrens to glistening mineral soil, to gravel, to rock fields, and to the great compound fractures of bedrock splintering through the skin of the hillside. The way climbs geologic folds, skirts rock dikes, ascends steep upthrusts, or sidles around escarpments. When it hurts you or beats you up, though, you don't really blame it. You blame the bastards who put it there.

Before I decided to thruhike I'd been one of those bastards—a trail maintainer. Once each month, for a year, I would drive four hours to meet twenty to thirty other members of Piedmont Appalachian Trail Hikers at a campground north of Mount Rogers, from which we'd fan out with chain saws and clippers and heavy mattocklike implements called Pulaskis. Sometimes we just groomed the trail, painted white blazes on trees, and cleared the fallen trees called "blowdowns." At other times we'd actually make new trail, rerouting and relocating short stretches of the footpath from valley to hill or road to meadow, painting out old blazes and adding new ones.

Maintainers and thruhikers are different creatures, and there is a kind of unspoken yin-yang war between the two that has existed ever since the early trail establishment pooh-poohed Earl Shaffer's first thruhike as a stunt. While thruhikers are mostly young, most maintainers are middle-aged or retired. They love hiking, of course; many are weekend backpackers and a few are former thruhikers, but by and large they are gardeners, not pilgrims. Most live conventional, rooted lives during the week. They come to the trail on weekends, proud to be responsible for keeping the way clear, for hiking up from the nearest road in all weathers to chainsaw a blowdown, or taking clippers to a tangled mass of greenbrier, or slashing away with a string trimmer where nettles and honeysuckle have encroached on the path. And just as thruhikers grouse about needlessly difficult sections of trail, maintainers grouse that the long-distance walkers take their work for granted.

The art of building mountain trails consists of clearing and hardening a narrow path across the forest floor without spoiling the surrounding woods, or throwing the whole equation of rain and runoff out of balance. A lot of thought and skill goes into the planning—it's not just whacking away with a hatchet. Build it too steep and too direct, without switchbacks or "water bars" to divert runoff, and water gullies down it like a creek with every rainstorm, turning treadway into a raw eroded ditch of sharp rocks and mud. Build it too flat and water stands on it, pooling in great sloppy quagmires around which hikers edge, trampling the surrounding undergrowth. Here the national trail organization takes the lead, setting standards, teaching classes on trail building, providing crew leaders skilled in wilderness construction techniques, and working with the Forest Service and Park Service to satisfy federal regulations.

My club maintained fifty miles of trail where it came down from the high country. North of there, along the Virginia–West Virginia border, the Allegheny Mountains run to the Cumberland Plateau of Tennessee from West Virginia and central Pennsylvania; south, the Blue Ridge stretches down from the Maryland border and bends around the New

River Basin. In between the trail crosses a series of rampartlike mountains and valleys, sometimes fifty or a hundred miles long; down the middle of this is the Great Valley of the Appalachians, a major geologic feature that extends from Canada's Saint Lawrence River to the hills of Alabama. Along that valley Daniel Boone once led pioneers out to Cumberland Gap, gateway to the American heartland, and later the Germans and Scotch-Irish came down it from the Potomac to settle the piedmont.

Here at last lay familiar trail, places where I'd spent a day grubbing out roots and vines only to learn over the course of a subsequent week of agony that I'd been elbow deep in poison ivy. Where I'd walked five miles with a can of white paint marking trees every twenty-five yards. Where a paid crew leader demonstrated over and over again the proper "bench and step" method of cutting a sidehill trail—digging a small "step" to stand on, then chopping into the hillside above it, scraping away the skin of forest duff to the durable mineral soil, clearing a gently sloping "bench" for the treadway, and then repeating this a few feet farther on. Where twenty of us had stood, shoulder to shoulder, swinging Pulaskis on a hot July afternoon, scoring the mountainside on a quarter-mile relocation that replaced a steep and eroded ridgeline climb with a wide, graded sidehill switchback.

Maintainers delight in the sense of belonging to a great enterprise, and in the challenge of engineering bridges and fords, building stone steps, solving problems of erosion and overuse, repairing shelter roofs, digging out pits for privies, and cutting new trail alongside the "shock troops" from the semiprofessional crews that the Appalachian Trail Conference employs each summer to help them. Several dozen such clubs fall under the loose umbrella of the ATC, ranging from college outing societies, where a handful of students and faculty members keep up a few miles of trail near their campus, to independent-minded institutions like the Appalachian Mountain Club and Potomac Appalachian Trail Club, each with thousands of active members working closely with the National Park Service and U.S. Forest Service to patrol and protect many hundreds of the trail's most heavily hiked miles.

When I walked through our section on my thruhike, a skin of dead leaves had already begun forming anew as the mud-raw scars of fresh trail construction took on the gray-brown leaf cover of forest floor. I approached a section I had dug myself: about ten feet long, the fruit of a full day's sweat and sore muscles. The crossing took a few seconds, and I did not linger.

This rivalry is that of the gardener with the cook, each essential, each certain of misunderstanding on the other's part. But at bottom it is the same dream. For the maintainers, this mountain garden runs two thousand miles, a dotted furrow on the contour map that yields year-round its crop of muddy tracks and braided bogwalks: scant produce, maybe, for the price in poison ivy, sore backs, and blistered hands. They pay it readily, and not as some vague patriotic due, but every month return, weaving the strands of trail and lane and bridle path and view into this single track that threads through stands of pine and poplar, fir and spruce—that binds two thousand miles of hopes, two million strides. A way imagined, longer still, unwinds beyond the miles they tend. To know it bides is recompense enough: a last walk out when detours dead-end; a road not taken; a coffered promise for the times of doubt.

24

White Blaze—Day 60
Friday, May 30, 1997 • Knot Maul Shelter • Virginia
Brushy Mountain • 539 miles hiked • 1,621 miles to go
Overcast, showers • Low 50, high 64
Elevation 2,880 feet

MY MOTHER-IN-LAW GREW UP ON a livestock farm in the mountains near the Virginia–West Virginia border, and she often recalls how most years, after her brothers had shorn the sheep when it turned warm in May, a spell of cold, rainy weather would set in, during which sheep would sicken and die. Mountain people call it the Sheep Rains, she says. And as I come down out of the high country of the Blue Ridge to hike north toward the Allegheny Plateau, across the Great Valley of Virginia, where I'd grown up, the Sheep Rains set in around me.

A wet day is manageable, but after days of chill late-spring rain and drizzle the land turns sodden and creeks begin to rise, racing and gurgling around rocks where the trail crosses, making fording difficult. Every time I step in a puddle or walk through high grass, cold water seeps through tiny cracks around the tongue of my boots, wicks into my socks, and squishes between my toes. Calluses on my water-shriveled feet turn soft and peel or blister off. My clothes are damp and smell of mildew and sweat. There is nowhere to dry out.

At one shelter I arrive to find the charred remains of a Bible in the fireplace. Ever since the trail dipped into Tennessee, some wilderness Gideon has been providing each shelter with a Tupperware tub containing a King James edition and religious pamphlets. They are large, solid, books printed on pulpy stock and bound in brown or blue leatherette. On this one, though, the leatherette has peeled back from the blackened edges of the boards, and fire has bitten large chunks out of the ash-brittle pages. It lies there amid the coals, sooty cans, and half-burned sticks in the hearth. Who would burn a Bible? I picture a thruhiker stumbling out of the Sheep Rains, wet, unhappy, hoping to get dry and warm but finding only the cold stone shelter and no wood to burn. Outside the rain pours down, soaking the forest, soaking all the fallen logs and sticks, the heavens conspiring to make for a miserable day and no kindling. And here, dry and smug in its Tupperware haven, this artifact of pious evangelism, this insistent intrusion upon the wilderness: *The hell with that. The hell with whoever put it here! I am not out here to be preached at. And if their God is making it rain on me all day, well, let's put their Bible to good use. Let's see how well it can warm cold hands. Let's see how well it burns.*

When I was a graduate student, years earlier, I'd often come across a young homeless man about my age wandering the streets and sidewalks of the college town muttering to himself. He stank. Every so often he would fall to his knees and pray. Then he'd get up, walk another couple of hundred yards, and fall to his knees again. Along the tree-lined avenues of a small southern college town such a display is hard to ignore. What was this? I thought. Was it some kind of pious performance, a con, a panhandler's stratagem? But his image stayed in my mind, and one day it made sense to me. It wasn't an act: the poor bastard heard voices—frightening voices, terrible voices. When they spoke he would fall to his knees and pray to God. *Deliver me from evil, Lord. Send these demons from me.* He would walk a little farther and the voices would come back. *Deliver me from evil, Lord.* Eventually he wasn't around town anymore. Was he taken off to a mental hospital? Was he chased out of town by the cops? Did the demons get him?

I don't hear voices, but during the past twenty years, when I wasn't engrossed in a project that required focus, sometimes a mental videotape would switch on and start playing over and over moments of my life from when I was a boy to the present day that haunt me: a conversation gone wrong, a missed opportunity, a moment of self-delusion, a cowardly act, a trust betrayed, a mistake made, a promise unfulfilled. These are *my* demons. Over the past few years they'd multiplied until I could no longer simply will myself to turn the machine off and get on with the business at hand. More and more I found myself raging at the obligations, the failures, the fact that I couldn't stop repeating myself, couldn't leave the demons behind. It began poisoning the accomplishments I took pride in, the beauty I saw, the friendships I valued, the people I loved.

That's one of the ways depression works, coming upon you gradually, like night. "Myself am hell," Satan says in *Paradise Lost.* He's right: hell is not a place. It's a darkness you carry with you, a darkness that burns. But for all that, mornings come, and with them hope. "I believe," begins the Apostles' Creed. "I do," vow husband and wife. "Yes," say Molly Bloom in *Ulysses*. I've come out here to lose myself, but I carry my small edition of psalms and stories to remind me that if hell follows me, well, each morning the dawn is here too. Who would burn a Bible?

I limp into Knot Maul Shelter late in the afternoon a few days later, soggy and cold, my left leg aching from shin splints, grateful for the break and full of notes for my trail-maintaining comrades the next time I meet them: fix this bridge, smooth out this switchback, replace this sign. In my mind I write out a detailed inventory of indignant complaints to send them. Instead, I sit down to read the shelter register. Next to it lies a dog-eared section of the *Appalachian Trail Data Book*, a bare-bones compilation of mileage, landmarks, road crossings, water sources, and shelters that many hikers carry. This one has been carefully annotated in a tiny precise hand. Clearly someone used it for record keeping, and would not have wanted to leave it in the shelter. But who?

I flip through it, looking for a name. None. I page through more carefully. Maybe if I could tell where the mystery hiker has stayed, and can when, I can identify him. I turn back a few pages. The entry reads:

5/27—Burned a Bible today!

The next day, a chill gray rain hides the view from Chestnut Knob Shelter. I mention the *Data Book* to one of the other hikers there.

"Here's the answer to your mystery," he says, and shows me the shelter register. In it, the precise hand has written:

> *If anyone found the AT Data Book I lost between here and Knot Maul shelter, I'd like to get it back. I will be staying in Bland two days from now, and will be leaving late in the day. Or send it ahead with a fast hiker. Thanks.—RockDancer*

RockDancer. I know him, all right—one of the hikers I met at the Kincorra hostel in Tennessee. He's about ten years older than me, a compact man with dark, thinning hair, a bushy beard, and round glasses. RockDancer, a Bible burner. But why? Perhaps I will ask him.

The rains continue, slowing me down, and two days later, after splashing across the several knee-deep crossings of Wolf Creek in my Tevas, I pull wet boots back on and slog the last miles to Bland through a downpour, with kettledrum rolls of thunder in the clouds above but never the crack and cymbal clash of a close strike. Thank you, Lord. Lightning scares the hell out of me, and a mountaintop is nowhere to be in a thunderstorm. Each time the thunder rolls around me I can't help picturing the knights questing for the Holy Grail in the Monty Python movie: *Oh, don't grovel,* God says. *Every time I try to talk to someone it's sorry this and forgive me that and I'm not worthy . . . it's like those miserable psalms. They're SO depressing. . . .* Fortunately, the trail here stays under cover, running along a heavily wooded mountainside on a narrow sidehill treadway that bends in and out of hollows and through "hells," as they're called, of lavender-bloomed rhododendron. The dripping limbs sometimes bow low across the path and I have to push through them, cool leafwater tracing down my face and branches scraping the pack.

Sunlight breaks through the clouds just as I reach the road and hitch a ride to town. After a week of the Sheep Rains, I am ready for a hot shower and a restaurant meal. At a motel near the interstate, where tractor-trailers howl down the valley toward the green wall of Walker Mountain, I learn that RockDancer has already gone. I check into my room and call home.

Cathy has been on her own about two months now, and at first I barely listen as she rattles on about her week. She has just finished filing our taxes. Then there is paperwork about the home equity loan we've taken out in the event that the savings run out—so many things to think about. Her office is being moved, and she's had to wrangle with an architect over new floor plans. At church this Sunday everyone had been asking her about me and about how she was doing, politely not quite saying what was on their minds: Is he coming back? When she went down to the church basement for coffee hour after the service, she walked over to her friend Victoria near the cookie table and asked how she was doing.

"Bad news," Victoria told her. "I've got breast cancer, and they operate Friday."

Cathy is not exactly sure what happened next.

"I remember thinking to myself that I had to try to stand up, and I just couldn't anymore," she says. "A part of me was glad—glad just to let go. It was like I was relieved that there was nothing I could do anymore. And the next thing I knew, Victoria and all of them were bending over me, asking if I was okay. I'd hit my head on the basement floor."

They took her to the emergency room, she says, even though she insisted she was okay. She had never fainted before.

"Everyone was so nice," she says. "Victoria and Daphne took me there and waited while they did all these tests on me, and Victoria insisted that I come home and stay with her family last night. When she had cancer to deal with!"

It is probably stress, the doctors decide. She should take some time off from work.

"Okay, I'm coming home," I say, quickly considering the logistics: Hitch a ride to Wytheville. Rent a car. I can be there by midnight, maybe.

"No," she says. "No, I don't want you doing that. You need to stay out there."

"Look, you were in the hospital. I'm coming home."

"I'm okay now," she murmurs. "I want you to *finish*. I want you to finish and then come back home. I don't want to have gone through all this shit for nothing."

Outside the motel room's door I notice that it's raining again.

25

I'D COME HOME to the magic mountains where Annie Dillard began her Tinker Creek pilgrimage some thirty years earlier, when I was a kid and she was one of many barely apprehended students moving madly through the small college campus where our family lived and my parents taught. The Roanoke Valley landscape that her book made famous—Tinker Creek, Brushy Mountain, Carvin's Creek, Tinker Mountain, McAfee Knob, Dead Man Mountain—was also the backdrop for my childhood. I had belonged there. We lived at the foot of Tinker Mountain, amid the clover lawns and ivy-swaddled colonnades of the college, rarely venturing into the hills. Now, as I walked along the ridges, looking down on the valley, the sun sometimes came out after rain and warmed the path, filling the air with a scent of piney humus, recalling other pine woods I'd known back then, when our family left the campus behind and summered at a cabin near the coast.

Most afternoons during those vacations I'd walk or ride my bike half a mile along a sandy lane to the roadside mailbox, through a still, shadowy pine forest. Several other lanes branched off from ours and disappeared into the gloom under the trees. As I carried the mail back to my parents I used to imagine dark, vine-choked ruins at the end of those lanes. On trees near the intersections, the property owners had nailed up pointer signs: OLIVER, MANCHESTER, JOEL, and over the years the trees grew, skewing the signs until the arrows pointed crazily at sky, or ground, or deep into the deerfly-tormented shadows of the pine-fragrant woods.

Signs, so inescapable in the valleys and plains and cities, mark the Appalachian Trail too, but like the skewed markers I remembered from that piney lane, something there is about the woods that does not love them. Paper disintegrates, wooden signs rot, plastic weathers sun-brittle and shatters, metal rusts. Like the trail itself, signs must be tended to assiduously or the forest soon obscures them.

Mostly, though, the trail is crafted to speak a wordless language that does not require printed instructions, and indeed is written only for those who know how to read it. Most common are the blazes, which employ a conventional vocabulary of color and shape and placement, and mark the trail so thoroughly that you need map and compass only when storms or fog envelop open mountaintops or deep northern snows fill up the woods and bury the marked tree trunks. Blazing used to mean hatcheting trees as you walked, like the hiker on Springer Mountain's bronze plaque. Even now, in a more mindful time, trail maintainers use paint scrapers to smooth patches of bark, on which white blazes are subsequently applied. Scrape too deep, though, or pick a thin-skinned species and such patches gall the tree, wounding or even killing it. Knotty scars often surround old blazes, where a tree has tried to heal over its wound. As paint flakes away and wounded trees become diseased and die off, a trail's blazes can disappear; within a decade little will remain but the forsaken path itself.

Somewhat more permanent are small anodized metal "A.T." diamonds that the original trailblazers nailed along the path in the 1930s and 1940s. But like the signs from my childhood, these became skewed as trees grew, they fell to the ground as nails rusted away, or they were removed during trail relocations. Only a handful remain now, reverently noted in the guidebooks like splinters of the True Cross.

Near road crossings—typically hidden from vandals a few hundred yards up the trail—clubs often plant kiosks and hang mileage signs, indicating the approximate distance to the next shelter or crossing. They carve or burn these signs into planks that weather silver-gray or turn moss-green from humidity. In the South they're afterthoughts, scattered unpredictably through the great national forests, often ignoring obvious landmarks in favor of obscure road or trail crossings. As the trail nears the mid-Atlantic, mileage signs become more common, intrusive, and chatty, like roadside historical markers. In New England, where trails are more rocky and permanent, signage is more regular, but even there the distances are almost always incorrect, since clubs reroute and change the trail while leaving signs alone.

At trailheads, and where private land impinges on federal rights-of-way, plastic or metal signs proliferate. A few are handmade billboards for hostels and pilgrim resorts, but most are government notices that politely request, or blandly announce, or threaten with steely menace: foot travel only, no horses, no ATVs, no hunting, violators subject to federal prosecution. Their tone and color and content vary from one district to another, between Forest Service and Park Service lands, and according to the maintaining club that posts them. Where government easements cut across private lands, landowners as if in answer slap yellow or white POSTED or NO TRESPASSING signs along the corridor boundaries, to keep traipsers passing by and discourage them from venturing off-trail to camp or forage.

Though small signs tend to cluster around trailheads and road crossings, the trail does not advertise itself to passing cars except at a few interstate overpasses. Unless you know to look, you'll pass it by and never notice the path that boots erode, the woods-hooded eye-white stare that's blazed upon a poplar trunk a few steps from the road. Nor is this accidental. Motorist attention isn't welcome. Women on solo thruhikes soon discover that creeps at highway waysides are far more threatening than bears or rock slides, and learn to band together with the day's hiking companions on the way down from the hills. The farther into the hills thruhikers get, the more they depend on maps and landmarks, and the safer they feel: robbers and drunks don't like climbs, and a case of Budweiser generally weighs too much to lug far up a mountain.

For something so massive to be invisible sounds ridiculous, but even in places like the Roanoke Valley, where hundreds of thousands of people live within a few miles of the trail, the sheer bother of mountains turns them into backdrops for the business of getting by in the world; no one looks up at them for more than a few seconds. As a kid, I'd stare for hours out the picture window of our house at the mountains, making up stories about how they came to be there and who lived on them, and why, and wonder what was on top, but by the time I moved back to the valley as an adult, after college, mountains were just part of the scenery. For three years my daily commute led me past a small sign where the trail came down from the ridges and crossed U.S. Route 11; every day I drove past it, remarked on it abstractly, and went on to an office at a newspaper, where my job was to write about more important things: crime, government, notable people, deaths, the price of real estate.

I knew the trail near Roanoke well. Two years earlier, I'd come there for my first serious overnight hike. I'd rented the backpack and borrowed the sleeping bag, heavy four-person dome tent, and rain jacket from my brother's canoe gear; I'd bought the hiking boots eight years earlier for dayhikes during our honeymoon trip to England. I arrived at Route 311 near Catawba to find the remnants of a tropical depression rolling in over the Virginia mountains. Thirty-six hours later and twenty miles farther north I came stumbling off the ridge, soaked to the bone, chafed fiery red where my rough canvas shorts sandpapered across my scrotum and the inside of my thighs, toenails blackening where they'd jammed up against the front of boots that didn't fit properly. I was miserable, and completely exhausted by the ordeal of trying to will an overweight, sedentary body over a couple of 1,000-foot climbs and a rocky ridgeline walk. The plastic trash bag I'd used to cover my pack had leaked during the hike, which left everything I carried soggy and weighing twice as much as normal. That night, in an old shelter, mice invaded the pack's top pocket, shredding the roll of toilet paper I'd brought, then neatly moving the shreds "downstairs" to the pack's main compartment, where they built a nest I had to shake out (along with the mice) in the morning. My inadequate sleeping pad left me with hips bruised from the hard wooden floor, on which I'd tossed, listening to rodents scurry and rain pour down. Dinner had been cold sardines, cheese, and Triscuit crackers.

Cathy had been relieved to see me after that first hike, glad I'd gotten the craziness out of my system. And for a month or two I'd thought I actually had. But I kept thinking back to it, especially that moment on the second day when the clouds lifted, the September sun broke through, and the scent of piney humus rose from the forest floor around me as I stumbled along the ridge. It was so beautiful, and I was dying. Suddenly nothing I did down below counted anymore. What mattered was the *now*: getting down from that damned beautiful hill, getting into some dry clothes, getting something cold to drink and something hot to eat, and some hydrocortisone for the rash.

This time, instead of walking *over* mountains that conspired against me to pull me back, I had come to lose myself and hide out, drifting *through* them like ragged clouds after a rain. Now the cold overcast of the Sheep Rains was giving way to the sweat and bugs of summer. Below me, in the valley, that place where I grew up looked impossibly distant.

26

White Blaze—Day 85
Wednesday, June 25, 1997 • Maupin Field Shelter • Virginia
Blue Ridge Mountains • 815 miles hiked • 1,345 miles to go
Sunny • Low 65, high 89
Elevation 2,720 feet

AT FIRST IT SOUNDS LIKE A CICADA, buzzing in the heavy summer air, only fierce and harsh. But as we walk up the gravel lane we see the timber rattlesnake curled there, shifting its coil in order to keep an eye on us, the buzzing insistent as we gather around. Don't tread on me! It is about four feet long, with mottled black-and-umber markings.

We are at the pilgrim resort I call Never-Never Land, where a handful of us have spent a day off the trail lounging on threadbare couches, reading, and slapping no-see-ums. Among the thruhikers is Rock-Dancer, he of the precise handwriting and the burned Bible. In fact, he's the one who's discovered the snake. He laughs nervously and takes a photo as we gather around it. He came upon it as he was leaving. When the snake coiled up in the lane and started rattling, he wasn't sure whether he could safely skirt it, so he retreated and went to get the rest of us. "Want to see a rattlesnake?" he'd asked, poking his head in the door of the porch.

Behind us, stumping up the driveway carrying a plastic tub and a broom, comes the Philosopher King, the gruff old despot who rules Never-Never Land. He's sixtyish, in denim overalls, and looks something like Tom Clancy with a reddish-gray Mohawk haircut.

"Never seen a rattler down here before," he says. He bends down with the tub and busily sweeps the snake into it. It strikes twice at the broomstick, the click of contact faintly audible.

Once it's safely inside, he leads the handful of hikers back down the driveway toward his cabin, carrying the snake in the tub. No, ain't going to kill it, he says. Going to release it a few miles away. As he walks it shifts and writhes in the tub, trapped and furious, the sound of its buzzing accompanying our little procession like maracas.

Never-Never Land hides behind a nondescript metal gate along the Blue Ridge Parkway, a couple of miles from the trail. At first, as you pick your way past the gate and walk down the narrow double-track lane, you might wonder if you've come to the right place. But once out of sight of the parkway you round a curve and you see the first sign. Then another. Like Burma-Shave ads from the 1950s, they flank the lane and provide a running commentary as you descend. Each announces itself in a different typeface and color. Some describe prohibitions and conditions (no computers, cell phones, electronics, newspaper reporters, dogs), and some are wisecracks ("Those found here after dark will be found here in the morning"). The tree-shadowed lane opens out to reveal a ramshackle grouping of sheds, cabins, and huts on the brow of a grassy hillside overlooking idle farmland. On the far side, half a mile distant and several hundred feet above the hollow, the parkway describes a wide bend around a mountain shoulder and the sound of squealing tires sometimes filters down. Some of the structures are old farm buildings; others are haphazardly nailed together out of vinyl, weathered planks, and aluminum. No electricity, phones, or running water link them to the modern world. The main building, fronted by a long glassed-in porch, bears a dozen or so signs. To the right lies a slab of concrete with two basketball backboards. Next to it stands an elaborate privy, raised like a sentry box five or six feet above ground level; a sign says that if you have to pee, you should use the fire hydrants beyond the basketball court, *not* the privy, which is for night soil only. The hydrants are pure whimsy, not otherwise functional, as the only running water is the creek at the bottom of the hollow. One shed contains a Volkswagen's half-dissected corpse. Near the main cabin stands a chicken coop, where hens scratch, roosters crow incessantly, and a sheepdog peers out from a doghouse beneath the coop as we approach. Beyond the coop stands a tree-shaded springhouse.

It looks like the ideal hiker hangout, and indeed it's been a legendary stop along the trail for years: bunks enough for several score of hikers, a wood-fired hot tub and sauna, a horseshoe pit, a spring-fed bathtub (cold and colder running water), shelves of paperbacks to read, a trap and clay pigeons, and a long tradition of hijinks and revelry. It operates on hiker donations and has an active alumni network. But unspoken rules (none of them on signs) govern the place. If the Philosopher King likes your company, or trusts you, the hospitality light switches on and the rules relax; if he doesn't, you are on your own and he watches with a wary eye. If you are using Never-Never Land as a shelter and leaving the next day, don't expect much acknowledgment. If, on the other hand, you choose to stay awhile, pitch in on chores, and enter into the spirit of the place, well, you never know what might happen.

Two of my old colleagues from Loon's Tribe, Dancing Bear and Icebox, have arrived a day ahead of me and are waiting here for friends. They started hiking together again a few hundred miles north of Damascus and are considering partnering up for the remainder of the trail. At dusk the day before, we'd sprawled around the living room by lamplight with two or three others, listening to the King's stories. Once you drew him out he had a wealth of them, which he told in a blunt, profane, sometimes hilarious deadpan; we repeated stories of our own, consumed sloppy joes that miraculously appeared from the propane stove and iron skillets of the kitchen, argued, laughed, and snacked on junk food. As darkness deepened around the hills, the King got up and announced that he was firing up the hot tub. An hour later half a dozen of us were out there, naked in the chill air of evening, laughing and splashing and joking like Walt Whitman's twenty-eight young men, and all so friendly.

But the longer I stayed there, the more I could only imagine what Never-Never Land was like when the first few classes of thruhikers discovered it in the early 1980s, when both they and the Philosopher King were making up the legend: lasting friendships, vivid moments, no signs, no traditions, no unspoken rules, nothing of the institution about it. That's what it was now, though—a kind of anti-institutional institution, a "don't miss" resort on the Pilgrims' Way where, despite the King's best efforts at keeping things unpredictable, much of the spontaneity had been stripped away as rules proliferated and hikers came to take it for granted. It had started to run on memories. Drunken hikers had forced the King to ban alcohol the year before. If you asked for a ride to nearby Waynesboro for groceries, he scowled at you and refused. What had once been there for the hikers was now there mostly for him. As long as the hikers kept it interesting, they were welcome, but this was his show, not an eleemosynary institution. It was like the place in the movie *Pinocchio* where all the bad little boys run off to when they skip school—an amusement park where they can eat whatever they want, and there are no rules, and all sorts of games to play, and in the end they turn into donkeys.

The Philosopher King drives off with the rattler in his van, and a few minutes later I follow RockDancer back up the lane to the parkway and the two miles back to the trail. Perhaps I will ask him about that burned Bible.

By now I've become used to the way thruhikers appear, disappear, and reappear. Dancing Bear, Icebox, Kilgore Trout, RockDancer—I'll leave behind those who are hurt, or ready for fun in town. I'll hike for a stretch, take a day or two off the trail myself, and then one or two of them will surprise me in the next town, or sign the shelter registers a day ahead of me. Then I'll follow, reading their register notes, until the next town or hostel stop, when I'll catch up and appear triumphantly, or hike by without stopping and leave them behind again.

This has been going on since the night I learned that Cathy had fainted. Minutes after we hung up, the sad eyes and gnomish smile of Kilgore Trout peered in from the open door of the motel room, and he offered to split the cost of the double with me. For two weeks the two of us kept about the same schedule, sometimes hiking together, sometimes a day or so apart, crossing the Great Valley of Virginia to the ramparts of the Allegheny Plateau, where the trail touches it north of Pearisburg, then turning back east across the valley again toward the Blue Ridge at Roanoke. Summer has come on with a rush. Suddenly wildflowers are all around—or maybe I just notice them more as the rains abate. Lavender rhododendron blooms cover the mountainsides near the ridgeline, sometimes offset by patches of white-and-pink mountain laurel lower down, or orange flame azaleas that fill the air with the scent of bubblegum. Now that the overstory has filled in, tiny white bloodroot petals litter the path, grasshoppers have consumed the toadshade trillium, squawroot clusters have browned and crumbled, ramps have yellowed and shriveled away. Succulents like nettles and jewelweed take their place under the trees, and bright shade-loving solitaries take root near fallen logs or around rocks: pink lady's slipper, cardinal flower, spring beauty, bird's-foot violet, jack-in-the-pulpit. Wet dells of Virginia bluebell, patches of wild columbine, and lawns of Allegheny foamflower abound. Bumblebees make beds of white-fringed phacelia buzz and stir like magic carpets. Whole hillsides are overspread by the broad, helicopterlike leaves of mayapple, or the round, shining rusty disks of galax. Brilliant bits of color peek through green groundcover: purple dwarf iris, fire pink, or oxeye daisies nodding at the edge of clearings.

For all that, I'm starting to wonder: Will I ever find my way out of Virginia? Already I've spent almost a month here and over three hundred miles teetering along ridgeline after rocky ridgeline. I expected it to feel like coming home, but the hiking feels monotonous, and a strange numbness has come over me: I've seen all this before. Some 150 more miles remain before I reach the Potomac River at Harpers Ferry. I'll never find my way out. I am leaving the deep forest, too. North of Roanoke, the trail closely parallels and often crosses the Blue Ridge Parkway, a narrow strip of national parkland running along the ridgetop above populous valleys. I leave Kilgore Trout behind in Roanoke, where a woman he knows from New Hampshire is flying down to meet him. Cathy has visited a few more times, and will meet me in Harpers Ferry in a couple of weeks, but with each week of hiking adding another hour or more to her drive, Harpers Ferry, a good seven hours from home, is about the outside range of weekend dates. We'll get together there one last time, we agree. After that, I'll be on my own, heading north.

I catch RockDancer about an hour north of Never-Never Land, and we fall into step together, talking as we hike to keep our minds off the bugs and the sweat of midsummer. This is a novelty for both of us. Until now, we've done most of our hiking solo. But it is pleasant, for a change, to carry on a running conversation as we pick our way across rock fields and around hillsides overgrown by kudzu vine. He is a small man—quiet, ruminating, ready to laugh but holding something back. I keep trying to reconcile this side of him to the side that burned the Bible. He says he's come to the trail from Boston at age forty-four, after a stint running computer systems—the last of a series of scientific or high-tech jobs he's held. Periodically, he explains, he gets restless and goes off adventuring.

"You got your *Data Book* back, didn't you?" I say. "After I got ahead of you in Pearisburg I left it in a shelter with a note for you."

He chuckles hesitantly when he discovers that I know about the incident with the Bible, both embarrassed and pleased that his scandalousness had been discovered.

"What can I say?" he says, shaking his head. "A truly horrible day. I didn't think it might hurt the feelings of other hikers. I was completely focused on whoever had been leaving the Bibles. The next night I found that a couple of others had been really upset and I felt pretty bad. I hope you were okay about it."

Afternoon has begun to give way to evening as we pound down the steep trail from Humpback Rocks, a scenic outcropping two miles from the next shelter. We didn't leave Never-Never Land until late morning, and now it looks like we'll be cooking dinner in the twilight by the time we reach shelter. Below the outcropping, where the Blue Ridge Parkway swings close to the ridgeline, we have to cross an extensive picnic area and visitors center. Through this section the trail sometimes crosses the parkway several times in a day, and is occasionally within earshot of traffic. For day-trippers, it means they can park their station wagons or RVs, set up a picnic lunch or a cookout, and walk a couple of miles along the Appalachian Trail. For thruhikers, used to long isolated stretches subsisting on peanut butter and noodles, it means "trail magic" and a chance to "yogi" like mad.

Trail magic usually means free food, though sometimes it simply refers to genuine kindness from people with a soft spot in their hearts for hikers. *Yogi-ing* is a thruhiker technique for provisioning without actually carrying food, as pioneered by Yogi the Bear—cleverly (and without quite begging) inspiring nonhikers to donate food. Certain thruhikers make an art of yogi-ing, perfecting a look and attitude that convey just the right combination of exhaustion, hunger, polite desperation, and harmless goodwill. When that fails, they sometimes resort to more shameless tactics, such as asking to buy food from picnickers, knowing full well that no decent picnicker would try to sell food to a starving traveler. They make a point of taking extended breaks at road crossings or picnic areas, where unsuspecting day-trippers are likely to see them and become curious. After that it's usually just a matter of smiling and conversing until cornucopian picnic baskets open and let forth their bounty.

RockDancer and I don't set out to yogi the two families grilling burgers and hot dogs in the picnic area; it just works out that way. The trail runs right past their picnic table, and RockDancer, walking a few yards ahead of me, pauses to refill his water bottle at a spigot. One of the men in the picnic party asks him where he's headed. "Maine," he says nonchalantly, surrendering to the inevitability of what comes next. The other man, the two women, and two of the children crowd near.

"What do you eat?" one of the women asks. We explain how we resupply in towns and carry trail food in between, how we try not to carry fresh fruits, vegetables, and meats that will spoil or that will weigh down our packs. Tonight, I say, I'll be having Lipton Noodles & Sauce, prepared with Squeeze Parkay and canned chicken mixed in, and Cajun spice sprinkled on top.

"We've cooked extra burgers tonight," she says. "Would you like some?"

They shouldn't have to ask twice, but for some reason I still have it in my mind that we must hurry on to the shelter before dark so we'll have time to cook before the bugs get too bad. "Thanks anyway," I say, and start making noises about needing to get moving up the trail.

"Are you sure?" one of the men says. "We've got plenty." RockDancer catches my eye and I realize what I'm doing.

"Well, okay," I say. "That's really nice of you."

We pay for our burgers and slaw and hot dogs and soda with the story of life on the trail: of mice and men and women, of bears and rattlers and other hazards, of walking through hot and cold weather, of boots, clothes, hiker hostels, trail towns, people we've met, of the high mountains, the hard climbs, of the where we are going and the when we are getting there. We explain about quitting jobs and leaving friends and family behind. Our currency is the humdrum business of walking we've gotten used to after nearly three months, suddenly precious when seen through eyes to which it isn't humdrum at all, but rather the sort of grand adventure one reads about—a story to live by. And really, as we tell our stories, and they become strange and wonderful to us again through the telling, the pickles and relish and potato salad are only a fringe benefit; the true payment is this audience through which we glimpse ourselves, if only for a moment, as we would like to be.

"When you hesitated after they offered food," RockDancer says later, as we waddle down to the shelter in the gathering dusk, "I thought I was going to have to strangle you."

27

THE BOTTOM LINKS of the trail's great Chain of Being belonged to the germs and animacula inhabiting the dust thruhikers breathed, the waters they drank, and the unrefrigerated food they ate. Here dwelt winter colds that got passed between friends, mystery pathogens such as the Damascus stomach bug, and more insidious atomies such as hantavirus, which could kill. Most notorious were the Lyme disease bacterium, carried by deer ticks, and the *Giardia lamblia* protozoan, a waterborne creepy-crawly responsible for the dreaded "beaver fever" that manifested itself in an advanced and persistent case of the shits. Curing either required doctors and strong drugs.

Already one hiker I knew, Barkeater, had gone off the trail after developing the telltale bull's-eye rash of Lyme disease. I'd heard of several cases of giardiasis, but no one I knew had succumbed yet, even though a few like RockDancer disdained filtering their water or treating it chemically, relying instead on boiling and a discerning nose. Though I used a filter, something had gotten to my guts north of Roanoke, forcing me off the trail for two days at a commercial campground. I spent them perspiring on my inflatable mattress while a sluggish breeze breathed through the mesh walls of my tent, where I'd retreated in order to escape swarming gnats and mosquitoes. My head throbbed. I had a low-grade fever, chills, and a wicked case of diarrhea that kept me hurrying back and forth between the tent, the men's room, and the soda machine. For two afternoons tractor-trailers howled and grumbled along the highway to Lynchburg, waking me up every time I started to doze. By the third day, though, I felt well enough to start hiking again, so apparently it wasn't giardiasis.

Farther up the chain of being, the arrival of summer meant that insects were our constant companions. Most annoying was the hovering cloud of eye-gnats dogfighting around my face as I walked, and it wasn't until a 2,000-miler taught me to dab 200-proof deet under the brim of my cap and pull it low over my eyes that I discouraged them. Otherwise, deet wasn't much good during the day, as it was quickly sweated off. Walking provided some protection from slow fliers like mosquitoes, but it only gave deerflies and horseflies the chance for boeuf on the hoof. Sometimes I must have looked like a nightclub dancer doing the Vogue, waving my arms around my head to knock them away or batter them senseless against my temples. One of the repeated satisfactions of fly-swarmed afternoons was finally crushing a persistent horsefly, dropping the carcass on the forest floor, and watching ants bear it away.

One kind of large, carnivorous fly I called the F-117 Stealth Biter. Unlike its cousins, it preferred hunting at dusk, and had perfected the art of a silent approach. When it succeeded in landing without my noticing, it would raise huge bleeding welts on my legs. My other nemeses were no-see-ums, the nearly invisible punkies that plagued open shelters on still summer nights when it was too clammy to retreat into a sleeping bag. Along with mosquitoes, they were the best argument for tenting. Next on my hate list, after the no-see-ums, were the small black biting flies I called "toe-see-ums," as they had a nasty habit of waiting until I'd taken my boots off at the end of the day and prospecting down into the sweaty soft area between my toes, where they would drill bloody pinprick-sized wounds.

Not all insects had a taste for hiker, of course. Along the high ridges south of the Shenandoah National Park I walked through groves of trees under attack from gypsy moth caterpillars. They would strip leaves from whole sections of forests. On a sunny day it sometimes sounded like it was raining in the forest as the sandlike shit of millions upon millions of tiny green worms dropped all around me. They dangled down on gossamer from the trees over the path by the hundreds, and as I walked I'd use my hiking sticks to scythe through them. The Rhymin' Worm composed a much-acclaimed stanza about this experience:

O Gypsy Moth, on silken thread,
Deep in the forest lush,
If you get in my face again
I'll turn you into mush.

Along with the whine of mosquitoes, warm weather filled low-lying woodlands with the grunting bellows of bullfrogs at dusk, and the creaks and teletype-like clacking of peepers and tree frogs late into the night. During the day, lizards and skinks rustled in the undergrowth along the trail, racing up trees or along downed trunks as I came near. This could be unnerving in snaky places, but I'd reassure myself that most snakes were harmless. When I reached central Virginia, though, every week or two I'd come across a timber rattler, after which the expression "rattled" took on more precise meaning for me.

The arrival of snake season in the mountains meant a noticeable dip in the ground-dwelling rodent population, which had been booming ever since the last subfreezing nights of the southern mountains. In the great national forests of Georgia, North Carolina, and southwestern Virginia, the ardent alarms of chipmunks were as common as birdcalls, and every hundred yards or so one would rustle across the trail in panic toward its burrow. Gray squirrels were more rare; they looked like the same greedy tree rats that raid suburban window feeders, but a gray squirrel in the wild is a completely different beast—wary, graceful, and silent. If you've ever seen a suburban squirrel frantically juke and stutterstep in front of an approaching car, only to run under its tires, you might wonder about the theory of natural selection. But watch a wild squirrel flee deep in the woods, and it becomes clear: this is where it belongs, where those frantic changes of direction become graceful flowing evasions along the fractal geometries of tree branches.

Probably the most dangerous wild animal on the Appalachian Trail was the "shelter mouse," which had the unfortunate habit of carrying nasty diseases like hantavirus. No outbreaks had been reported among trail hikers, but every shelter had its residents, and each night as I listened to them scamper along the rafters I tried not to think of potential disease vectors. Pitching a tent away from heavily trafficked areas helped some but was no sure protection, as mice sometimes gnawed through the nylon and invaded. They were at their worst in the shelters, though, protected from predators and close to a ready supply of food. While most thruhikers didn't worry about bears or snakes, every evening they went to great lengths protecting themselves and their gear against mice. The little bastards would chew through the most expensive "bomb-proof" Cordura nylon backpack pocket to investigate anything that smelled like peanut butter. Tiny tooth holes appeared in my tent one night after I'd left a candy bar wrapper inside it, even though I'd rolled the tent up in its stuff sack and left it lying inches from me in the shelter. Another mouse chewed through the accessory pouch to my pack, where I kept my snacks during the day, when I hung it overnight too close to a wall. You couldn't fight it: the only way to keep your backpack intact was to remove your food sack each night, along with all your garbage, and open up all the pockets and zippers so that mice could investigate the pockets without tearing holes in them.

Then you had to hang your food. Shelters were invariably decorated by several makeshift contraptions for this purpose—empty metal cans, inverted, each with a hole punched through its bottom and hung by a string like a bell. But instead of a clapper, what dangled beneath the open mouth of the can was another short length of string from which was suspended a twig, like a miniature trapeze, around which the cords of food bags could be secured. I sometimes pictured a particularly bold mouse swinging from one trapeze to another, like a circus acrobat. Mice performed amazing stunts anyway, running upside down along shelter rafters and down thin cords to the food bags dangling below. In theory, our acrobat would arrive at the inverted can and discover that his claws couldn't grip the metal, realize that he'd fall off as soon as his weight was committed, and, frustrated by human ingenuity, would retreat chastened, or exact his revenge by scampering over the heads of sleeping thruhikers, causing them to wake up and curse in the middle of the night. In practice, mouse trapezes worked most of the time, but in some shelters the mice had wised up and learned to wait until after dark, when they'd fling themselves through the air from the rafters with the greatest of ease, either snagging the bags on the way down or thumping to the floor only to climb back up and try again. Unless a hiker heard the noise and woke up to evict them, they eventually succeeded and helped themselves to whatever wasn't sealed in metal or glass.

One shelter north of Pearisburg had acquired its own resident mousetrap, a ginger tomcat that thruhikers named Yogi. The register was full of stories about Yogi, who generally showed up an hour before sunset and wandered around begging food. I had never seen a cat eat an M&M, but reportedly Yogi had acquired the taste. Late that night I woke up thirsty and fumbled around by my sleeping bag for a water bottle. Failing to find it, I switched on my headlight. In the periphery of my vision I saw glowing eyes, and I whipped around to shine my light at Yogi the cat, sphinxlike and unblinking, staring at us from the picnic table in front of the shelter. The mice lay low.

As we moved from the wilderness to the more populous and frequented woodlands of the Blue Ridge Parkway and the Shenandoah National Park, larger forest animals became more evident. Here for the first time I saw foxes slink across the trail and glimpsed a bobcat, head held high as it paraded across a creek bed with a rabbit dangling in its mouth. Near campgrounds in the Shenandoah National Park, for the first time deer came close, unafraid. I'd heard them startle and whistle in the southern forests, and had seen hoofprints, but now in ones and pairs they stared blankly at us from behind trees, sometimes bolting nervously a few feet and pausing again to stare, close enough for us to see the ticks bloating on their shoulders and snouts. With the approach of evening, they moved slowly up from the forest toward the parking areas, where campers sometimes fed them illegally. At one wayside parking lot, near a snack bar, a doe begged food, tottering from car window to car window like a streetwalker.

I didn't see any more bears, but I saw bear scat, and all the trash cans had been "bear-proofed" with heavy metal tops to discourage garbage foraging. The guidebooks said that Shenandoah National Park averaged one bear for every square mile within its boundaries, one of the densest black bear populations in the United States. In the wildest parts of the great southern forests, the day was rare and memorable when hikers saw bear, or surprised deer coming over a rise—and for good reason: hunting season. They were wild there, and on their guard. But here in the Shenandoah, which spread out for miles on either side of Skyline Drive, park rangers kept hunters out, and visitors could not be prevented from feeding the animals; deer and bear could kick back, relax, and let the creatures closest to the top of the Great Chain congratulate themselves on having preserved this wilderness as they drove through in their sport-utility vehicles.

28

White Blaze—Day 90
Monday, June 30, 1997 • Shenandoah National Park • Virginia
Blue Ridge Mountains • 843 miles hiked • 1,317 miles to go
Sunny • Low 58, high 76
Elevation 2,250 feet

A NEW CROWD of hikers has begun overtaking me: Tonic, Mossman, Trail Snail, Mr. Clean, Pushcart, Wildflower, Fiddlehead, the Hiking Viking, and others. Everyone's pushing to reach Front Royal, at the Shenandoah's northern boundary, by July Fourth; many of them plan to get a ride from there to Washington, for Independence Day fireworks and a much-rumored "Hempfest" planned somewhere around the Capitol Mall. It means averaging about twenty miles a day. Even over the racetrack paths of the park, that's a lot of hiking.

When a large group of thruhikers bands together, a strange dynamic develops that a hiker I met later called "catch-up-and-keep-up." The pace most comfortable for a group's fastest, most impatient members tends to become the pace for the whole group, until at last the slower hikers give up. "I feel like Big Miles today," someone says. "Come on, you can do it! Catch up to us at Loft Mountain." And off they go, pounding twenty miles down the trail, free and happy, leaving others to follow as they can. Weaker or older hikers determined to keep up must start early or finish late, or else take shortcuts. After eight hundred miles, we're all in terrific aerobic shape; on any given day, any of us can hike all day and into the night. Keeping such a pace up day after day is another matter, though. Younger bodies recover more quickly, stronger muscles have more reserves, and constantly playing catch-up wears on the soul.

My friend Kilgore Trout should have learned his lesson in North Carolina, when he'd hiked a twenty-mile day to catch a companion; the next morning, stiff from the exertion, he'd slipped on a loose rock and rolled his ankle, nearly breaking it. The injury had slowed him down until he reached the hostel in Tennessee, where he'd taken nine days off the trail to recuperate. Now he's bought new boots and has joined a group of exuberant younger hikers whose company clearly delights him. Soon his feet start sweating in the new boots, though, exacerbating a bad fit, and by the end of the first twenty-mile day he's worn big blisters on the bottoms of his feet. The next morning he asks Tonic, a young woman with emergency medical technician certification, to puncture the blisters for him surgically and then help him bandage his feet. He is going to keep up if it kills him.

"Mr. Worm," he says, grimacing, as I walk up while he's bandaging the feet.

"Mr. Trout," I reply. Ever since we shared the room in Bland, just after I learned about Cathy's fainting spell, we have ritually greeted each other this way. That night, as the Sheep Rains came down outside the motel room, I'd unburdened myself to him. He'd listened to me talk about having walked out on her, how it kept holding me back and tearing at me as I walked, how I just wanted to hide out in the mountains. He'd nodded like he knew what I was talking about.

Was he married? I'd asked. He had been. His wife had died the previous fall, after an illness. He'd dreamed of hiking the trail ever since he'd discovered it as a kid, but while his wife had been alive she hadn't been well enough for such things: she'd undergone lots of back surgery and had no feeling in parts of her legs, so hiking with her was out of the question. The idea of a thruhike was relegated to "someday," if he could ever find the time. Of course he never did, and before long he was in his mid-forties. Then she died, and he ran across a book about thruhiking that brought the old dream back. He was forty-five, he was lonely, it was way past time to change jobs, he had no debts and plenty of money. Why not? Around Christmas, about the same time as me, he'd decided to thruhike.

Later that evening, he'd called home to New Hampshire. "Your kids?" I'd asked.

"No kids," he said. "My neighbor . . . well . . . my girlfriend. Girlfriend: now that's a concept that's *way* too strange for words." He chuckled. "I have a date. This is crazy, I know. But she's flying down here from New Hampshire, and we're going to spend the weekend in Roanoke. The only thing is, she doesn't drive, so when we get near Roanoke I have to find some way to get to the airport and rent a car."

We'd hiked more or less on the same schedule for two weeks after that, though we'd rarely walked together. Keeping pace with another hiker requires conscious effort. Kilgore Trout liked to hike with headphones on, in rhythm with the music, listening to local radio stations. Every hour or so one of us would rest or admire a view, and the other would catch up, and stop for a minute to chat and compare notes. On the last day before he went off the trail at Roanoke, we surprised a wild hen turkey as we started up a shale-shingled hillside. It bounced up from the scrub and started to run, but instead of exploding into flight, as turkeys usually do, it began weaving around strangely, moving erratically up the trail.

"Will you look at that!" Kilgore Trout had said, pointing downhill, where the hen had come from. Five poults, tiny dappled fuzzballs, trooped in the opposite direction while the hen did her best to draw us away.

Now Mr. Trout is in pain again, the boots turning his feet into raw meat, but he churns out twenty-mile days with the rest of us. He's keeping up.

RockDancer is keeping up too, but it wears on him. Part of that may simply be his haircut: in Waynesboro he shaved his beard and buzzed his head military-style, and with his glasses he looks frail and Gandhi-like.

From casual references and hints, he's let me know he is gay. Did other people on the trail know he was out? Some of them, he said. He didn't make a point of announcing it. If it felt important, he mentioned it. If not, he didn't. It made for some awkward moments when young male hikers started boasting about their exploits with women, but while there weren't many other gay men on the beaten path, he'd found that most thruhikers accepted him readily enough after they knew. Still, he said with a laugh, it was hard finding gay bars in most towns.

"I was thinking, as we hiked yesterday," he'd said, the day after we left Never-Never land, "that when I'm hiking with someone it really helps me motivate myself to push onward. This next stretch, through Maryland and Pennsylvania and New Jersey and New York, is going to be tough in the middle of summer. Maybe it would be good if we partnered up."

"Interesting idea," I'd said, not sure what to think. At various points I'd thought about suggesting the same thing to Bigfoot, or Kilgore Trout. But I hadn't considered RockDancer. Frankly, the prospect of formally partnering with a gay man made me a little uneasy. I didn't want to rule it out, because I enjoyed hiking and talking with him, but I wanted to think about it. "Maybe a group of three or four of us who keep about the same pace should get together," I'd suggested. "I think Kilgore Trout is probably only a day or so back, and I think Jiggs is a little ahead of us. We could be the 'Over Forty Crew,' or something."

It felt like a pretty lame evasion. But now RockDancer's with the rest of us, pounding out twenty-mile days through the Shenandoah, keeping up.

He's been fastidious about hiking past every white blaze, walking every foot of the trail. Many of the others have begun to blue-blaze past steep or boring sections. And in the Shenandoah, there is a blue blaze that no one can miss: Skyline Drive itself—rock-free, gently graded, posted with a low speed limit that makes the passing cars less fearsome, with the added bonus of superb overlooks every mile or so. RockDancer leaves camp alone in the morning, retracing his steps to the point where he's left the trail; the rest of us amble down to Skyline Drive for breakfast at the Loft Mountain Wayside grill, then blue-blaze up the highway to the next trail crossing, a mile north along Skyline Drive.

After two days of this, RockDancer falls off the pace, slowing down after a long blistery hike in the rain while the rest of us hurry northward on a twenty-three-mile slackpack. Kilgore Trout and I are still aiming to keep up, but daylight starts to slip away on us. One day we take a wrong turn, climbing a quarter of a mile up to an overlook only to discover that the path dead-ends and there are no white blazes. As dusk nears, we run along the stony trail as it chevrons down the mountain to the gap, cursing our mistake and retracing our steps. Crows circle around the rocky overlook we've just left, and one of them starts laughing at us: HAW . . . HAW . . . HAWWW . . . HAW!

"I think I need a vacation from my vacation," Kilgore Trout says the next evening as he doctors his feet. We agree that we'll split a motel room in Front Royal on July 4. But he hikes out early that morning, and when I reach Front Royal that afternoon, another hiker tells me that Mr. Trout has caught a ride to Washington. After that, the hiker says, he may go off the trail, heading home to New Hampshire. For good? I ask. The hiker doesn't know. The others? They've all scattered. For all my catch-up, I haven't kept up.

It is almost two months since I entered Virginia, and I still have fifty miles to go before I escape.

29

WHEN I CAUGHT MYSELF STARTING the same page of *Democratic Vistas* for a fourth time, I gave up, put *The Portable Walt Whitman* away, and tried to keep from falling asleep on the bench in the morning sun. A faint breeze came up from the Potomac, blew past me, then across the Mall near the reflecting pool in front of the Capitol Building. Mid-July heat hadn't set in for the day yet in Washington, but I could feel it coming. A jogger crunched toward me up the gravel from the direction of the Washington Monument, scattering the pigeons near my bench, and he glanced incuriously at my backpack for a moment before pushing on around the loop for a last half mile before work. The pigeons returned, prospecting through the pebbles along the walk.

The ride in that morning was dreamlike as I drifted in the air-conditioned silence of a commuter train coach through the Maryland suburbs northwest of Washington. The day before I'd been sweating on a mountain ridgeline, as usual, descending through old Civil War earthworks and the heat of midafternoon to a bridge across the stairstepped rapids of the Shenandoah River and arrive at the tiny, museumlike town of Harpers Ferry, West Virginia. I'd spent a night, awakened early that morning, and caught the six o'clock train in. An hour later I was buying a sticky bun at Au Bon Pain in Union Station, drinking a cup of Colombian supremo with cream and sugar, and watching thousands of shoppers and travelers pass by. I could have been a million miles from the trail.

Most of the people in the station around me were overweight, like I'd been before the hike—fat jiggling around their hips or on their bellies, rippling under their arms, rubbing between their legs, swelling their necks and jaws and jowls. Four of every five carried the soft, mobile integument that came from too much time behind the wheel and in front of the TV.

The trail had changed us physically. By now younger male thruhikers had taken on the ropy, knotty musculature of cyclists and distance runners, but with great spadelike calf muscles. Most older men had become thin and bony. Midlifers, like me, though still a little thick around the middle, had lean, muscular legs. Most of the older women had dropped off the trail by now or turned to section hiking; younger female thruhikers, much to their dismay, typically hadn't lost much weight but had gained muscle under their body fat, which gave their skin a kind of firmness and glow like a ripe apricot. I'd lost forty pounds, and my size 44 pants hung so loose around my waist they had to be gathered by a strap.

After three months of hiking, the smells were foreign too: cologne and perfume, the waft of soap and shampoo, cigarette reek, the detergent tang of freshly laundered cotton. We'd become almost inured to our own stink. All our clothes, even after washing, carried a lingering stench of dried sweat and wood smoke, polyester fibers chemically bonding to the oils of daily exertion.

Most of all, though, our conversation had changed: everything revolved around the trail, and gear, and who was where, and getting to Maine. Sometimes, as I shared a shelter with weekend hikers or passed sightseers at an overlook, I'd listen to what they talked about: computers, the bull market, mutual funds, real estate as a long-term investment, the president's economic policies, sluggishness in the Asian markets, emerging growth and high-technology funds. I hadn't picked up a newspaper since April. Out on the beaten path we were no longer a part of the world that showered every morning, put on fresh clothes, and took in the financial news. When we'd first started, we'd transcended that world, devoting our lives to some superior virtue, far above the sedentary, TV-watching world of dayhikers and sightseers. After three months of pilgrimage, though, we were no closer to enlightenment than when we started. And, with a shock, we came to realize that to the rest of the world we weren't much more than curiosities, or we simply didn't exist. We didn't matter.

"There were so fucking many people," a Canadian thruhiker named Goose had said to me two days earlier. He'd yellow-blazed up to Harpers

Ferry and from there to Washington for the Fourth of July festivities. Some weeks earlier I'd hiked north with him and his friend Wishbone for a couple of days. Goose was, hands down, the foulest-mouthed thruhiker I'd met, and his main aim in Washington was getting drunk and stoned at the hemp rally. As a Canadian, he'd also been fascinated by the crowds and the celebration.

"We never did find fucking Hempfest on the Fourth!" He laughed. "But it was all pretty interesting. And I got laid that night. Crazy! The day after, I went sightseeing and then came back to Harpers Ferry and started hiking south, doing the section I skipped. Wishbone was broke and headed home to Orlando. He's off the trail. It was one hell of a crazy few days. There were so fucking many people there that night you couldn't find anybody."

So fucking many people.

I imagined the Mall sweltering and crowded, the fireworks pinwheeling beyond the obelisk, the bursts of sound rolling muted up Pierre L'Enfant's vast open avenues moments after the flash, the smoke from shellbursts lighting up like great drifting palm trees behind the pinwheels. Today no throngs filled the expanses, only small crowds huddling near the museums and milling along the tree-shaded sidewalks, and a few families crossing from one row of museums and galleries to another. Walk signals shrilled from traffic lights in the direction of the Carillon, and for no reason the pigeons near me startled up into the air, forming a single undulating shoal as they swung off toward the East Wing of the National Gallery. A helicopter passed beyond the Washington Monument in the direction of the White House. I thought of all the hikers I'd met over the first three months, all of the pilgrim faces on Polaroid photos in the official trail album back at the Appalachian Trail Conference's office in Harpers Ferry—in the four hundreds by the time I stopped by to register. Probably more people were here on the empty Mall on a sluggish July morning than I'd seen during all of the last three months.

I tried to imagine what Cathy's Fourth of July had been like, seven hours away. We'd talked about it the last time we met, when she drove up for a weekend before I entered Shenandoah Park and took me off the trail for a day. Her community band was preparing for its final concert of the season later that week: patriotic music for the Fourth. Her friends had rallied around her after her trip to the emergency room, gathering for several "girls' nights out" at restaurants and movies. She was getting better at bathing the dog and mowing the lawn, though she'd accidentally filled the mower with camping fuel one day.

Telling her about my hike was futile now. The first month, while everything was new, writing a long letter hadn't been hard. I'd felt like a stranger to the trail and could describe it much as one might describe a trip to an exotic vacation spot. But now I'd entered so deeply into its rhythms and rituals that I didn't know what to say anymore. Sure, I could explain about blue-blazing, and pilgrim resorts, and trail romances, and friends I'd made only to lose at the next town. But they didn't mean anything if you weren't a part of this world, and I knew that. What had become impossible to communicate was the compulsive rhythm of the hike, the joy of finding familiar faces in the evening when I came to camp, the shared ordeal. She could listen politely and try to understand, but it wasn't real to her—it wasn't like waking up in the morning, having to get to work while somehow taking the dog to the vet and getting the oil changed in the car and the checkbook balanced.

So we'd tried to enjoy ourselves on our day off. We'd driven down from the mountains, through the Shenandoah Valley, and rented a motel room in Waynesboro. We discussed plans: she and her parents would meet me on the trail for my birthday in a couple of weeks, near Harpers Ferry, and we'd celebrate and take some time off. Then I wouldn't see her again until October, after I finished the hike. That afternoon we swam in the motel pool, wandered around Waynesboro, ate dinner at an Italian restaurant, and watched *Batman and Robin* at the theater downtown. As I held her that night, my body felt unfamiliar and frightening to me without all the weight and bulk I'd grown accustomed to over the years, as if I didn't belong to it anymore.

The Carillon rang the hour: eleven. Time for me to wander back toward Union Station to catch my train south. Plans had changed. Cathy's parents had hatched the plot a week earlier. They'd tricked her into letting me know they wanted to talk with me, apparently something to do with getting my boots resoled. When I'd called up from a pay phone in the Shenandoah Park, they'd outlined the details. Cathy's boss had invited them to attend an award ceremony where Cathy would be named Employee of the Year in the state government department where she worked. She would be honored in front of hundreds of employees, praised by the state cabinet secretary who ran the department, awarded a plaque, and given extra vacation time. She didn't know a thing about it. Her parents had asked if I wanted to come home for it, if they could get me off the trail? Yes, I did. A few credit card calls later and I'd arranged to get from Harpers Ferry to Washington and booked a train south from Washington to Clifton Forge, Virginia, where they'd pick me up and drive me down to North Carolina with them. We'd show up the next morning as she got the award. Oh, she would be surprised!

I shouldered my pack, boots and hiking poles dangling from the back, and some of the tourists throwing pennies in the reflecting pool turned to stare at me. Time to leave my home on the trail for my home in the suburbs, to see her one last time. Then I would come back, cross over the Potomac, cross the Mason-Dixon line, walk into the northern Appalachians, and start the second half.

THREE
SEA LEVEL

I bequeath myself to the dirt to grow from the grass I love,
If you want me again look for me under your boot-soles.
—Walt Whitman, "Song of Myself"

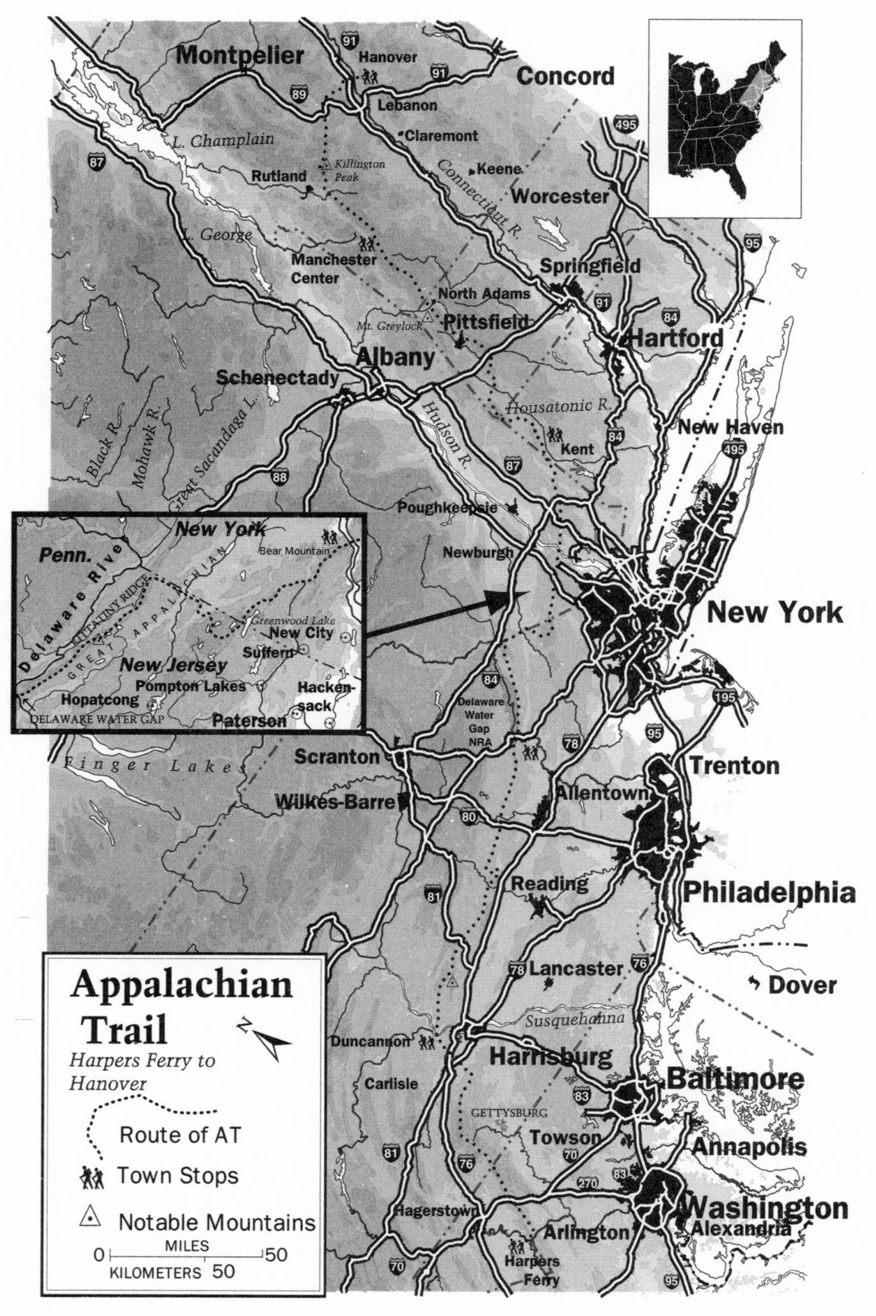

Appalachian Trail
Harpers Ferry to Hanover
Route of AT
Town Stops
Notable Mountains
0 MILES 50
KILOMETERS 50
Montpelier
Hanover
Lebanon
Concord
Claremont
L. Champlain
Killington Peak
Rutland
Keene
Connecticut R.
Worcester
L. George
Manchester Center
Springfield
North Adams
Mt. Greylock
Pittsfield
Hartford
Albany
Schenectady
Housatonic R.
New Haven
Kent
Hudson R.
Black R.
Mohawk R.
Great Sacandaga L.
Poughkeepsie
Newburgh
New York
Penn.
Delaware River
Bear Mountain
Kittatinny Ridge
Great Appalachian
Greenwood Lake
New City
Suffern
New Jersey
Pompton Lakes
Hackensack
Hopatcong
Delaware Water Gap
Paterson
Delaware Water Gap NRA
Finger Lakes
Scranton
Trenton
Wilkes-Barre
Allentown
Reading
Philadelphia
Lancaster
Dover
Susquehanna
Duncannon
Harrisburg
Carlisle
Baltimore
Gettysburg
Towson
Annapolis
Hagerstown
Washington
Arlington
Alexandria
Harpers Ferry

30

White Blaze—Day 109
Friday, July 18, 1997 • Pine Grove Furnace State Park • Pennsylvania
South Mountain (Blue Ridge) • 1,073 miles hiked • 1,087 miles to go
Sunny • Low 76, high 98
Elevation 877 feet

APRIL, MAY, JUNE, MOST OF JULY, and I've only gotten halfway. At this rate I'll get to Katahdin in November, after the mountain closes for the season. Closing date for Baxter State Park in Maine is October 15, just under three months from now. Twelve weeks, eleven hundred miles, and if I can hike about a hundred miles a week, I'll finish with a week to spare. It means walking faster: for the first half of the hike I've averaged only seventy miles a week.

Tomorrow morning I'll pass a signpost in the middle of the woods—the official midpoint, give or take a couple of miles. Today, like a sailor crossing the equator, I undergo the traditional initiation rite: an ice cream orgy outside the camp store here at Pine Grove Furnace. The preferred brand, Ben & Jerry's, isn't available, but the store carries half gallons of Hershey's, which will do for ritual purposes. As an initiate, I must pack away a full half-gallon in one sitting without getting sick or going blind from headache.

Maybe it would mean more if I had company. I've arrived alone, late in the afternoon, after most of a week chasing RockDancer, who got several days ahead of me while I went home. If I catch him, I've decided to accept his offer of partnering up for the latter part of the hike, if he's still game. But he's a day or two ahead of me, and I'm dragging now after four straight days of Big Miles with the temperature near one hundred degrees. There's a hostel here at the state park that promises a shower and a clean set of sheets. First, I have an appointment with a box of mint chocolate chip.

After I've consumed the last spoonful of chlorophyll-green goop and semisweet chocolate bits, the counter clerk—my only witness—rewards me with a small wooden spoon imprinted with the words "Half Gallon Club." I'm now a member in good standing.

"And it's my birthday today too," I say.

"Happy birthday," she says. "I guess you don't want any cake."

I reel up the grassy slope toward the hostel, dragging my pack: not quite sick from the gluttony, but ready to lie down.

Ironmasters Mansion Hostel, a Revolutionary War–era building near the old charcoal-fired blast furnace around which the park is built, is not air-conditioned. Inside, the doors have been propped open with electric fans, which hum and buzz and make the magazines flutter on the table of the common room. A small, dark-haired woman about eleven months pregnant comes out of the kitchen when the door jingles, and signs me in. Unlike many of the informal hiker hostels along the trail, Ironmasters belongs to a national youth hostel network that takes in all sorts of travelers, not just hikers. Its caretakers live there as part of their compensation, and kids run around the place yelling while the woman sweats and tries to keep from passing out in the hundred-degree heat. After I've paid, she calls over one of the little dark-haired boys, who can't be more than six, and tells him to take me to the sleeping quarters on the second floor, to which she clearly doesn't want to climb. He whines that he's playing with his friend but eventually gives in and leads me on a practiced tour of the building, playing back a script of information about the telephones and showers, pointing out a secret hideaway where escaped slaves sheltered before the Civil War, and leading me to the bunkroom. A while later I hear him out on the deck behind the building, shouting at some arriving hikers. "Hey, you wanna stay at a *hostel*?"

They do not: a wise choice. The box springs sag under the mattress, which hurts my back, and a fan blows clammy air all night, forcing me either to huddle sweating under my sheet or lie chilled on top of it. About three in the morning the fire alarm goes off, a false alert caused by a power surge; the caretaker couple shouts to each other in the hallway for fifteen minutes as they track down the problem, waking everybody again and making me wonder if we'll have to evacuate the building. Half an hour later the alarm goes off a second time.

I've come to the end of the Blue Ridge, the nearly continuous seam of weathered Precambrian quartzite rocks jutting above the limestone of the Great Valley. North of Pine Grove Furnace, the ridge terminates in a final sharp upthrust, and the trail swings across the Great Valley and the fields of Cumberland County, near Boiling Springs, toward the stony "Ridge and Valley Province" of the central Appalachians. On the map, this geologic region looks like a series of long, fractured furrows east of the Allegheny Plateau pivoting around Harrisburg and running northeast toward the Delaware Water Gap. Blue Mountain is the most prominent of these, a narrow, stony highland overlooking a valley of neat Germanic farms and towns built around eighteenth-century mills and forges.

The Mason-Dixon line now lies behind me, and I'm just a few miles from Gettysburg. Ever since I reached Harpers Ferry, over a week ago, I've had a sense of walking across countryside worn down by the coming and going of people as much as the workings of wind and water on the old mountains. The forests here have taken root along neglected ridges and hillsides once scraped bare by railroads, charcoal burners, and lumberjacks, rocks making them unsuitable for more cultivated uses. The spreading forests of the South are behind me.

I've been walking in a kind of stupor through the shimmering July heat, averaging about sixteen miles a day, focused only on pounding out the miles and catching RockDancer. There's no word in the shelter registers about Kilgore Trout, and I can only figure that he's off the trail. Three more days will take me to the Susquehanna River and the town of Duncannon, then on through eastern Pennsylvania to the Delaware Water Gap by the first of August. My goal is New Hampshire by September 1, then the last push to Maine. As I leave the Blue Ridge, coming down out of the woods toward the open farmland of the Great Valley, the air fills with the smell of mown hay and manure from a dairy farm. Just before I break out of the sweltering green woods for the last time and into the open, sun-parched valley, I see the season's first red leaves on some of the low bushes and undergrowth near the trail.

31

ON A MAP, BOUNDARIES APPEAR arbitrary: one state or county simply gives way to another. On foot, though, you realize that most boundaries follow landforms, often the same landforms that the trail follows. Usually, these mark places no one wants to be—no-man's-lands, thresholds between here and there, us and them, home and away—typically in the middle of a river or creek, or along the rocky crest of a ridge. Over the years the trail's builders sought out these inconvenient places and lobbied the government to claim or buy them, so that now most of it runs along federally owned easements. A few private landowners still hold out, refusing the government's offers, but it isn't the sort of rich real estate worth shedding blood over. It's no-man's-land, after all.

Not so the Mason-Dixon line. Like most boundaries that people fight and die for, it came from a surveyor's map, not natural landforms. Surveyed in 1765, the line separated the small farms and mill towns of William Penn's settlement from the slave-worked fields of Lord Baltimore's. The Civil War might never have been fought had chattel slavery stayed tucked away south of the Potomac and east of the mountains. But as the West opened up and slave-owning interests sought to project their power into that borderless frontier, two economic systems faced off over the surveyors' lines of places like Kansas and Nebraska. When Lincoln in late 1862 proposed freeing the slaves to Congress, he appealed not so much to morality as to economics: a sovereign Confederacy would destroy the Union's organic wholeness, the natural flow of commerce from the heartland down the rivers to the sea; artificial boundaries would not last. It's no wonder that some of the war's bloodiest battles, including Gettysburg and Antietam, were fought within marching distance of the Mason-Dixon line. When it was time to fight, though, the armies went looking for ridges and rivers to fortify. A surveyed line has no strategic value.

Though the trail's actual halfway point lies near Pine Grove Furnace, which is two days north of the line, the metal catwalk over the Potomac at Harpers Ferry, which is two days south of it, marks a more important waypoint for hikers. It is a real threshold, that old town: a convergence of East and West, mountain and piedmont, North and South, past and present. Civil War reenacters in butternut and blue lounge around its brick streets and eighteenth-century buildings chatting amiably, sweating in wool uniforms, and teasing wide-eyed children. Shuttle buses from the National Historic Park Visitors Center ply narrow Shenandoah Street, discharging sightseers and day-trippers. "We got fla-*min*-gos in Harpers Ferry," one shuttle driver crows to the tourists trapped on her bus, "only ours ain't pink," and she points to where a great blue heron stands motionless in a creek. Backpackers and thruhikers drift through the wandering sightseers, on their way north into Maryland and Pennsylvania or south into Virginia. A tall, white-haired woman in a Victorian-era dress leads a candlelight "ghost tour" of the old town at twilight.

Ghosts inhabit the town, all right. Some will argue that while the fighting started at Fort Sumter, South Carolina, the Civil War really began at Harpers Ferry when John Brown polarized abolitionists and secessionists with his attempt to start a slave revolt in 1859 by taking over the armory there. Until the years shortly before the Civil War it had been prosperous, located at the confluence of the Potomac and Shenandoah Rivers. Meriwether Lewis began his expedition into the West from Harpers Ferry, setting out from there to meet William Clark; settlers turned south from there up the Great Valley or, later, west along the Chesapeake and Ohio Canal to the Mississippi basin. With the coming of railroads and the subsequent decline of river travel, Harpers Ferry declined too—at least until the fighting broke out in 1861, and the threshold between North and South became worth dying for. Over the course of the war it changed hands in skirmishes and sieges, and figured in the battle plans of both armies at the bloody fight at nearby Sharpsburg. After the war, it was gradually forsaken. Potomac floods damaged many of the old buildings, which were not replaced. Trains still came through on the Baltimore & Ohio tracks, keeping the area from dying completely, but just barely. When the National Park Service took over parts of Harpers Ferry and the surrounding battlefields at midcentury, only a kind of ghost town haunted the bottom of the hill.

A living town remains at the top, though, and that's where the Appalachian Trail Conference has its headquarters, in a two-story building near the apex of the old high street. It's a quirky office: originally an 1892 temperance hall, later a soda shop, the town opera house, a combination gas station and automobile dealership, a sock mill, apartments, a gift shop, and a private residence. In 1976, when the ATC bought it, it served only as the meeting place for the Harpers Ferry Cooking Club. But it was within a morning's drive of Washington, D.C., where the headquarters had formerly been located, and the trail itself passed through town.

Today, a climb up the spiral staircase to the second floor of the ATC building reveals offices of ATC staffers who coordinate work with trail-maintaining clubs and the federal government, raise money, and advocate the trail in various official and unofficial venues. Downstairs, volunteers and paid staff members sell books and trail paraphernalia, pass out literature, and deal with the public. They also welcome thruhikers, and when the northbound crowd comes through in midsummer the air downstairs grows ripe with hiker stink as dozens of white-blaze pilgrims stop by to be photographed for posterity, pick up packages, lounge around on the couches, and read through the registers.

That's how I'd come through, as a hiker among other hikers, on the threshold between north and south after the early summer push through the Shenandoah. Then I'd left to go home. Four days later I'd come back as a tourist, with Cathy and her parents and the old dog. We'd explored the town and the surrounding countryside for two days, on the threshold between beginning and ending. And then I'd put my hiking clothes back on, shouldered my pack, and crossed it.

Back home, the secret plot had gone off without a hitch. I'd sneaked into the house after Cathy left for work, greeted the very excited dog, dressed in a baggy business suit, and then had driven her parents to the meeting room where the awards were taking place. An accomplice from her office spirited us into a corridor near the meeting room, where we waited as the state cabinet secretary played up the suspense, praised several runners-up, and read testimonials from co-workers about the winner. Then he announced Cathy's name, called her up front, talked about the importance of her work, and ushered in her parents as the gathering burst into applause. Once they were at the podium with her I peered around the doorway and watched her, flushed and beaming, near tears at it all. And then her boss mentioned how she had been doing all this while supporting her husband, who was walking the Appalachian Trail, and motioned for me to come out. She choked, laughing in little chuckling gasps. It was like the medal ceremony in *Star Wars*.

When it was time to say good-bye for the last time in Harpers Ferry, Cathy and I took a few minutes alone together near the engine house where John Brown had made his stand. From there, at the rocky point between the two rivers, the trail crossed the Potomac into Maryland along an abandoned railroad trestle branching off of the CSX main line. On the far side, next to a rail tunnel through the rocky walls of the gorge, it swung down from the tracks on metal steps and ran east along the old C&O Canal towpath that paralleled the Potomac. Her parents held back the dog. We spent a few minutes just listening to the voice of the rivers and watching them join and mingle in the rocky gorge. Some Canada geese dabbled around in eddies behind ruined bridge abutments, from which a couple of young vacationers dangled their feet in the water on the Shenandoah side.

Maybe I should have felt some overwhelming emotion, but I just wanted to start. This was the fifth time, now, that we'd said good-bye to each other at a trailhead, with Cathy playing the dutiful spouse resolved to carry on and me playing the adventurer bidding his heart farewell and pushing forth. We'd both gotten a little sick of the roles. When we said good-bye, she could get back to dealing with the mess I'd handed her, and I could go hide out in the hills again, trying to figure out why, trying to finish what I'd started.

Only the old dog choked up, wheezing and hacking at the end of her leash. The dog knew that the backpack and hiking sticks and sour-smelling polyester clothes meant I planned to walk away again, and this time, by damn, she intended to go along. She gasped and whined as Cathy's father reeled in the leash and I started across the bridge. Just as

I began descending on the far side, a long freight train howled from the tunnel, filling the air of the river gorge with the screaming and slamming of metal on metal.

32

White Blaze—Day 112
Monday, July 21, 1997 • Duncannon, Pennsylvania
Susquehanna River • 1,118 miles hiked • 1,042 miles to go
Hazy • Low 67, high 92
Elevation 400 feet

"UH-OH! FRESH MEAT!" says the woman with the road-map face at the bar of the Doyle Hotel. As I close the door behind me, a couple of other regulars glance up at me from the boxy-looking bar, laugh roughly, and go back to their Monday afternoon cocktails and cigarettes.

I've caught up to Icebox and Dancing Bear again. They wave at me from a corner, where they've stashed their packs and are digging through mail-drop packages.

"Where do you check in?" I say.

"See the bartender," Icebox says, and giggles as I gape around. The place looks like a Woolworth's lunch counter with hard liquor behind the counter and beer on tap. "Rooms won't be ready for a couple hours," he says, "so you may as well stay here with us and have a Yuengling."

Yuengling's Black & Tan is the local brew of choice. The bar looks like someone renovated it about the time Ronald Reagan was elected president, but through the door I can see that the rest of the Doyle hasn't gotten much beyond the Herbert Hoover era. It's a don't-miss tradition for thruhikers, with cheap rooms, cheap beer, sandwiches, breakfast, and a clientele of regulars that make the crowd on TV's *Cheers* look like overachievers. It was built around the turn of the century, when the river and railroad kept Duncannon alive, but the hotel, like the town, has been sliding downhill since the Depression. In recent years new owners have made halfhearted efforts at renovation, and several rooms on the second floor show evidence of work, but no one would mistake it for picturesque. The rooms up the creaking wooden staircase cost fifteen dollars, which is a deal as long as you don't plan on reading in bed: they lack air-conditioning and window screens, so turning on the naked bulb over the sagging mattress and box springs means inviting in every insect within a mile. The alternative is closing the window sash and suffocating in the stifling July heat along the river. Rooms on each floor share a small, grubby hallway bathroom equipped with a clawfoot tub, faded mirror, commode, and sink.

As I'm climbing the stairs to my room, a couple of thruhikers slip through a window along the landing onto a wooden balcony, where they start cooking dinner on their backpacking stoves—something that could easily ignite the whole firetrap hotel. I look out my third-floor window to see if I could survive a jump. Maybe—there are some bushes below me.

Only the first-floor bar is air-conditioned, and that's where a regular rotation of bartenders, women who look to be near retirement age, tend to regulars and sometimes sit down with a cigarette to join the ebb and flow of conversation. In most small-town saloons, conversation stops and suspicious stares come our way when we arrive, but at the Doyle thruhikers are part of a passing show, and the crowd at the bar ignores us and carries on its own little soap opera, leaving us to eavesdrop: *He just lost his job, didn't he? Damn straight. Where's he get the money from? I'd like to know. Is she getting some on the side? What do you think? I heard they had a fight and her cancer is spreading. That boy of hers has a good job in*

Harrisburg now. That's what she says, at least. Oh, I bet he does! Smile when you say that, you son of a bitch.

Leaving them there, I walk up the street to the post office to pick up the package of supplies Cathy has mailed me. The clerk hands me the box, and a postcard with a picture of Waynesboro, Pennsylvania. It's dated July 18, the day I'd arrived at Pine Grove Furnace:

> Hey Rhyming Worm: I got back on the trail and was, I think, 1 day behind you at Waynesboro, when the blisters wouldn't let me go on again. Have decided to go home, heal up, flip-flop. Should be leaving Katahdin about Aug. 15—will see you somewhere along the way. Happy Hiking!
>
> —Kilgore Trout

So he'd made it back to the trail! For some reason, as I lug my box back through town to the Doyle, this makes me happy. The last time I'd seen Mr. Trout he'd been making all the noises that thruhikers make when they're about to give up. Now he was going to do a "flip-flop" hike, driving up to Maine in August and hiking south from there, finishing his hike near the Mason-Dixon line, rather than on Mount Katahdin. He had abandoned the catch-up-and-keep-up game.

The next morning I spend a few minutes sponging off in the clawfoot tub, wash my hair with "strawberry essence" shampoo that a thruhiker has left behind, haul my pack downstairs, and order breakfast in the bar. I'm waiting to meet a friend.

I'd written Dinty from Harpers Ferry, and he'd promised to intercept me so we could "do lunch" when I got to Duncannon, a couple of hours from his home in State College. The last time we'd seen each other I'd been overweight, clean-shaven, professorial in my glasses and a polo shirt, and sick from stress and a case of bronchitis: I was his editor. Now I'm tanned and fit, slightly grimy from a week of hiking despite my bath and strawberry essence shampoo, wearing a stained olive-green nylon shirt and baggy nylon khaki zip-leg pants; my hair is unkempt, I sport a scratchy-looking salt-and-pepper beard, and I have taken to wearing disposable contact lenses.

The regulars on the morning shift have already started on beer and Bloody Marys when I arrive, about eight-thirty. The woman behind the bar disappears into a back room and reappears a few minutes later with a big plate of scrambled eggs, bacon, and toast. Icebox and Dancing Bear show up a while later, dump some leftover food in the hiker box, and stop by to talk. We trade news about other thruhikers. I learn that Bigfoot is in town, meeting a friend. The Virginia Six-Pack, the slack-packing expedition organized by the Princess and the Pea, has collapsed. Too many interruptions, from all reports—too much money spent in town, too many side trips to the beach and to hotels. Several members of the Six-Pack ran out of cash, while the others ran out of motivation. D-Bear is wistful. The girl he liked was among the Six-Pack, and he'd hoped the acquaintance would turn into something more than mere trail fellowship. But they're all off the trail now.

A few minutes later, I'm watching one of the hotel regulars surreptitiously pick through the box of discarded hiker food when Dinty pushes open the door and stands there awkwardly, taken aback by the utter shabbiness of the place. I've told him I'm staying at an old hotel, but he's obviously envisioned a desk clerk, an elevator, and a lobby phone, not this dusty Formica barroom filled with early-morning drunks. He looks right past me.

"Dinty, over here," I say, and he swings around, startled.

"Robert?" he says, grinning strangely and coming over to shake my hand.

I'd been Dinty's editor for two books of nonfiction. He'd just put the finishing touches on his second book when I left him in the awkward position of a publishing "orphan"—a writer without an editor to run interference for his writing once the publicists and book marketers got their hands on it. For most of our editorial relationship I'd been the one with all the answers—cheerleader, coach, collaborator, and consultant. Now, all of a sudden, I've become a hobo at a cheap hotel, fishing for a free lunch—or at least that's how I feel. Yet he's pleased to find me fit and hopeful again, and is honestly fascinated by this strange pilgrimage I've taken and what it has done to me.

We eat lunch at a truck stop, and Dinty watches with amusement as my appetite kicks in and I dispatch a large second breakfast of an omelet, sausages, coffee, orange juice, and hash brown potatoes at ten-thirty. Another thruhiker eating there figures that I've somehow yogied my way into some trail magic and sidles up to say hello, hoping to share. I play dumb, wave distractedly, and go on with the conversation until he drifts away. Dinty and I talk about my hike and about his book. He shows me the bound proof. The publisher has convinced him to change the title to one that's more marketable, and he likes it pretty well. He's been given the chance to speak to the book salesmen who will be pitching it to stores, and by all accounts it went well. The publicist seems certain she can get him on national morning talk shows, like *Today*, which will give the book credibility.

After nearly four months away from my job, the Rhymin' Worm draws back and watches Robert the Editor glibly discuss print runs and book tours and promotion budgets, in a truck-stop booth, in sweat-stained hiking clothes and Tevas. Everything sounds so great, and Dinty is so quietly excited. I try not to listen to the weary, cynical inner voice, the voice that says that the new title condescends to a wise, heartfelt book, that the talk at sales conference is a bone tossed Dinty's way rather than a commitment to spend money on advertising and promotion, that the vague assurances about television have been made knowing full well it will be an uphill battle for a writer neither famous nor controversial enough to excite the morning shows. *Shut up*, I tell myself. *Don't think that way. You quit. You gave up. If you cared so much, why didn't you stay and fight? Maybe it will all work out the way they say it will.*

33

PEOPLE PREPARE FOR THRUHIKES differently. Some just show up and start walking. Some plan for years. Some improvise every detail. And then there are those like Hatman and Happy Feet, a married couple who'd been roughly on the same pace as me since Georgia, and who I'd found myself sharing shelters with nearly every evening for the past week. They were about my age, they hiked about my pace, we'd started about the same time, we hailed from the South, and we had about the same level of education. So we should have had a lot in common. But they drove me up the wall.

Hatman was a tall, inquisitive man with a touch of gray and a slightly distracted air. He was an engineer who took his trail name from the strange homemade headgear he sometimes wore, a thick foam-rubber disk about the circumference of a toilet seat, with a hole cut in the center that he could jam down over the top of his head to shade him like a sombrero in sun or rain. Happy Feet, his wife, was a fit, competent woman with sandy-brown hair who deferred to Hatman in public, letting him do most of the talking and offering her opinion or comment when he turned to see what she thought. He did this assiduously, and hiking with them was like hiking with a committee—Hatman constantly observing and analyzing what was going on around him, talking about it at length to frame the issue clearly, and turning to Happy Feet for consultation regarding the proper action or answer.

They had undertaken the challenge of the thruhike as you might imagine an engineer would—as a problem to be solved. How do we hike the A.T. from coordinate X,Y (Springer Mountain) to coordinate x,y (Katahdin) as efficiently as possible without sacrificing (1) reasonable comfort, (2) palatable food, and (3) cleanliness? And how do we remain in close proximity without getting on each other's nerves? They appeared to have worked it out. The first thing I noticed was that, incredibly, they made a ritual of showering every day, carrying with them a portable shower bag that could be hung from a tree limb, and using every possible hostel or hotel to clean up; this was a challenge to be met even in the worst weather. Watching them recoil at the prospect of the Doyle and its grimy clawfoot tubs had delighted me. They also cooked elaborate meals, carefully planned according to caloric content and nutritional value; often while the rest of us were boiling noodles or unwrapping Pop-Tarts, they would bake breads and cakes using a backpacker's oven, a portable dome that fit over a hiking stove. And each day they pushed steadily and systematically north.

What was wrong with that? Nothing. They were always pleasant and considerate, never criticized me or my habits, and were genuinely interested in my plans. But eventually the fastidiousness, organization, unceasing questions, discussion, and analysis began driving me quietly nuts. It was like sharing a daily arts-and-crafts class with Martha Stewart.

We had become locked into a similar schedule, though, and I had a vision of listening to them atomize every detail of the hike for the next thousand miles, all the way to Katahdin. If I slowed down for a day and let them go ahead, I'd be at the mercy of their pace, constantly holding back so as not to overtake them. The only solution, then, was to push ahead and leave them behind. But that was hard too, because I couldn't hike any faster than they did, and doing so would mean exhausting myself, risking injury or heatstroke.

As we neared Reading and Allentown, more and more I sensed we were walking through a narrow margin of woods above suburban lawns and strip malls. Road crossings came more frequently, which often meant negotiating busy highways between towns and cities. Shelters, even the new ones, showed signs of wear and abuse by weekend campers, day hikers, and teenage mischief. Most of those near roads had been assigned part- or full-time caretakers to make sure that they weren't abused. The 501 Shelter, a few hundred feet off the road from Pennsylvania Route 501, was a good example. More like a cabin or a hostel than the usual lean-to, it featured a Plexiglas skylight, doors, tables and chairs, bunks, a stock of magazines and books, a solar shower, and a nearby caretaker's house that offered iron-saturated well water from a spigot; you could buy soft drinks and ice cream sandwiches from the caretaker.

RockDancer had not been there yet—I'd passed him in Duncannon, apparently. After I'd left town, and realized he wasn't ahead of me anymore, I'd slowed down on a rainy day and only hiked three miles, hoping he would catch up. Instead, Hatman and Happy Feet had arrived. I couldn't afford to hike three-mile days and still keep to my hundred-mile-a-week schedule, so the next day I pushed on again, passing the threshold north of Swatara Gap, at which there were fewer than a thousand miles left to walk. If RockDancer caught me, I'd talk about partnering up. If not, I'd just keep counting down the miles.

From the time I'd left Harpers Ferry, my mood had been growing worse and worse. Maybe missing RockDancer was good: this whole dog days transit of the mid-Atlantic had me feeling so numb and antisocial that no one would want to hike with me. I kept it to myself, mostly, but in the sun and haze I found I wasn't even bothering to stop when I reached scenic overlooks. The springs had dried up, and the heat made the ridge crests shimmer and the eye-gnats swarm. I found myself plotting ways to lose Hatman and Happy Feet, and after about a week the occasion presented itself. They were, as usual, off to a late start, baking an elaborate coffee cake on the picnic table outside the hostel we'd just shared. If the map was right, today would be what I called a "'tweener"—a day in which shelters were spaced so that you either had to hike short, dawdling eight miles to the first one, or long, battling the rocks for nearly twenty miles to the second. In between, at the foot of Blue Mountain, lay a campsite that promised good water and a way off the ridge on a day in which the temperature was supposed to be in the nineties. Unless I missed my guess, that was as far as Hatman and Happy Feet would get. Me? I'd hike long.

By midafternoon I needed a break and stopped for lunch at the newly constructed Allentown Shelter, near the crest of Blue Mountain. A day hiker was there already, eating lunch before returning to Hawk Mountain, a famous ornithological sanctuary located a few miles south, on the route of the thousands of hawks that migrate along the Appalachian ridges each fall. We talked about hawk migration season, and hawks we'd seen while hiking. Then I heard someone's boots approaching the shelter. *Damn,* I thought: *The Hatman cometh.* But no, it wasn't them. We broke off our conversation abruptly. This guy was by himself, and absolutely naked except for his backpack and hiking boots.

"Hello," he said nonchalantly, as the day hiker and I flushed and looked away. He was wiry—mid-twenties, maybe—with metal-rimmed glasses and curly hair. He took off his pack and climbed into the shelter, where he rested against the rear wall, behind where I was sitting.

"Hot today, isn't it?" he said.

"Yeah," I said.

"Hey, if it bothers you guys that I'm naked, just let me know and I'll put something on," he said.

"Yeah," I said, facing stonily forward. The day hiker looked away. The naked guy chuckled, obviously enjoying the fact that he'd freaked us out.

"You're thruhiking?" he said.

"Yeah."

"Many thruhikers go in for naked hiking?"

"Couldn't really say," I said, still not looking at him. He chuckled again. This was ridiculous. It *did* bother me, talking to some son of a bitch who got his kicks shocking people. Some wilderness experience!

"Hey, gotta go," I said, and slung my pack on without looking back, waved to the day hiker, and stormed off down the trail, getting madder and madder with each step. Son of a bitch!

Three miles later, I was still mad. It wasn't so much that the guy had been naked. Thruhikers go naked to swim in creeks and rivers, and some of them brag of stripping down to hike on hot days in deserted areas. Back on the summer solstice there had even been talk of a "National Nude Hiking Day," though I hadn't participated and hadn't seen other thruhikers going naked either. But this wasn't a deserted section of the A.T.; it was a heavily hiked section close to a city, crossed by numerous roads. I'd already passed three day hikers today and a troop of Scouts. What bothered me wasn't so much the man's nakedness as his wish to impose it on others, his exhibitionism. It was the sort of thing you expected of flashers at a city park, not on the Appalachian Trail. Maybe that was the problem now. It didn't feel wild anymore. A few minutes later some teenage kids on mountain bikes passed going the other direction—mountain bikes are forbidden on the trail, but who was going to enforce it?

"Not supposed to be riding those on the A.T.!" I said.

"Fuck you, asshole!" one of the kids said, and the other shot me the bird.

I'll bet that's their car, I said to myself a mile farther on, when I came to the parking area at Pennsylvania 309 and saw a decrepit Jeep CJ with bike racks on the back. By now I was feeling so mean that I considered letting the air out of the tires and making the bastards sweat in the sun. But maybe it wasn't their car. So I pushed on, slipping and scrambling back and forth over a rocky spine called the Knife Edge, finishing off most of my water in the heat as I wrapped up twenty miles of sweat, rocks, and bad karma.

The sun was low when I crossed one final road, a mile from the shelter. It was a gravel gamelands route, with five or six cars parked in a scrubby lot to one side. I saw the taillights flicker on one of the pickup trucks, and as I got closer I noticed it was rocking slightly. Please, not today, I thought. But sure enough, a high school girl straddled her paramour on the bench seat and rocked back and forth while he held on to the steering wheel. They didn't see me, so I just slipped past the lot and back onto the trail farther on.

As I drifted toward sleep that night, rereading some of the psalms that sing of slaughter, destruction, and divine vengeance, it occurred to me that what I'd felt today wasn't so far from the kind of rage you feel when you're trapped in traffic. For the last four months, I'd been more or less alone whenever I wanted to be. But now, as I walked toward sea level, toward New York City and the heart of the mid-Atlantic, the trail sometimes seemed little more than a suburban greenway, trammeled in by development. For the first time there were just too many people.

34

White Blaze—Day 121
Wednesday, July 30, 1997 • Lehigh Gap • Pennsylvania
Ridge and Valley Province • 1,232 miles hiked • 928 miles to go
Sunny • Low 54, high 81
Elevation 400 feet

I HELP MYSELF TO BLUEBERRIES for breakfast. They grow wild along the trail, in low bushes about ankle-high, and as I approach Lehigh Gap across the grassy crest of Blue Mountain the bushes spread profusely for many yards on both sides of the path, beckoning a hungry hiker to reach down, strip a cluster from their leaves, pop the handful into his mouth, and hike on, spitting out stems, barely missing a stride. Moist and sweet and refreshing in the early morning sun, they occupy my attention fully, and pretty soon I'm not thinking about how angry I am, or how far I have to hike today to stay ahead of Hatman. Just blueberries.

Actually, I'm going long again: twenty-five miles, to be exact. It will be my longest day yet, if everything works out. I'll make up the time lost in the rain north of Duncannon, keep to my hundred-miles-a-week pace, leave Hatman and Happy Feet a full day behind me, and be on schedule to make the Delaware Water Gap by tomorrow night. Once there, I can take a day off and visit a writer I know who's invited me to her farm. By then, I'll have less than nine hundred miles to go. Blueberries, blueberries, blueberries.

As I descend Blue Mountain at Lehigh Gap, into the shimmering heat where the Lehigh River cuts through the ridge at Palmerton, I come upon a kiosk with official notices on it. One of them is a federal environmental bulletin informing the public that because of heavy metal contamination, the entire area on both sides of the gap has been designated an EPA Superfund Site. Yes, it rings a bell: the Palmerton Superfund Site, a notorious environmental disaster area where, over the course of several decades, a zinc smelter devastated the surrounding countryside with heavy metal fumes. Blueberries, blueberries, blueberries—and I've been eating them!

The north side of the gap reminds me of the description of Mordor, the hellish home of all things corrupt in Tolkien's *Lord of the Rings*. The ridge of Blue Mountain, which stretches down from near the Delaware River, thirty miles away, stops abruptly there in a rocky jumble of scree, talus, and boulders, plunging a thousand feet to the river. The rocks are stained and oxidized by the fumes that belched from the smeltery until it closed in the late sixties, and the cliff side appears absolutely barren of life: no trees, no bushes, even very few weeds. The climb out soon becomes a rock scramble, following blazes and arrows painted on the stone itself—the kind of hand-over-foot hoisting and teetering that I haven't encountered since southern Virginia. Only this scramble goes on for almost two miles. At times, perched precariously on an outcropping, the weight of my backpack threatening to tip me off the rocks and send me tumbling down a precipice, my adrenaline kicks in and my heart races. I am absolutely alone here. It would be so easy to fall and break an arm, a leg, or worse.

In a frightening sort of way, climbing through this dead land matches any spectacle I've encountered on the entire hike—slatelike river curving beneath me, city huddled gray and comatose on its banks, moan of trains and cry of ambulances rising from the distance, heat shimmering up off rocks, wind sighing over the ridge. Like a flood, a forest fire, or a storm it offers the sublime of devastation rather than creation. Atop the ridge lies a volcanoscape of dead trees that cover the west side like skeletons of fallen soldiers after a battle. The living essence has moved on, leaving only the bones. I hike north nearly a mile along the contaminated crest before finding any living trees large enough to cast a shadow over the trail.

Another day in no-man's-land. Soon I'll be in New Jersey.

35

WALKING THE TRAIL sometimes reminded me of walking the streets of New York on my twice-yearly business trips there. Whether gazing at the variety of life around me, or marveling at the immense scale of things, or simply putting my head down and drawing into my own angry shell, always I had the sense of drifting through almost unseen, able to watch and take the world in but (as long as I looked where I stepped) not letting it touch me. And just as I might pause in the city for news, food, or human contact at a magazine stand or in front of a sidewalk vendor, I would come down to the trail towns and highway crossings for a day or two to taste the world at the foot of the hill, for reassurance that it was still there. Once that world began to bind me to it again, I could shoulder my pack and leave it behind, as a New Yorker might vanish into a crowd to avoid meeting an unpleasant acquaintance.

It's easy to get ignored in New York. That's what frightens the outsider. When I would come to the city on business I'd find myself almost holding my breath, much as a swimmer might, to keep from breathing it all in and drowning. The outsiders who came in and flourished grew gills, learning to breathe its denser, richer atmosphere, to move quickly and unconsciously through it all. I doubted I ever would. You have to keep a strong sense of who you are, or where you're going and what you need to do, as a shark keeps swimming to stay alive; stop, freeze, doubt, hesitate, and you risk losing yourself. No one will notice, either: it's no place for pilgrims. Sometimes as I read my battered book of Whitman, I tried to imagine what it was like when he grew up in Brooklyn during the 1820s, when much of Manhattan north of Central Park was semi-rural. Even then things moved incredibly fast. In his lifetime Whitman saw New York grow from a compact, bustling port clustered around Wall Street to one of the world's great, sprawling cities.

Why don't we imagine Whitman the city boy—the Nooyawker? Why do we see instead the "Good Gray Poet" singing of the open road? As day by day I drew nearer to his city, it occurred to me that perhaps he wrote of that road when he too was drowning there—just another struggling wordsmith bouncing from day job to day job well into his thirties, paying the bills as a journalist, a schoolteacher, a printer, a storekeeper, a building contractor, a real estate speculator. Except that Whitman looked around and saw how the whole world had come to those rocky islands on the Hudson, how they encompassed so much more than just the old Dutch colony, how he could find the open road on Broadway. It became his story to tell. The great poem "Song of Myself" burns with the fire of his desperation and loneliness as he tries to tell it, to articulate the ways in which he is more than just a journeyman from Brooklyn, the ways that he too is connected to the wonderousness of the continent, of the world.

But what if no one had noticed? What if Whitman had poured all of himself into what was initially a slender volume only to see it disappear without acknowledgment? What if the most famous American man of letters of his day, Ralph Waldo Emerson, hadn't read the copy Whitman mailed him, if he hadn't sent back a letter with the kind of endorsement that no one could ignore? Suppose Whitman had gotten no response at all. Would he, as an old man, have looked back fondly and benevolently on that huge, faceless, humming city that he couldn't escape? Would he have given in to his depression, his loneliness, and ended up the jour printer he describes, eyes blurred with a manuscript, or the suicide sprawled on the bloody floor of a bedroom?

When I had been an editor, I remembered, I'd spent a significant part of my time saying no. Each day dozens of letters and manuscripts came in for me to look at or report on—sometimes too many to look at carefully, much less publish. Part of my job was sifting the gold from the gravel, and sending the gravel back. Publishing is a business, after all, and the idea is to make money. Most writers, deep in their hearts, dream of both fame *and* fortune, so they can usually accept the general notion (though rarely the specific case) that editors reject books they don't think will sell. And so editors write rejection letters. Such a letter is a courtesy: it acknowledges the recipient, saying, "I don't want what you have to offer, but I have at least considered it." One person offers, another person politely refuses. As I drew into myself, though, I found it harder and harder to write those letters—found myself increasingly unwilling to say, confidently and dispassionately, "No." Instead, as the joy in my work drained away, anger took its place—anger at bad writers who saw me as their ticket to ride, anger at good writers whose dreams I could only disappoint, anger at co-workers who didn't embrace my ideas, anger at friends who needed my rescue when I myself was drowning, anger at rivals who challenged my judgment when I no longer felt confident about it myself. And so, more and more often, instead of allowing that fearful anger to sweep me away, I ran from it, drifting past the people reaching out to me as I might drift through a city. Instead of saying no, unable to force myself to complete the human transaction, I simply said nothing.

Now, as I followed the trail, returning to New York on foot, turning things over in my head, I came to realize that what I'd done was far worse than saying no. Being ignored wounds more deeply than being refused—perhaps it hurts less sharply at first, but it leaves an infection that spreads more profoundly and terribly. Being ignored means you don't count, you aren't even worth acknowledging, you don't even show up on the radar. When Andy Warhol joked that in the future everyone will be famous for fifteen minutes, he got it exactly wrong. In the future, everyone will be ignored. You won't matter unless you *can't* be ignored. And so fame becomes our national pastime.

Anonymity and alienation, the diseases of the modern heart, made Whitman's voice powerful, and sent him out seeking in his imagination across the unfolding continent to tell the story of the extraordinary in each of us. He could never have written such things half a century earlier: he needed to feel lost amid the crowds of a great city so that, instead of raging against anonymity and failure, he went searching out kinship. *I am not alone*, he cries, *because all of this is in me, and I am in it*. A brave cry, certainly.

36

White Blaze—Day 124
Saturday, August 2, 1997 • Delaware Water Gap • Pennsylvania
Kittatinny Mountain • 1,267 miles hiked • 893 miles to go
Showers • Low 66, high 87
Elevation 320 feet

"AREN'T YOU TERRIBLY worried about bears?" It is one of the standard questions thruhikers get, and usually I dismiss it, saying that bears are as scared of hikers as we are of them. But oddly enough, if what the rangers and ridge runners at Delaware Water Gap say is true, it's worth worrying about for the next three days in New Jersey.

"Jersey bears will mug you if you aren't careful," joked one of the ridge runners at a church potluck dinner two nights ago. "Think about it for a minute: all the bears from this whole state, and a good part of southern New York, get squeezed into the Delaware Water Gap National Recreation Area, Worthington State Forest, and High Point State Park. That's a strip maybe forty miles long and three miles wide. Hunting's illegal. And people don't know any better so they feed 'em. Then you've got a lot of bears in a small area, they're not afraid of people, and they know you've got food. You figure it out."

I get ready to leave Delaware Water Gap and with it most of the pilgrims I've been hiking with since Harpers Ferry. Hatman and Happy Feet are tented out back and have come in for the showers. Skywalker, a thin young red-haired kid, lies sweating and miserable on his sleeping bag on one of the couches in the hostel, having contracted giardiasis. After a few minutes he jerks upright, surges to the bathroom, and starts puking. I've been contemplating some sandwiches a friend has made for me, even though it isn't noon yet, but this convinces me to take them outside to a picnic table in front of the hostel. Then RockDancer shows up, his arms full of packages.

"You look like you've hit the lotto," I say, and he laughs.

"Some friends knew I'd be here. They said they'd be sending me treats, but I didn't expect all this."

We catch up on each other's progress. He went off the trail at Duncannon to visit friends and came back with a much lighter load that has made a real difference in how fast and far he can hike. He arrived this morning just in time to pick up packages, and plans to spend a couple of days here. I consider mentioning his idea of partnering, but it will mean losing another couple of days at the hostel, and falling behind Hatman and Happy Feet. I feel the frustration of the last week coming back. So I say nothing, pack up, and head out to cross the Delaware.

The next morning I surprise two dog-sized adolescent bear cubs near the trail. They run crashing off into the undergrowth as I approach. Momma is not to be seen. Fifteen miles north, I spend an uneasy night at Brink Road Shelter after reading in the register that Mr. Clean, a Buddha-like "ultralight" hiker whom I'd met in Virginia, has actually been chased by a large bear here. I put my food and my backpack in one of the bear-proof metal boxes provided near the shelter by the local trail club, and wake up several times that night when things go *bump*. Fortunately, if the bumps are bears, they leave me alone.

Even without the bears, Kittatinny Ridge is surprisingly wild and beautiful—hardly what I expect of New Jersey. It has none of the feel of grown-over wasteland that I sensed in parts of Pennsylvania. Only the frequent day hikers and weekenders, and the occasional bakery or tavern at a road crossing, hint at the major population centers nearby. More weekenders than thruhikers pass me during the next couple of days, and I began to see occasional southbounders. They've started in Maine in June and expect to finish at Springer in November or December. Unlike the clusters of northbounders, southbounders mostly travel and camp alone or in pairs, and they say they've been passing northbounders for about a month now. In another week or two they expect to have moved through the pack and begin enjoying a much more solitary thruhike for the rest of the way. We are apparently the tail end of the northbound pack, and will be among the last to finish before winter closes in.

"Think you'll make it?" they ask.

"If I can keep hiking hundred-mile weeks," I say. So far, I'm pretty much on schedule. But I'm in a lull between groups of northbounders—many of those I'd seen at Delaware Water Gap are, I figure, a day or so behind me. Another group, including Icebox, Dancing Bear, and a few others, are a day or so ahead. The only thruhiker on a pace with me is "Trip," a laid-back guitar-carrying West Virginian, blond and bearded like a California surf hippie but with a low, knowing drawl. His great joys on the trail are yogi-ing and hitting on women: he'll often hang out at road crossings waiting for someone to ask the usual questions, and has mastered the art of talking himself into near-instant intimacy with anyone. I've never seen him playing his guitar—one of those portable "backpacker" models—and ask him about it one day.

"I don't play very well." He laughs. "But it's a good way to meet women." He's the only thruhiker I've met who keeps what can only be called a "little black book" for the names and numbers of women he meets along the way. An inveterate yellow-blazer, he's always appearing where you don't expect him. I imagine he'll keep popping up all the way to Maine. By now I've yellow-blazed too—skipping the last six miles into Delaware Water Gap after one last truly horrible Pennsylvania day. I don't have much room to feel superior. Purity just hasn't seemed like much of an issue lately.

Eventually, after passing the obelisk-topped High Point, New Jersey's tallest mountain at 1,803 feet, the trail leaves Kittatinny Ridge and turns southeast, running down the state line toward New York City. Down, down, gradually toward sea level. I leave Trip working his magic on a church outing group that discovers it needs some camping advice. Down, down the trail leads, down into the Great Appalachian Valley one last time—the same valley that stretches back to Pennsylvania, through Virginia and into Tennessee and Alabama. Here the trail leads through grassy swamplands, green even in the dry heart of summer, and runs along puncheon bridges over bogs, and past fields of summer corn. At the center of the valley stretches a vast open wetland, once a commercial sod farm, now taken over by the U.S. Fish and Wildlife Service as a bird sanctuary. The trail skirts canals and locks and sluiceways on an old railroad bed, squares around mazes of cattails and reeds and chattering fields alive with birds. From there it climbs two ridges, Pochuck and Wawayanda Mountains, sometimes winding along suburban roads, sometimes climbing steep ridge fronts. All the time it nears New York City, the place on earth you least expect to find it heading.

The trail does not lead all the way into Manhattan, thank God. On top of Bellvale Mountain, overlooking Greenwood Lake, it stops running southeast toward the city, turns sharply northeast, toward New England, and roughly parallels the Hudson River along a low ridge about twenty-five miles from Yonkers. Six days after setting out from the Delaware Water Gap I make the turn and climb a high glacier-scraped outcropping known as Prospect Rock. Below me stretches the deep blue lake, ringed by camps and vacation cottages, plied by sailboats and speedboats and summer vacationers there for an afternoon in the sun. The day has dawned unexpectedly clear and crisp for early August. I look at the far ridge beyond the lake, where something glints in the morning sun. At first I think it is a rock on the top of the ridge, then I realize it's a building . . . no, two buildings. The upper stories of the World Trade Center. And suddenly, as if in an hallucination, I realize that a single wooded ridge lies between me and a panorama of Manhattan. There, farther to the north, are the midtown skyscrapers—Empire State Building, Chrysler Building, Citicorp Building, and dozens of less famous towers—jutting up in the distance, forty-five miles away, the trees on the ridgeline beyond Greenwood Lake sprouting crazily up between them.

37

IN APRIL OF 1921, a prominent woman suffrage activist named Jesse Stubbs, wife of an obscure U.S. Department of Labor bureaucrat and former New England forester, killed herself by jumping from a bridge into the East River of New York City. Afterward her husband withdrew to the home of a friend in New Jersey, where, three months later, he wrote an article for an architectural journal in which he imagined a giant striding down out of the high mountains of New Hampshire, across the forester's old stomping ground, Vermont's Green Mountains and Massachusetts' Berkshires, and surveying "the crowded east—a chain of smoky bee-hive cities extending from Boston to Washington." The giant also sees "vast areas of secluded forests, pastoral lands, and water courses, which, with proper facilities and protection, could be made to serve as the breath of a real life for the toilers in the bee-hive cities." This natural sanatorium promises to mend the fractures of modernity—"a resource that could save thousands of lives. The sufferers of tuberculosis, anemia and insanity go through the whole strata of human society. Most of them are helpless, even those economically well off. They occur in the cities and right in the skyline belt. For the farmers, and especially the wives of the farmers, are by no means escaping the grinding-down process of our modern life. . . . They need acres, not medicine."

With broad strokes this dreamy pipe-smoking disciple of Theodore Roosevelt and Gifford Pinchot sketched out "An Appalachian Trail: A Project in Regional Planning," the proposal that inspired the present-day trail. His name was Benton MacKaye, and the whole thing was one of those schemes we'd jeer today: a crackpot's windmill tilt—utopia upon a mountain ridge. But his America was that which built the steel roads heading west, the Brooklyn Bridge, that armed a million men to end a war—a bull moose of a land that blundered forth impervious to pain, just as T.R. shrugged off a gunman's bullet. Anything seemed possible. Against "the high powered tension of the economic scramble" he posited communities of backwoods campers. At a time of warring isms, here was campism rather than communism: "in essence a retreat from profit. Cooperation replaces antagonism, trust replaces suspicion, emulation replaces competition."

Within sight of the Manhattan skyline, then, the Appalachian Trail was born in the imagination of a dreamy Massachusetts Yankee, who'd been reflecting on walks taken in the Vermont hills that were more real than city life. Shortly after MacKaye proposed the project, hiking enthusiasts from the city began figuring how the trails that they were then marking out in the newly acquired Harriman State Park could link up with MacKaye's master plan—most of which had not gotten off the printed page and into the woods. A New York hiker and outdoors columnist named Raymond Torrey championed the obscure proposal in his columns and helped bring blue-sky types like MacKaye together with practical-minded trail cutters and organizers into a precursor of today's Appalachian Trail Conference. Harriman Park's chief engineer, Major William Welch, was the ATC's first chairman. Had it not been for hikers who loved the Hudson Highlands trails, the A.T. idea might never have gotten *on* the ground, so to speak.

But that doesn't make hiking through in August any more fun. Unlike New Jersey, the trail through downstate New York feels worn and overused. Small roads and freeways crisscross it, trash litters the road crossings, dingy old shelters from the 1930s sag in overused state parks, the woods have been stripped of burnable firewood, springs and all but the foulest creeks dry up in the heat of the dog days, and you begin to think that the route was chosen for maximum aggravation, as it climbs steeply over rocky glacial hillocks called roches moutonnées instead of taking the easy way around them. New York has craggy and beautiful mountains farther north, notably the Catskills and Adirondacks, but the Hudson Highlands barely rise much above 1,200 or 1,300 feet.

At Bear Mountain State Park, where the trail descends to within sight of the Hudson River's estuarine waters, thousands of day-trippers come in cars or on buses for summer afternoons. They wander around Hessian Lake, feed the ducks and geese, run laughing along the lakeshore, pedal paddleboats, and grill lunch next to lawn chairs. Inline skaters race around on the pavement near the Bear Mountain Inn, once an exclusive Gilded Age retreat, now a state-run inn and restaurant. Traffic cops direct cars around the crowded driveway, pointing them toward parking areas and bullying them away from the entrance to the inn. Boomboxes thump. Kids yell. Thruhikers disappear into this mass of summer visitors, gathering in small knots under the trees outside the inn, or eating overpriced cheeseburgers in the cafeteria.

From the inn, the A.T. blazes lead through the crowds by the lake to a pedestrian tunnel running under U.S. Route 9W. Emerging on the other side, hikers arrive at the gates of Trailside, a zoo and nature trail connected to Bear Mountain Park. The gate attendant waves them through—since the trail passes through the zoo, hikers are admitted free during its hours of operation—and thruhikers wander through with their trail grime and backpacks and hiking poles, drawing stares from the Dads 'n' Lads. The animals, mostly crippled or rescued wildlife, drowse in the August heat, hiding in out-of-the-way corners of their pens. Then, about halfway through, hikers come to a bronze statue: Walt Whitman, reaching out as if to shake hands. Underneath is an inscription from his "Song of the Open Road":

Afoot and light hearted I take to the open road,
Healthy, free, the world before me,
The long brown path before me, leading wherever I choose.

Here, cast in bronze, stands an idea, at the very lowest point of the Appalachian Trail: here, a mere 124 feet above the sea level of the nearby Hudson River, are the words of a poet who told a story about America.

And once upon a time some other city boys heard that story—city boys who in turn dreamed of walking out of the city into the hills and finding the high road themselves, just as Whitman had, even though he never completely left Brooklyn. And today, a little over a century after Whitman's death, the white-blaze pilgrims file past the statue, down from the hills where they've retreated, where they've been looking for something they have a hard time explaining. They're walking the high road those city boys opened, the foundations of which reach down to sea level here at Bear Mountain. Would Whitman have approved of the modern Pilgrims' Way, with its resorts and traditions and rituals? Who knows?

But he would have understood the search.

38

White Blaze—Day 149
Wednesday, August 27, 1997 • Manchester Center • Vermont
Green Mountains • 1,625 miles hiked • 535 miles to go
Partly cloudy, showers • Low 57, high 73
Elevation 800 feet

FOR THE LAST FEW HOURS, Mass's dog, Tagalong, has circulated through the community room at Zion Episcopal Church, greeting everyone, begging food, and exploring. She isn't supposed to be here: the posted rules of the makeshift hostel clearly say NO DOGS ALLOWED. No one says anything. They're all watching Jackie Chan in *Supercop*, which someone has rented from the Manchester Center video store. They don't start playing it until near midnight, at which point, when it's clear no one from the church office plans to check up on the hikers, Mass sneaks Tagalong in the back door for the night.

About twenty of us, northbounders and southbounders alike, have spread our gear across the terrazzo floor here. Labor Day weekend is just ahead, but even after three weeks that have taken me from sea level at the Hudson northward through the Taconics of Connecticut and the Berkshires of Massachusetts and into the Green Mountains of Vermont, I haven't left the *dies caniculares* and its discontents behind. I try to sleep but end up spending two hours with my eyes screwed shut, unable to tune out Jackie Chan's stilted dialogue as he plays a Hong Kong cop teamed up with a lovely mainland police agent aiming to bust an international drug ring. Tagalong freelances around the large room and sometimes out of sight through the kitchen door to other parts of the building, returning when Mass calls, but not for long. Complaining would mean confronting Mass, a big, loud, brawny guy with a lot of friends in the room. Eventually, around two o'clock in the morning, the credits began rolling over the blooper outtakes of Chan's stunts, the VCR gets switched off, and everyone drops off to sleep.

A few hours later the church secretary lets us know she's pissed off: "No, I'm sorry, we can't have this." She's dealt with hikers before. I blink at her from my sleeping bag in the early-morning light to see Mass frantically grabbing to leash Tagalong, the secretary glaring at him from the middle of the room, hands on hips. "Get the dog out now. You know the rules. No dogs in the building."

"She was tied out all night," he lies. "She just got loose from her rope and came in here this morning when someone went out the door. I was going to put her—"

"Take her out now," the secretary says, not buying it.

"Shit," he mutters after she departs, as he pulls on his shorts and takes Tagalong out. A few minutes later he packs up and heads out. Love me, love my dog. I go back to sleep. Before long, another woman from the church's office comes back to the community room and clears her throat.

"Someone had a dog in here last night?" she asks.

"I think so," one of the hikers says.

"Oh there's no doubt," she says. "Who was it?"

"He's gone," I say.

"Well, his dog left something behind, upstairs in the children's playroom," she says. "Who's going to clean it up? Cleaning up after dogs is not in my job description."

We are all rolling our eyes—this is exactly the sort of dumb stuff that gets hikers banned from places where they've been welcome. Since I was baptized at an Episcopal church a month before I started my hike, I feel vaguely proprietary, and step forward. She shows me some paper towels and a bucket of soapy water, and I climb the stairs to the second floor. There, surrounded by alphabet blocks and rubber balls, in solitary splendor dead center on the wooden nursery floor, reposes Tagalong's fresh, warm turd.

◆◆◆

Only a few thousand people actually live in Manchester Center; along with the nearby mail stops of Manchester Depot and the village of Manchester proper, it is now peopled largely by the name-brand residents of our global Main Street: Anne Klein, Ben & Jerry, the Brooks Brothers, Burberry, Calvin Klein, Christian Dior, Donna Karan, Georgina Von Etzdorf, Georgio Armani, Levi Strauss, J. Peterman, Liz Claiborne, Orvis, Ralph Lauren, Tommy Hilfiger, Dexter, Baccarat, Crabtree & Evelyn. The business of Manchester Center is outlet shopping. The cars of bargain hunters and tourists queue up in the streets all day long, from ski season in the winter to camp season in summer and leaf-peeping time in the fall. Although there's a good camping store in town, and a few outlets offer reasonable buys on synthetic fleece clothing, the main reason most Gore-Tex pilgrims come to Manchester Center is to visit the shrine of Zion, the last good resupply point before New Hampshire.

Like other church-run hostels I've visited, Zion Episcopal welcomes hikers without trying to proselytize them—a good thing, too, because there are not many churchy types hiking the Appalachian Trail. Of the twenty-odd limping, blister-footed pilgrims, I'm the only one who shows up at noon for the midweek healing service.

I don't know what to expect, having only seen television shows of fundamentalist faith healers overcome by the power of the blood. Surely Episcopalians will be different. And, indeed, there are no choirs singing Glory, Hallelujah, in the decorous, echo-heavy sanctuary. A middle-aged man helps an old woman on crutches up the aisle. The church secretary shows up. Another two or three people in dressy clothes sit near the front. One is missing an arm. That is all. Eventually an elderly Episcopal priest in white vestments limps to the front of the church. He works his way slowly through the liturgy, pausing while we read the appropriate responses from the prayer book. Then he sits down heavily and, looking off vacantly toward a stained glass window at one side of the church, begins a rambling sermon that tells the story of a nineteenth-century missionary who persevered despite tremendous physical handicaps. As he broods his way through the story, I realize he is crying. He collects himself, and after several readings from the prayer book, he asks everyone up to the altar rail.

One by one, he asks us what sort of healing we seek. The old lady suffers from arthritis. One of the men has a degenerative nerve disease. Someone has high blood pressure. He asks us to join him and lay hands upon each sick person while he prays aloud for their healing. Finally it is my turn. I feel out of place—these people are truly sick, and I'm well enough to have walked sixteen hundred miles. I'm just sore and tired and unhappy.

"What prayer may I say for you?" he asks.

"My knee sometimes hurts me and I'm afraid it will keep me from finishing my hike," I say. "Also I am a little depressed."

It sounds so trivial. Then his hand is on my forehead, and the hands of the other people—people I don't even know—are on my shoulders.

"I lay my hands upon you in the name of the Father, and of the Son, and of the Holy Spirit," he says, "beseeching our Lord Jesus Christ to sustain you with his presence, to drive away all sickness of body and spirit, especially those injuries that would prevent you from completing your journey, and the sadness that afflicts you, and to give you that victory of life and peace which will enable you to serve him both now and evermore."

After the service we stand around trading pleasantries for a few minutes: the priest is visiting from another parish and doesn't know much about the trail or the hiker hostel nearby. Though I've showered that morning, my clothes still smell, and I am painfully aware of my stink, but no one says a thing or draws back. He asks the usual questions about food, and bears, and snakes, and then we shake hands and I leave, and set off for town to get a haircut and do my laundry.

Tonic and Mossman have arrived ahead of me. They came to town about the same time as me on Tuesday afternoon, and like me they've taken Wednesday off to prepare for the last push through the Green Mountains to Hanover, New Hampshire. We met back in the Shenandoah: Tonic had treated Kilgore Trout's blisters during that grinding week of catch-up-and-keep-up. I've been just behind them since Delaware Water Gap, and have stayed with them at a monastery at Bear Mountain and a motel room in Connecticut. Mossman is a trim, compactly muscled man with kinky copper-blond hair that has just started to recede, a mischievous grin, a stubbled boxer's face, and a heavy tan from his work as a landscaper in Florida. He favors sleeveless shirts. Tonic is nearly his height and usually wears a tank top that reveals strong, long-muscled shoulders and arms; she has a wide forehead, large bright eyes under short-cropped brown hair, and a heart-shaped face. She's from Colorado, where she's been working as an EMT and waiting tables near a ski resort. Both of them are around thirty. They met in Damascus, fell in love in southwestern Virginia, and will finish the trail together.

After the service I run into them several times in town as I shop, gorge myself at McDonald's, buy a book on Teddy Roosevelt, and wash my laundry. They've recently caught up to a friend of Tonic's, "Broken Arrow," a woman who was hiking to Katahdin from Connecticut; that night we all walk in the rain to a pizza restaurant, and then go to the movies together. Afterward, I stop on the way back to the hostel to call Cathy and make some other phone calls.

I've spent the morning poring over the mileage charts, trying to predict when I'll finish. My knee has hurt me for the last week, but the day off has helped it, so I stop worrying about it and start thinking about the final push to Maine. From here to Katahdin there are no relatives or friends to take me off the trail; the only people I know in Maine are a married couple from my graduate school days with whom I haven't spoken or corresponded in nearly ten years. Still, even without help, it looks as if I might be able to make it by the tenth of October if I can average a little better than twelve miles a day for the next forty-four days, which appears possible. That includes two more days off: one in Gorham, New Hampshire, after I cross the White Mountains, and one in Monson, Maine, before I begin the final hike through the desolate forest land known as the "Hundred-Mile Wilderness" to Katahdin. It's time to start thinking about how to get home at the end of the hike. I've always assumed I'll be coming home by myself, on a bus or train, but now Cathy is thinking about using some extra vacation and flying up to meet me.

"When will you be finishing?" she says.

"I don't know for sure," I say. "Right now I'm shooting for sometime around the first week of October—maybe as late as the tenth."

"I can get a good airfare for the two of us if I buy thirty days in advance."

"I'll call you from New Hampshire," I say. "I'll have a better idea by then. You should still have time."

After we finish talking, I call down to "Wingfoot" Bruce, the guidebook editor in North Carolina, hoping he will have information about a hostel a few days north of here that has mysteriously closed, but where I've shipped some replacement boots. No, he says—no idea about that. But have we heard that a thruhiker has died in the White Mountains?

His trail name was Gator Boy, Wingfoot says. He'd been on the trail since Harpers Ferry, doing a flip-flop thruhike after graduating from college this spring: Harpers Ferry to Katahdin, then Harpers Ferry to Springer. He'd come back to the trail after attending a rock concert, and collapsed a week ago near one of the peaks on Franconia Ridge. A lot of rumors are flying around, and Wingfoot wants to put them to rest: it wasn't drug-related, or carelessness; Gator Boy apparently died from a hidden medical condition—brain lesions—that led to seizures as he climbed Mount Lincoln.

That's still about two weeks north of me. Suddenly it isn't so far.

39

EVERYWHERE THROUGH Connecticut, Massachusetts, and Vermont, the roads teemed with off-road brawn—gleaming, spotless four-wheeling mudmobiles suitable for the harshest backwoods Forest Service bogway but that would never get any closer to the wilderness than the blacktop out of town that crossed the Appalachian Trail, or maybe a leaf-peeping expedition as the fall colors changed. A hiker hitching a ride was better off waiting for the old pickup truck, or the AMC sedan with the drunk behind the wheel. Fortunately, there were plenty of kindred spirits around to offset the anxious SUV owners. One driver, Kampfire, who'd been one of the slackpack evangelists down at the campground in Tennessee, had spent the rest of the summer following the pack of northbound hikers like an Inuit following the caribou, offering rides to and from the trail (donations accepted, thank you) and joining in the off-trail celebrations. He was in New England now, and he periodically posted his pager number at kiosks along the trail and bulletin boards in hostels.

Just as Gator Boy had, a lot of the younger thruhikers caught rides to the big Phish concert in Maine—the "Went," as it was called. It was a daylong spectacle at a decommissioned air force base in the wilds of Maine that the band had rented out, with private security, so its fans could have an uninhibited concert experience. Many Phish fans had been followers of the Grateful Dead, or were at least peripherally connected to the Deadhead culture that trailed the band from venue to venue. With the death of Jerry Garcia in 1995, the lifestyle had died hard, and rather than give it up some began to follow Phish and other groups much as they'd followed the Dead. A lot of hikers were fans too. I'd seen half a dozen I knew gathering at a town in Connecticut to catch a ride to the Went. It had been a regular feature of trail conversation for weeks.

Once I asked Dancing Bear, who'd been to several dozen Dead concerts and took his name from his tattoo of one of the Dead's icons, what the connection was. Part of it was freedom, he said. But you had to like hiking too—it wasn't just a party on the trail. There wasn't a huge drug scene here, though certainly there was plenty of "green-blazing," particularly in the first month. He'd never really gotten in a group discussion with any of the other Deadheads about what brought them out here. But from what he'd seen, there had always been this "hippie kind of thing" going on out on the trail—whether it was the freedom or the challenge or the low cost of living, he wouldn't even want to guess.

Well, here's a guess. As the Dead toured, and their fans followed, they offered a mythology and narrative about spontaneity, community, and living the moment in an age when those things aren't much rewarded. It wasn't a considered philosophy or a formally structured set of beliefs, but it was a mythology and a story to live by just the same. The trail offered a mythology too, and the walk north promised a narrative, one that spoke to many of the same things. It took a little more work getting from place to place, and it was harder to stay wasted on the way, but the appeal wasn't so different.

LIKE THE APPALACHIAN TRAIL, Vermont's Long Trail begins in the middle of nowhere, at the crest of East Mountain on the Vermont-Massachusetts line, and ends in the middle of nowhere, at the Canadian border, 265 miles farther north. Also like the A.T., white blazes mark its route, and though the two trails share the same path for over a hundred miles, Vermont's trail maintainers, the Green Mountain Club, could perhaps be forgiven if they showed a pronounced chauvinism for their own. After all, though the A.T. might be the most famous long-distance American hiking trail, it wasn't the first. That distinction belongs to the Long Trail, which inspired Benton MacKaye to imagine its far longer sibling. Other lengthy trails existed in New England before the Green Mountain Club started digging treadway in 1910, but historians Laura and Guy Waterman have called the Long Trail "the first conception of a long-distance hiking trail as the ultimate expression of mountain walking."

To thruhikers, the change is mostly superficial: A.T. signs become scarce at road crossings and shelters, L.T. signs proliferate. Welcome to Vermont. Welcome to the Long Trail. And welcome to the beginning of the end. That was the real change: soon we were among the first really formidable mountains—the ski resort peaks of Stratton and Killington—that we'd seen since south of the Shenandoah. And by late August the Long Trail was where the long hot summer began giving way to the New England fall, and the idea of reaching Maine became real.

40

White Blaze—Day 153
Sunday, August 31, 1997 • Kent Pond, Vermont
Green Mountains • 1,676 miles hiked • 484 miles to go
Partly cloudy • Low 52, high 70
Elevation 1,535 feet

MOSSMAN GRINS AND GREETS ME, affecting his git-down-funky-soul-brother voice, clowning for Tonic's benefit and his own amusement. "Yo! Mister Rhymin' Worm!"

They have been trading off with a Walkman and headphones for several days. This morning is Tonic's turn, but Mossman can't quit talking about an NPR interview he'd heard earlier, where some inner-city kids had talked about their "crimey cousins," and how hard it was to stay out of trouble. He turns to Tonic, who is a few steps back.

"Yo, crimey! Whassup?" he said.

"Mossman, you're insane," she says, shoving him playfully as she comes up to him along the trail.

"I'm crimey," he says, wrestling briefly with her.

"You're crazy!" Tonic says, laughing.

Broken Arrow comes around the bend and laughs awkwardly at the horseplay. She's a third party here, and it makes for some tricky moments. She and Tonic were best friends before the hike, and had intended to thruhike together until Broken Arrow fractured an ankle just before flying to Georgia. She stayed home in a cast for most of the summer. Tonic hiked north on her own. Mossman hadn't been part of the plans.

We've been together since Manchester Center, three days earlier, and suddenly, after fifteen hundred miles, I find myself beginning to wonder if maybe I've found the group I'll stay with the rest of the way to Katahdin. We've tented or sheltered together several times as we work our way north through the birch forests and goldenrod-clad fields of the Green Mountains. Last night we camped a couple of miles apart—I kept going after they stopped along a likely looking stream—but they catch me this morning at the Governor Clement Shelter before I leave, and Mossman is horsing around with Tonic while I pack up.

She's trying to get him to quit so she can hear a news report on her headphones. But he jostles her again. Whatsa matter, crimey?

"C'mon Mossman, hey . . . oh my God, she died. Princess Diana's dead."

Her car has crashed, Tonic says, standing motionless. She was being chased by photographers and her car crashed.

It's so strange to have this news in the middle of the woods. We are still talking about it ten miles farther along the trail, at McGrath's Irish

Pub in the Inn at Long Trail, north of Killington Peak, where we stop for lunch and a few beers that afternoon. Occasionally a special report, "Death of a Princess," flashes on the large-screen television. Millions are grieving. They were going one hundred miles an hour when they lost control. A hundred miles an hour, Mossman says, shaking his head. Can you imagine?

Sure, I can imagine. *If it bleeds, it leads*. That's what a local television newsman I knew used to say at the bar with the other journalists after work, mocking his own profession, back when I worked at a newspaper. What a story.

I thought of Gator Boy, the young hiker who died in the mountains I'd soon be climbing. That too would be news: a young hiker dies mysteriously on a rugged mountain, alone on the famous Appalachian Trail, but it would never make headlines anywhere except the local paper, and in his hometown, where he would be more than just another name. His life had come much closer to mine than the famous princess, yet what did I know of him? Earlier I'd passed a register in which, with childlike lines and letters, he'd drawn a picture of a hiker with an alligator head, jumping along the ridgeline. "Gator Boy, hip-hopping peak to peak," it said. He had been very happy, apparently.

By now we've all had a few beers and no one much feels like hiking any more. But rooms at the inn are out of our price range, the nearby state park is full with Labor Day weekend campers, and the next shelter is too far away, so we yellow blaze a mile down the road to a deli half a mile from the trail, buy some dinner and some beer, carry it into the woods along the A.T., and sneak into a wooded area where camping is forbidden. That evening we sit drinking beers on a swampy island at the edge of a wide pond, watching the sun set through late-summer haze as cumulonimbus clouds march across the red western sky and the darkness spreads over the water. From here, the trail leaves the Green Mountains, turning east, away from the Long Trail, toward New Hampshire and the Whites, toward Maine and Katahdin. The next morning, Labor Day, September first, cries of loons on the pond wake us at dawn.

TWO DAYS LATER, Back at the Steeplejack's house, they are making a stone soup. Before we'd slackpacked away that morning, everyone had chipped in a few bucks, and a thruhiker named Kadiddle took charge of the menu: eggplant parmesan, pasta with steamed vegetables, bread, roasted garlic, and wine. Now, as darkness falls over the parking lot outside the Hanover Food Co-Op, Mossman, Tonic, Broken Arrow, and several others wander around waiting for the Steeplejack's van to arrive and take us back twenty miles so we can join the others for the big dinner.

"The Steeplejack" is not a trail name: he is the genuine article, a hulking, gruff, Irish contractor who has made a small fortune repairing historic clock towers, domes, and church steeples across the mid-Atlantic and New England. A few years back he'd bought a farm in the Vermont hill country, between the Green Mountains and the Connecticut River Valley. He'd trucked his gear and tools up to the huge old three-floor New England barn and filled it with his ladders, ropes, scaffolds, and tools. He'd parked his Jaguar sedan in the driveway of the old farmhouse across the highway, rebuilt the kitchen, added a deck and a hot tub looking out over the grassy backyard and the creek behind the house. But he wasn't married anymore when he bought the place, and he sometimes rattled around it when he wasn't away on a job. He'd done some hiking himself, and had started noticing the regular stream of hikers crossing the road a few hundred yards south of the house. One day a few of them asked to sleep in his red barn, he invited them over to the house, and suddenly there was a new stop along the Pilgrims' Way.

"Can you believe this guy?" we'd said as we hiked east toward the Connecticut River Valley through leafy birch groves shot through with the yellow of coming fall. He opens up his house, his barn, his kitchen.

He gives keys to his work vans to thruhikers he barely knows, allowing them to go off for groceries in Woodstock, to slackpack each other for miles in all directions. In return he asks for a little gas money for the vans, an hour of manual labor at the barn, and nothing else other than good humor, responsible behavior, and good stories from the trail. Need some trail magic? The Steeplejack is the genuine article.

We've already spent one night at the Steeplejack's, arriving early Tuesday, dropping our packs at the house, and pushing on halfway to Hanover before stopping to be picked up and shuttled back. We'd stopped in the pricey residential town of Woodstock for groceries and beer and brought it back to the house, where we'd showered off and cleaned up for the first time in a week. The others had tented out on the lawn. With rain threatening, I'd chosen to roll out my sleeping bag and mattresses on the second floor of the barn, which I'd had all to myself, surrounded only by the great ghostly ladders and ropes looming in the musty emptiness. That night the rain had rattled down on the roof, chasing away the silence of the darkened barn.

Now we arrive to find a sudden impromptu convocation of thruhikers that has gathered nearly everyone on the trail between Sherburne Pass, twenty miles to the west, and Hanover, twenty miles to the east. Fall is coming. It has snapped cool the last week as we've hiked north from Massachusetts, and it feels good to be inside for a change, pack off, boots off, clean and rosy from a hot shower, drowsing in a comfortable chair as the windows fog over from the steaming pots. RockDancer is here, and surprised to see me. He figured I was two days ahead. I may seem to be here now, I explain, but I'm really at the co-op parking lot in Hanover, twenty miles farther north, where the Steeplejack's slackpack van picked us up earlier. Several southbounders are staying too, two of whom have been off the trail for a while with the Steeplejack, doing work for him and keeping the house open to thruhikers when he's away. The Steeplejack's girlfriend, a massage therapist in Woodstock, shows up. Soon there are nearly twenty of us.

And what are we celebrating? Only the end of the summer, the beginning of fall, the changing of the leaves, the companionship of a season's walking, and the unexpected gift of a stranger's hospitality. Now, as we try to steel ourselves to hike the last 450 miles—the last big push north through the Whites, the Mahoosucs, the Bigelows, the Hundred Miles—for one night we solitary pilgrims became a loud, joyous congregation. Hikers swirl around the first floor of the house, phoning home, drinking beer and wine, and demolishing the remaining food. A Van Morrison CD plays on the boom box. The Steeplejack recounts to several avid listeners a story of how Bob Vila and his *This Old House* show had come to film a historic church he was restoring, but had departed in a huff when the Steeplejack kept correcting Vila on-camera.

RockDancer and I sit back in the TV room and spend a few minutes catching up, comparing hikes. "You know," he says, "this is probably what Never-Never Land was like in the beginning, before it became an institution."

He's right: this was what I'd hoped that pilgrim resort back in Virginia would be when I showed up back there in June—an impromptu gathering with no rituals, no unwritten rules, and no favorites played. Surely it can't last. Surely, by next year, the Steeplejack will tire of the demands of hikers, the wear and tear on equipment, home, and grounds. Or, if he formalizes things and makes it a regular pilgrim resort, allowing it to be listed in the guidebooks, surely next year's thruhikers will take it for granted, push the limits of his hospitality, and begin to treat it like any other traditional stop along the way. The magic is right here, right now—it will never be like this again.

A while later I wobble back to the barn through a cold mist and pick my way through the dark interior, with its hulking shapes and the sound of rain scattering on the roof one floor up. I am a little drunk, but deeply happy with myself, with my hike, and with the world of the trail. A week of hiking with friends who enjoy my company, a week when the world's tragedy and sorrow is forgotten while we glory in the beautiful rolling landscape of Vermont on the cusp of fall: this is the Pilgrims' Way at its best, a stone soup where everyone contributes something. The taste is indescribable.

FEW EARLY DEPARTURES TAKE place that next morning. Rock-Dancer shoulders his pack on the front porch, says good-bye, and heads back down the road to the trail. By then it is nearly eleven. Time to get moving, I think. Only no one is ready to move, and Hanover is twenty miles away—twenty miles I've already walked. I can only wait. I sit around on the deck in the chill, talking to Tonic and Broken Arrow. They're going to take another day off the trail in Hanover.

Another day in Hanover? We'd spent most of yesterday there after slackpacking in. We'd shopped, eaten at a pizzeria, and picked up our mail. My business there is finished. I'm rested, well fed, resupplied, and ready to go. Another day in Hanover?

They don't want it to end!

No one does. By now we have been out here on the trail for five months. Gone are the out-of-shape dreamers who blistered themselves off the trail in the first week, gone are the college-age kids out looking for a rolling town-to-town party, gone are the talkers and dabblers, the recreational backpackers who came looking for inspiring vistas, those who set themselves a meaningless endurance challenge. They have dropped by the wayside—at Neels Gap, at Fontana Dam, at Hot Springs, at Damascus, at Harpers Ferry, at Delaware Water Gap. Those remaining, though they might never say so, have come out here looking for a community of kindred spirits and a part of themselves that seeks something they don't really understand. And now, as the end draws into sight, though perhaps no closer to finding what they're after, they don't want the searching to end. They don't ever want to stop dreaming of reaching Katahdin.

On and on the morning lingers, and the waiting stretches into early afternoon—a chill, blustery day of cold air direct from Quebec. No one at the Steeplejack's can be persuaded to move. Finally one of the authorized slackpack drivers agrees to drive to Hanover in one of the vans. He lacks a valid driver's license, and the van's insurance has lapsed, but, okay, he'll do it if we don't mind dropping off a couple of hikers in Woodstock for massage appointments at the office of the Steeplejack's girlfriend. I pile my gear in along with that of Tonic, Mossman, Broken Arrow, Hiker Ned and his wife, Sweet Pee, and a couple of others. We rattle sickeningly across the Vermont back roads, finally ending near the green of Dartmouth College, where one of the campus fraternities allows thruhikers to sleep in the basement.

Mossman asks me if I'm going to be in town tonight. I tell him I don't know.

I wander down the street to Everything But Anchovies and order a pizza. While I wait, I recalculate my schedule, but the guidebook offers no real help on this question.

I've been hiking with Tonic and Mossman and Broken Arrow for the last week, and it has been the best week of the hike. Maybe they'll get sick of me, but then, maybe we'll just become better friends. Maybe RockDancer will catch up. We can see this through together. So we'll finish a week later, two weeks later. What difference will that make? The gates to Maine's Baxter State Park close on October 15, but for years thruhikers have found ways to climb Katahdin after the park officially shuts down. It might mean getting snowed on, but I'll be picking up my winter gear in a week. I can handle it. I'll just phone Cathy, tell her I'll be two weeks late, and that will be that. Just two more weeks, I'll tell her.

Or I can leave the others behind, hike out tonight, stay at the shelter north of Hanover, leave early the next morning, push on into the Whites by next week, and arrive in Maine on schedule.

After eating a large pizza I stop at the Ben & Jerry's scoop shop. Two thruhikers, Time to Fly and the Texas Ramen Shaman, stand outside, and wave happily to see me. They ask if I'm staying in town, if I'm going to the movies with them tonight. I tell them I don't know.

"Better decide, bro," Time to Fly says. "You're burning daylight."

By now it's after three. I go into the shop, order a banana split, and linger over it, looking out the window at the students passing back and forth. Freshman orientation begins this week.

I look at my watch. Time to fly, all right. Time to go if I still want to get anywhere. Time to go home.

All spring, all summer I've tried to keep from thinking about going home. After all, home was where I'd become so desperate I couldn't allow myself to feel anything anymore—not love, not compassion, not happiness, not pride, not excitement, only anger and remorse. Mostly, I didn't allow myself to feel, period. For feeling I came out here, where I could feel happy about a long day's walk, a breathtaking view, the wheeling progress of seasons, new friends, the wild things in the forest.

But I can't stay out here forever. None of us can. We can only make it last a few more weeks, or start repeating ourselves. What we had at the Steeplejack's last night can't be frozen in time. It will be different tomorrow. Hell, next year it might not even be there, and we'll have to go looking for the next place, all the while telling stories of the Steeplejack's, and the way it used to be.

Time to go home. Time to find out how much of what I've found here I can bring back. The old dog will be glad to see me. But it's Cathy I miss, Cathy I've left so hurt and so confused, Cathy who loves me even after I've poured out all of this midlife angst on her and made her doubt her own heart, Cathy who is there for me, whatever else was wrong with my life. Sure, she's angry with me for this, and not letting me forget that I should feel guilty hasn't made the walk north any easier, but she hasn't cut me off and turned away either. I think of the handful of times we've seen each other since April Fools' Day. Each time it has felt so good to see her. Each time it has felt so bad to leave. And each time I have made myself think only about getting back to the trail, where I can just walk.

Time to go home. There will be a lot of pieces to pick up. It will be hard.

I just have to get to Katahdin first.

Four

MONADNOCK

In such manner had each of the orogenies of the Appalachians cannibalized the products of previous pulses, and now we were left with this old mountain range, by weather almost wholly destroyed, but nonetheless containing in a traceable and unarguable way the rock of its ancestral mountains.

—John McPhee, In Suspect Terrain

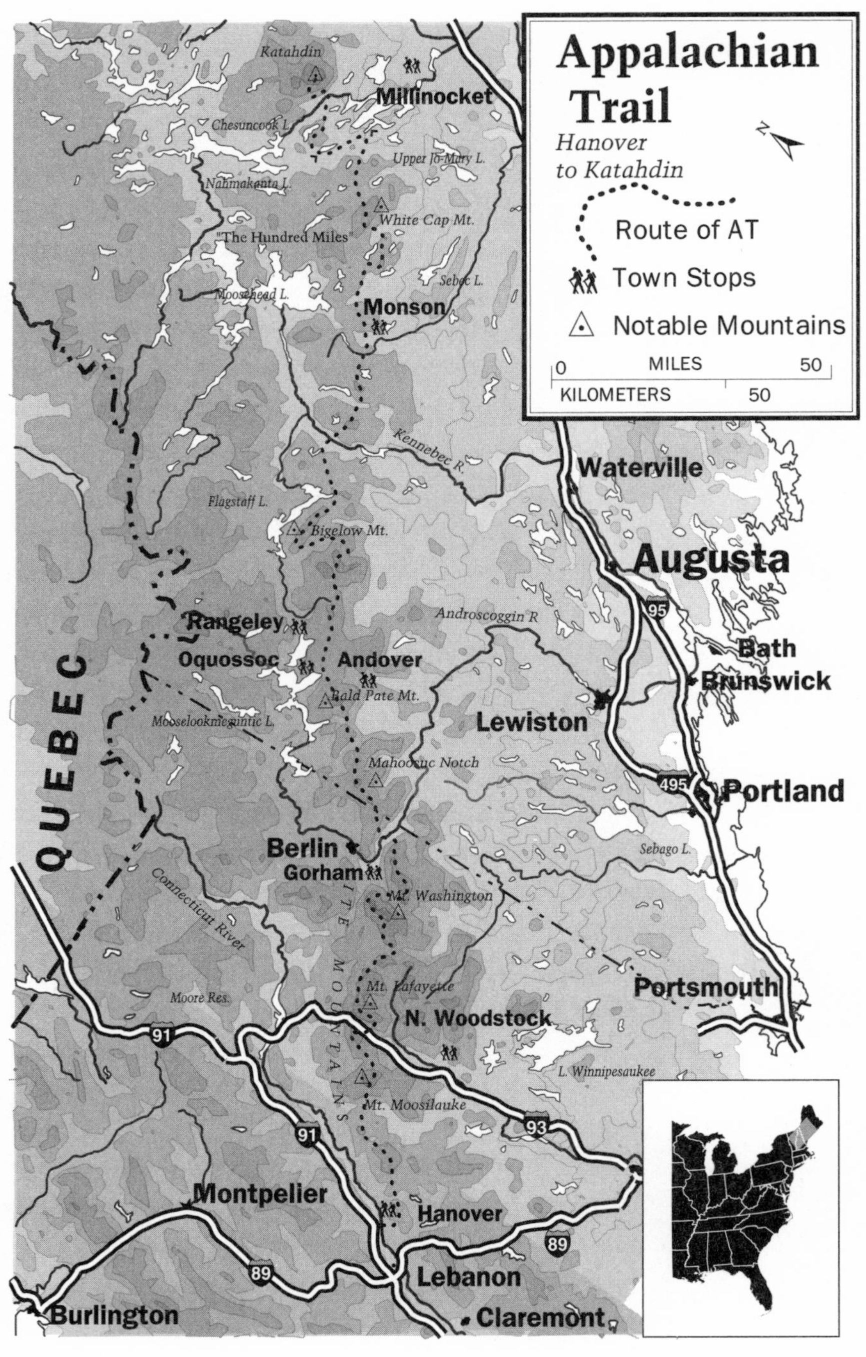

Appalachian Trail
Hanover to Katahdin
Route of AT
Town Stops
Notable Mountains
0
MILES
50
KILOMETERS
50
Katahdin
Millinocket
Chesuncook L.
Upper Jo-Mary L.
Nahmakanta L.
White Cap Mt.
"The Hundred Miles"
Sebec L.
Moosehead L.
Monson
Kennebec R.
Waterville
Flagstaff L.
Bigelow Mt.
Augusta
95
Androscoggin R
Rangeley
Oquossoc
Andover
Bath
Brunswick
Bald Pate Mt.
Mooselookmeguntic L.
Lewiston
QUEBEC
Mahoosuc Notch
495
Portland
Berlin
Gorham
Sebago L.
Connecticut River
Mt. Washington
Portsmouth
Moore Res.
Mt. Lafayette
N. Woodstock
91
L. Winnipesaukee
Mt. Moosilauke
93
91
Montpelier
Hanover
89
89
Lebanon
Burlington
Claremont

41

YES, THEY ARE ANCIENT, the Appalachians. Old as the hills. Older, really, for the hills we know today are what has not washed away during the 500 million years since colliding continents first crumpled into Himalayan-sized waves of rocky folds, the lineaments of which today's geologists can only infer. As they piece together from fragments of rock a picture-puzzle of mountains primeval, it's as if a portrait of a departed ancestor emerges. Though its spirit still haunts the hills, only its bones remain as the old ridges of bedrock and quartzite, its teeth as the massive monadnocks like Georgia's Stone Mountain and Maine's Katahdin.

Geologists still feud about that ancestor, and how exactly it manifested itself, and what precisely gave rise to it. Their lexicon dizzies the casual student with terms like *block faulting*, *subduction zones*, *plate tectonics*, *island arcs*, and the mountain-building episodes they call *orogenies*. The old arguments employed terms like *geosynclines* and *peneplains* and the *geographical cycle of erosion*. They are not wholly discredited, but most theories now favor the idea of continental collisions. They tell you that a supercontinent called Pangaea formed when the Ocean of Iapetus was slammed shut as North Africa began a 250-million-year-long train wreck into the eastern seaboard, before rending open again to form the Atlantic Ocean we now know. Today's Appalachians are the eroded remnants of the train wreck, still jutting up through younger rock to remind us just how long ago it all was.

It's hard not to gain at least a little appreciation for the geologists and their stories during a thruhike, when the slate folds and quartz dikes and granitic intrusions are constantly calling themselves to your attention. The guidebooks offer shorthand discussions of theories, and consider shales and schists and basalts as if they're common knowledge. Some of it eventually sinks in. Hikers who seventeen hundred miles earlier couldn't tell mica from Mickey Mouse find themselves pausing to admire rock formations and speculate on how they got to be there.

The mountains of the south—the Blue Ridge, the Smokies, the Nantahalas, the Unakas, the Black Mountains—wear their age decorously, hiding it under wrinkled skins of topsoil and trees. Their rounded contours and time-sculpted edges are cracked and worn like old leather. But north of Delaware Water Gap and into New England and Canada, the Appalachians show the stony cicatrix of recent Ice Age glaciation, which scored and carved the old mountains into a kind of grotesque imitation of youth, like an aging movie star whose skin the plastic surgeons have stretched paper-tight over sharp cheekbones and bony eye sockets. Glacier-graven notches and cirques coil around the peaks, cutting spectacularly through granite and bedrock, scattering moraines and erratics and eskers at their feet. And, from the White Mountains on north, the hills often rise above treeline, the elevations at which little lives other than lichens, moss, and a few backpackers.

Treeline, which climate rather than altitude determines, occurs where the mountains poke up into a part of the atmosphere at which arctic conditions prevail. In New Hampshire, that's around 4,000 feet above sea level. Farther north, in central Maine and southeastern Canada, it ranges from 3,000 to 3,500 feet; in the South, none of the mountains—not even Clingmans Dome or Mount Mitchell, the two highest mountains east of the Mississippi—rise into the arctic zone. Above treeline you find plants and animals common to the arctic tundra of northern Canada. Between the high ridges, the swampy valleys and glacial passes known as "notches" are often temperate and protected. Northbound thruhikers, having spent four months under the summer's green canopy, two of those four in the low ridges of the mid-Atlantic, can't wait to climb up where they can see again.

Below treeline the terrain of upcountry New England often becomes boggy, and in the White Mountain National Forest moose sometimes splash through shallow ponds and swamps near low sections of trail. As I'd moved into those uplands, I'd expected rocks and waterfalls, not swamps. Glaciers have gouged out hundreds of ponds and kettles and valleys, which later filled in with sediment. Many of the creeks flow from beaver ponds, and often the trail descends from a granite hillside to a rush-ringed marsh of grass and shallow water. Rivers and mountain streams begin here, running over water-smoothed stones and around erratic boulders deposited as the glaciers retreated through the hills.

Since mid-June I've been carrying summer gear: a light sleeping bag meant for temperatures above fifty degrees, light clothes, and an eleven-ounce fuel bottle since I don't cook much in hot weather. Now, though, as I approach the White Mountains in September, it's time to reequip for winter. The Whites may not be as lofty as the Smokies or some the high country of North Carolina and Tennessee, but the weather they catch makes them a lot more dangerous to hike through, particularly since many of them rise above treeline onto the glacier-stripped ridgelines, where nothing at all stands between a hiker and winter winds sweeping down out of Canada.

Every year hundreds of unprepared hikers, climbers, and skiers in the White Mountains get caught above treeline in arctic weather, which can descend during any season. Every year it surprises people. Nearly every year someone dies. During the year I was on the trail, Appalachian Mountain Club crews went out over fifty times on White Mountain search-and-rescue missions. Already, three weeks earlier, Gator Boy had died on Mount Lincoln when the time bomb in his brain went off; as I passed through Hanover I'd heard rumors of two day hikers who'd followed their dog off a cliff in the July fog, one of whom had also died; and an elderly man had recently died of a heart attack on Franconia Ridge. Each time, Appalachian Mountain Club search crews went out to find the injured, or the dead, and begin the labor of manhandling them down from the ancient and barren world above treeline to places more amenable to the usual business of living and dying.

42

White Blaze—Day 164
Thursday, September 11, 1997 • Franconia Notch • New Hampshire
White Mountains • 1,788 miles hiked • 372 miles to go
Overcast • Low 51, high 64
Elevation 1,450 feet

I'M LIGHTHEADED AND slightly drunk from three or four beers when I call Cathy after dinner from a gas station phone booth in North Woodstock, New Hampshire. The last week has seen me hike out of Hanover, leaving Tonic and Mossman and Broken Arrow and the others behind, and push into the Whites, on my own again. I've been above treeline for the first time, and watched as the yellows of early fall begin mixing with reds and oranges in the high country. Even though I'm carrying fifty pounds of gear and supplies again, I've been hiking powerfully, feeling like an unbreakable machine, and keeping near my hundred-miles-a-week pace despite terrain that has gotten tough. By this time next month I expect to be finished.

This good news goes undelivered. Cathy gasps and cries out as soon as she hears my voice: for the last three days she has been trying frantically to locate me on the trail, with no luck. It has been a horrible week.

Our last phone call had been when I was on my way out of Hanover, pushing north to finish sooner rather than later. "I'm ready to come home," I'd said. "I'm ready to finish this."

We'd talked about what came next, after the trail, and as I was about to hang up I described to her an idea I'd had for a research project. No more hiking, but it might involve some travel, and maybe coming back here to New Hampshire to search through some library papers.

Later she begins dwelling on this, and it grows and darkens in her imagination. This is how my idea to hike the trail began, as a small notion, a simple wish to do some backpacking that perverted itself into this huge obsession for which I abandoned a career, put marriage and home and savings at risk, saddled her with the job of making sure it is all still there six months later, and went running into the woods with no real plan other than heading north. And what will stop me from doing it again, and again? If not a thruhike, then something equally impractical, equally destructive? But by the time her questions take shape, I am back in the woods. She tries to leave messages, but I don't get them, and she doesn't know exactly where I'll be next.

Then, that weekend, Princess Diana's funeral plays itself out on television, and despite herself Cathy watches it, live from London: the princess her own age, whose fairy-tale wedding had taken place when Cathy had been a student abroad in France and England. She'd watched the wedding back then, only to see it slowly come apart in the tabloids as the years passed. She'd read the stories of a young woman forced into a straitjacket of expectations; a princess whose prince turned out to be distant, unsympathetic, and eager to divorce her for another woman; a celebrity who despite beauty and glamour battled eating disorders, depression, doubt. It all ends in that horrible crash and the slow ambulance ride to the hospital as life bleeds away, just at the moment when the woman may be taking charge, letting go the ragged shreds of the fairy tale to live outside the golden cage. Elton John sings "Good-bye England's Rose," the flowers pile up outside the gates, and

Cathy sits on the bed watching and weeping, unable to help herself, unable to find me, unable to do anything except wait for my next call.

We talk for over an hour; I sober up quickly. I want to be home too. I lay out my plans for finishing the hike: four more weeks. I'll call from Mount Washington, from the town of Gorham on the other side of the White Mountains, and from the towns of Rangely, Caratunk, and Monson in Maine. Go ahead and make reservations, I say. I'll be there.

Leaving North Woodstock the next morning, I try to put the phone call behind me. Going home now won't solve anything, any more than it would have when she fainted in June. *I don't want to have gone through all this shit for nothing,* she'd said back then. I still have hiking to do, and I need to finish, to get this behind me, behind both of us.

As I hitchhike out of town, I keep glancing at the weather. A heavy overcast has set in, and I am about to tackle Franconia Ridge, a climb of nearly 3,800 feet to the summit of Mount Lafayette, and a long, exposed walk above treeline. Down in the notch it's warm and muggy, but that won't be the case on the ridgeline.

At least I'm ready now. After seventeen hundred miles of hiking, I'm fit enough, and equipment doesn't mean so much now—I'm confident in a way I wasn't back in the spring, on those subfreezing nights in North Carolina. That counts for a lot, but not everything: warm clothes are indeed required. One night, before I entered the Whites or got my winter gear in the mail, the temperature fell into the forties and I lay shivering in a shelter with all my clothes on, my silvered plastic emergency blanket draped over the summer bag, unable to get warm. I've lost about seventy pounds of body fat by this time, and my built-in insulation layer is gone. About four o'clock in the morning, when I looked at the tiny thermometer-compass dangling from the zipper of my backpack, it read thirty-eight degrees. Using the formula that each additional thousand feet of altitude means a temperature drop of three degrees, I figured that on Mount Washington, the highest summit in New England at 6,288 feet, it was twenty-five degrees, not counting windchill.

But now I was looking forward to the Whites too much to let them scare me. And I'd gotten inside information.

Descending steeply toward Wachipauka Pond just before the first climb up Mount Moosilauke into the Whites, I'd seen a hiker coming toward me from the bottom of the hill. He stopped and raised his hiking poles triumphantly.

"Is that the Rhyming Worm?" he shouted.

"Mr. Trout?"

"Mr. Worm!"

I pounded down the steep fifty yards of trail and we clapped hands around each other's shoulders and did the "How the hell have you been?" business. After he'd written me in Duncannon, we'd traded one more set of letters, and he'd laid out his southbound schedule. This was right about where it would have put him. But deep down I'd wondered if he would really come back.

We camped near there that night, working our way through the underbrush around Wachipauka Pond along a faint trail, trying to find any sort of small clearing where we could pitch tents. Some local fishermen passed us and glared at us for intruding on their domain, but finally we found a couple of scooped-out leafy spots near the water, dropped our packs and began rolling out the tents in a light mist of rain.

"So," I said. "You've climbed Katahdin?"

"I've climbed Katahdin," he said, grinning. "It's really there. They didn't lie to you."

He looked great. He looked happy. The last time I'd seen him, he'd been turning his feet into hamburger trying to keep up with the under-thirty crowd in Virginia. "You looked miserable in the Shenandoah."

"My feet were cooking," he said. "I needed some time off the trail. I came back down there in Virginia and I nearly caught you before the blisters got too bad."

He never got those boots broken in, though. He finally had to get a new pair. I told him I wished I'd known, I'd have waited. He said the way his feet were, he wasn't going much farther. They were now a size and a half larger than when he'd started. "I finally got some Sundowners my size, extra wide, and they feel good."

He had been hiking on and off with southbound thruhikers since leaving Katahdin about a month earlier, and had found the experience quite different from going north with the pack. He mentioned a few southbounders' names, all of whom I'd somehow missed. He kept meeting northbounders he knew, which was fun, but going south was mostly solitary. Still, he found himself feeling stronger and hiking more efficiently and consistently with each week. Now he was through the high mountains, and looking forward to making better time over the gentler trails between New Hampshire and Maryland.

We cooked dinner in the woods by the pond, talking about people we knew, what we'd seen, what we had to look forward to, what was behind us: RockDancer was probably a day or so back, along with Mossman and Tonic; he shouldn't miss the Steeplejack's. Bigfoot, Dancing Bear, Icebox, Trail Snail, and several other familiar names were a day or two ahead of me. Mr. Trout warned about the mountains of southern Maine, which had been surprisingly hard—the most difficult hiking of the whole trail for him—and he offered tips on getting through the Appalachian Mountain Club's fee-based shelter-and-hut system without going broke.

"Now you've just got to finish," I said. "If anyone deserves to finish, it's you."

"I was going to say the same thing," he said. "Except the tough part's ahead of you."

After dinner, to celebrate our meeting, he cooked a pot of chocolate pudding on his backpacking stove. Rain was coming down harder now, drifting in from over the pond, and we each retreated into our tents to finish it off, continuing our conversation late into the evening, disembodied voices in the rain-fragrant night.

Now, climbing out of Franconia Notch, I think of Mr. Trout's advice. But I also think of Gator Boy, who died making this same climb. 3,800 feet in six miles—only Mount Moosilauke matches it on the AT for sustained climbing, and only the ascent up Katahdin surpasses it. As the trail steepens, the weather worsens.

Hills have a kind of gravity to them that can overwhelm you if you're not ready. As you climb a steep, tree-mantled hill, the horizon draws in above you, shutting off the view and all sense of moving forward through space. It becomes just you and gravity. You look up and ahead, your pulse pounds in your ears, your nose runs, your legs feel leaden, the horizon of the hill looms over you, and rather than let it stagger you, you focus instead on some tree or rock in the middle distance, until the whole hillside pivots around that fixed point with each stride, the distant trees capering up and down and side to side, as if you're not moving at all, as if you're pinned to the hillside while the trees and rocks dance.

Keep at it, though, keep pushing, rest every few minutes, and eventually you begin to notice a change in the quality of light, an opening out, as if gravity has lessened and the sky has come back. Now, perhaps, you take the time to look up, away from the path, to peer through the trees, where suddenly you have a sense of distance, of other hills rising around you. As the light increases, the trail itself changes too, becoming stony, the bones of the hill splintering through the stubbled skin of dirt and shrubs and wind-stunted trees. Then the horizon that had closed you in seems to flee far away, miles and miles from you. The forest duff and mineral soil of the footpath give way to bare rock that juts out from the tree cover. Time and gravity seem ready to release you and let you hurry away toward the horizon.

I try to find a rhythm of breathing, walking, and planting my hiking poles. For the first few miles, I ascend through a hardwood forest of red and sugar maples, birch, beech, oak, and basswood, mixed with a few large pines and spruces. Yellow, orange, and red leaves from stressed or diseased trees drift down and rustle underfoot, and even the healthy trees show signs of turning. By the time I leave the Whites in a week, the colors will be all around me. Every quarter mile or so the woods echo with the shrill rattlesnakelike scolding of red squirrels, unhappy with this creature moving through their forest. About an hour into the climb the way steepens even more, and black spruce and balsam fir start to replace the maple and oak as the trail enters the boreal zone, still interspersed with birch and aspen. Needles begin to cover the ground, softening the sound of footsteps and filling the air with their acidic, piney scent. Near 4,000 feet, the trail leads even more steeply up, into the gray cloak of clouds atop the ridge. The air turns chill and raw. I make lunch at Liberty Spring Tentsite, refilling my water bottle at the spring, fixing a couple sandwiches of peanut butter and raisins wrapped up in flour tortillas, and put them in a Ziploc bag in the top pocket of my pack.

The campsite consists of a caretaker's heavy canvas tent staked down on a wooden platform, a spring, and several wooden sleeping platforms tucked away in the bushes. This had been Gator Boy's last camp three weeks earlier—he'd hiked up from Franconia Notch after spending the weekend at the Phish concert in Maine about the time I was in the Berkshire Hills of Massachusetts. I try to picture it: he felt sick after his climb and complained to the campsite's caretaker of migraine headaches. Must be dehydration, he told the caretaker, and the next morning, the twentieth, he felt a little better, and resisted the suggestion that he go back down the mountain. He was strong—a ski instructor, in fact—and he was in shape: he'd hiked eighty days and almost eight hundred miles already to get here. He would push on. He probably refilled his water bottle at Liberty Spring, as I was doing now, and continued on up the ridge.

By now the yellow birch leaves are gone and the evergreens appear shrunken and gnarled, some not much more than ten feet tall. Like

Japanese bonsai, they have been trimmed back and dwarfed by the unrelenting wind and ice that blasted and froze their new growth each winter. Botanists call the effect "krummholz," or "crooked wood," and it means I've entered the high subalpine zone. Sure enough, the path turns stony, the light increases around me even through the drizzle and overcast, a chill wind seethes through the rattling limbs, and I come up through the krummholz to the crest of the ridge. Small juncos and sparrows flit through the branches around me. Here the krummholz grows only shoulder-high.

From Liberty Spring the trail runs for almost a mile along a level glacier-raked section of ridgeline, somewhat sheltered from the wind by krummholz, before it begins its final two-mile climb along a narrow rock-tumbled spine to Mount Lincoln, and a mile farther to Mount Lafayette. Rain is in the air, and the wind whistles through the branches; I don my Gore-Tex jacket and stuff my fleece sweater under the hood of my pack, where I can grab it without opening the pack, tighten down the rain cover, and move above treeline.

Temperatures have been in the forties, but the wind streams hard out of the east, driving the chill factor down into the twenties. I hardly notice the rain: the wind is the thing, numbing my hands, working through the zippers and gaps of my jacket, singing against the hood that I've drawn tight over my head, whipping against my bare legs as I work my way rock to rock along the craggy ridge. The trail is marked by tumbled granite cairns, which appear through the fog like human figures, and blazes become scarce. It ascends steeply again, first to Little Haystack, then to the rockpile top of Mount Lincoln. Near the summit of Lincoln, I find a sheltered spot where I can take off my pack, pull on my rain pants, my fleece sweater, my polypropylene balaclava mask, and my mittens. The chill is getting to me. These are all my warm clothes except my long underwear. I eat two sandwiches and drink some water, but if I want to stay warm I have to keep moving, or bundle up in sleeping bag and tent.

Mount Lincoln doesn't even look much like a distinct peak when you reach it, just an upthrust of ridgeline rocks on the way up to Lafayette. Somewhere around here Gator Boy had lain down, unable to push himself farther. The headache had gotten too bad. He felt sick. The weather was still fair, and he snapped a couple of pictures with his camera: the blue sky, the rugged above-treeline beauty of Franconia Ridge. He pulled out his sleeping bag and got in: even in good weather, he knew, he had to stay warm up here. You could die up here if you weren't careful. Sometime later a family out for a hike came upon him in his sleeping bag and talked to him, then continued on, reporting to the caretaker at Liberty Springs that they'd encountered a hiker in trouble up on Mount Lincoln. The caretaker radioed the search-and-rescue team at nearby Greenleaf Hut, and they all went up after Gator Boy. He was still lucid when they arrived, but not long afterward a seizure hit; he lost consciousness and could not be revived.

The autopsy revealed a tumor in the center of his brain, about the size of a walnut. His name was Jacob Cram.

The wind picks up, and even in my winter gear I feel it. My massive pack, with the rain cover drawn around it, acts like a big sail, the wind hitting it at right angles and sometimes staggering me as I move up toward the summit, bracing myself with the hiking poles. Though I've cinched the rain cover as tight as possible, it balloons out to leeward, like a sailboat's genoa. My clothes flap and snap in the wind, and occasional bits of sleet sting my exposed face when I pull the balaclava down so I can breathe more easily. Atop the stony crown of Lafayette I find the ruined foundations of a nineteenth-century "summit house," and nearby a sign pointing down the ridge, away from the AT, to the Greenleaf Hut lodge.

Weighed down by stones, behind some rocks that shield it from the wind, lies a bouquet of blue flowers in a plastic wrapper. For Gator Boy, I guess, though he never quite made it here. But it is just too cold to linger now, to think about it, and him: a chill gray afternoon where the cairns fade into the clouds only a few dozen feet away, the temperature dropping and the wind picking up.

43

WHITE MOUNTAIN NATIONAL FOREST marks, more or less, the end of the New England of chrome-bright SUVs and ice cream counterculture and sitcom-quaint country inns. To its north lies the New England of Frost and Wyeth, not that of Longfellow or Rockwell. Here begin the North Woods that even at the end of the millennium spread largely uninterrupted into Maine, Quebec, across the Saint Lawrence, and on up the meridians to the arctic tundra. Winters get fierce enough that the idea of living year-round in an isolated backwoods cabin isn't a romantic lifestyle choice, it's freaking daft: towns are where people come home to at day's end from work out in forests, and lumber yards, and mills. Sure, there's tourism and leaf-peeping in the fall, and traffic to the great playground of the Whites themselves, but most of the summer cabins for Bostonians and New Yorkers are up in Maine; like French Canada, northern New Hampshire still feels rough as the granite at its bones.

The Whites signal that threshold, and hikers and campers have walked into them looking for wilderness since early in the Victorian era. In the years after northern New England's colonial farm economy crashed, when more convenient pasturelands opened in states to the south and west and hillside fields reverted to forest, early visitors like Thoreau regaled city dwellers with accounts of explorations in search of the sublime. After the Civil War, the first guidebooks appeared and the first hiking and outing clubs formed, promising alpine majesty to anyone with the time and means to journey into the high country. They said little about the going or the getting there. Rather than today's detailed trail descriptions, old guidebooks mostly gushed about the grandeur of summits and the magnificent views. Soon the fresh-air lovers who climbed up to see them firsthand began building primitive huts and shelters high on the ridges near popular camping spots, particularly the springs and tarns above treeline.

The early twentieth century had seen trails worm through the Whites, as the newly established U.S. Forest Service began acquiring land. The trail system grew with it, until by the time MacKaye's disciples arrived, spreading the gospel of the A.T., an established system of linked through paths already boasted its own proud constituency of hikers and maintainers. Even today, where the A.T. runs along those routes, the signs still announce the historic trail names, with A.T. blazes often hard to spot. The rough shelters grew into enclosed primitive lodges, or "huts," which, a century later, make up an elaborate system of hostelries run by the Appalachian Mountain Club. Each is maintained by a year-round caretaker; during the summer paid college-age "croos" staff them, packing in supplies and working as kitchen patrol, entertainment, musclepower, and guides to wayward hikers. Some of the huts can accommodate over a hundred people. Helicopters or croo "Sherpas" deliver bulk supplies and haul out trash. Visitors use the bunkrooms as base camps for excursions, or hike from hut to hut through the Whites, above treeline much of the time, without having to load up an expedition-weight pack. At $50 or more a night, and with reservations required, prices are a little steep for thruhikers.

At the center of this webwork of ridgeline trails and huts looms Mount Washington, rising fortresslike in the morning sun from fog banks that blanket the above-treeline summits of the Presidential Range. Sometimes a hollow wailing cry rings out in the morning air, and salt-and-pepper clouds of steam and smoke signify the Mount Washington Cog Railway, which since the Civil War has shuttled day-trippers and campers to hotels and lodges at the summit, mounting incrementally up the massive sloping shoulder of the mountain's northwest flank. Three great antennas from a weather station and visitor center on the summit glint crownlike in the sun, and as you near it you can discern silhouettes of the buildings. Benton MacKaye imagined the Appalachian Trail terminating here, the highest point in New England, but Maine boosters prevailed, extending the footpath to Katahdin.

Lucky for the A.T. Ending on Mount Washington would be like ending on the observation deck of the World Trade Center. Even though it's not a national park, more people visit the Whites every year than visit Yellowstone and Yosemite combined, and it seems as if most eventually end up at Mount Washington, arriving by railway or by car. With mountain huts often booked solid through the summer, thruhikers without money or reservations must either stay in their basements on a "work for stay" basis or descend to camping areas below treeline. Most popular of all are the three huts in the Presidentials near Mount Washington: Mizpah, Lakes of the Clouds, and Madison Springs.

I had come through on a Sunday, after the last day of the season, when Lakes of the Clouds Hut stood mostly empty in its high, stony saddle near the two minuscule spring-fed alpine "lakes" that gave it its name. Once the "croo" shooed away the last day hikers and backpackers, they set to work cleaning up and shutting the hut down for the winter. It had been full on that last night, but about eight thruhikers had managed to lodge there, either agreeing to work in the morning for the night's stay in the "dungeon" below the main floor or sleeping on the porch and hoping they wouldn't be noticed amid the end-of-season confusion. One lovestruck pilgrim had been hanging around for four days, waiting for a young woman with the trail name of "Beer Gurl," whom I'd seen in North Woodstock keeping company with another male thruhiker and showing no sign of wanting to hurry north.

No one was hurrying anywhere anymore. A strange spell comes over northbound thruhikers as they enter the Whites, as if the immensity of geologic time all around them has finally begun to work its slow sorcery in these magic mountains, and as long as they stay here they have all the time in the world. The summerlong catch-up-and-keep-up games have exhausted them, and now they begin to understand that the trail won't lead north forever. As I neared the top of Mount Washington, following the cairns carefully up a long jumble of rocks that sometimes showed signs of rearrangement into rough steps, I saw someone looking down from an outcropping in the gray cloud above me.

"All right!" he shouted. "The Worm!" And he raised his arms triumphantly. Bigfoot! Back in Hanover he'd been about a week ahead of me. I'd read in the registers about his encounters with pack-stealing bears and a wicked case of giardiasis, and now we finally had a chance to swap stories. I'd found the food bag I'd given him, bear-shredded, on an eastern Pennsylvania ridge. He'd been here a couple of days already, having spent one night at Lakes of the Clouds, and illegally "stealth camping" above treeline another. He'd joined the hut croo for a season-ending blowout, among other less formal celebrations, and was hugely happy. "I've been up Washington a couple of times already," he said, laughing. "This morning a couple of us hiked up naked at dawn and mooned the cog railway" (a long-standing thruhiker tradition). He and his hiking partners planned to dawdle around in the Whites until their supplies ran out.

"I figure I'll finish in late November," Bigfoot said, only half-joking. "Climb Katahdin in the snow—now *that* would be cool. I'll just call up my mom and say, 'It's gotten really hard, and it's going to take me a month longer than I thought. And would you mind sending another check?'" He chuckled at the thought. Mom was great—she'd understand.

It *would* be cool to climb Katahdin in the snow, if that didn't mean battling a blizzard, with windchills down below zero. For that was the only flaw in these plans: time might seem to move more slowly here, but the progress of the seasons rolled on unaffected. Winter was coming. You could feel it in the chill atop Mount Washington. Already I'd seen sleet on Mount Lafayette and snow flurries on South Kinsman

Mountain. There was always an element of danger in these mountains, but winter magnified it. RockDancer, who had hiked the Whites for years, had been extremely nervous about high-country weather in late September and October. But right now we felt invincible, hardened by five months on the trail, able to power up the mile-high ascents and steep rocky notches of the Whites more easily than we'd crossed the rolling foothills of Georgia. The worst was behind us.

44

White Blaze—Day 173
Saturday, September 20, 1997 • Baldpate Mountain Lean-to • Maine
Mahoosuc Range • 1,895 miles hiked • 265 miles to go
Rain • Low 35, high 66
Elevation 2,640 feet

SOMETHING IS WRONG.

I stop for lunch at Baldpate Shelter a little after one o'clock, before a cold front arrives. A heavy, humid fog lies across the hillside—the tail end of a warm air mass, and I can tell something is coming. But something's wrong with me, too.

A good lunch, maybe that's what's needed. I have lots of food left. I boil a pan of water—half of which I use for ramen noodles, the other half for coffee with sugar and nondairy creamer—and fix myself two large peanut butter and raisin tortillas, following up with a hunk of cheese, a Snickers bar, and some dried apricots. I should go, I tell myself. A system is coming in, and I'm on the wrong side of Baldpate. Just three and a half miles to the next lean-to, including a steep thousand-foot "up" above treeline to the first crest, a second short, steep up to the second, and then a steep drop down below treeline to the shelter. No good getting caught above treeline in a storm; best get over before it hits. Better go. Better go. Better go.

I can't. Something's wrong.

Yesterday I hiked five miles, only three of them on the trail, through Mahoosuc Notch and up Mahoosuc Arm to Speck Pond. Today I've come another six miles in about five hours. I have no strength left, and as I sit here in the shelter I feel myself getting chilled, the cold seeping into my hands, my arms, my feet. Better go. Or better get into the sleeping bag.

A hard rattle of rain hits the roof. The front has arrived. All around me trees start thrashing as the rolling mass of cold air piles in from Canada and whistles around the eaves of the shelter, leaves tumbling down with the first real fall weather system to hit the north woods. Back at Mount Washington, the temperature will be plunging into the twenties tonight, winds gusting over eighty miles an hour. Baldpate is lower and not as exposed, but it has to be nasty up there too. The spray and rattle on the shelter roof intensifies. The warm fog vanishes and a pervasive chill sweeps in as the dew point plummets. Well, that decides it. I'm not going over Baldpate in this. I pull out the sleeping bag, unroll the mattress, and set up for a long afternoon in the shelter. My teeth start chattering before I finish. Within a few minutes I'm wrapped up, listening to rain and watching the trees whipping and bowing in the wind. My legs cramp with cold, and I try to brace them against the shelter walls. I find myself thinking of the bouquet of blue flowers up on Mount Lafayette on that raw day nine days earlier. At least I'm not dying. But God, I'm tired, and my own body, which felt like such a machine as I pushed through the Whites, just isn't working anymore. Almost breaking my leg the other day—that had been a sign. I should have taken another day off, maybe two. But no.

I could think only of food. Back in Gorham I'd found an offer too good to resist at Dunkin' Donuts: a dozen donuts and a cup of coffee for three bucks and some change. I'd eaten all twelve right there—two honey glazed, two Bavarian cream, two Boston cream, two jelly, two coconut, and two apples 'n' spice. A nice light breakfast that took the edge off my appetite. I noticed a couple of people staring at me. They hurriedly looked away. Well, what did they expect, putting a donut shop next to the post office?

The Whites were behind me. Ninety-nine miles in nine days was no record, but respectable considering the steepness of the terrain and my pack heavy with winter gear. Bigfoot and the others were still back in the Whites, taking it easy. I'd fallen below my pace of a hundred miles per week, but now I could pick it up again. In three weeks I'd be finished.

I'd come into town happy but completely exhausted. For the previous two days, since leaving the Presidentials, the feeling of exhaustion had dragged at me. I told myself that a day off, along with some town food, would get me going again. Gorham was an unpretentious little town on the edge of timber country, and Hikers Paradise, one of several low-rent pilgrim resorts in town, offered a good place to rest and eat cheap food. For a few dollars extra the owner, Bruno, his wife, Mary Ann, and Bruce—a bearlike three-hundred-pounder who lived at the hostel and shuttled hikers around the area—cooked chicken or sausages or steaks on a bank of grills, and then passed around massive helpings of home-cooked mashed potatoes, vegetables, and salads. Bruno delighted in teasing hikers: after they'd brought their grilled meats into the dining area, he would lock the doors theatrically and announce that no one could leave until we'd eaten all the salad.

And Paradise offered slackpacking. At four the next morning I found myself escaping down the hostel's rickety back stairs with only lunch, snacks, maps, and a few emergency items in my pack, and stumbling across the parking lot to the dining room, where Bruce prepared a breakfast of scrambled eggs, heaps of skillet-fried potatoes topped with salsa and sour cream, sausage, buttered toast, and juice and coffee for me, then led me out to a little Toyota hatchback that he drove buzzing into the blind night. We spun through the deserted streets of the paper-mill town of Berlin and out onto a graveled logging road that led off into the woods for twenty miles, toward the Mahoosucs.

Bruce was a Mainer, with the gruff accent of someone who lived "up" in the hilly western part of the state. Despite his bulk he'd hiked and explored all of the mountains between Gorham and Katahdin, and knew them intimately. He'd happened upon Hikers Paradise a year or two earlier, and had worked out a congenial arrangement, living there and helping Bruno and Mary Ann manage the hikers. He was a student of backwoods history, and during that hour drive into the dawn he talked about the timber and paper industry that dominated the Maine backcountry, the techniques of logging, and the management of the backcountry rivers and streams. As late as the 1970s, loggers still used rivers and streams to get timber to the mills in Maine, he said, and only in the last few decades had that practice given way to logging roads and big trucks. It was one reason so much of Maine remained so wild—rivers, not roads, had moved lumber to mill.

"This is all private paper-company land, you know," Bruce said, as the small car worked its way carefully along the road. "Used to be they kept it gated, and you could only go in if you knew someone. But now they open it up so people can use it, figure that's one of the best ways of keeping the government from taking it."

A porcupine ambled across the road in front of us and into the woods, the first I'd seen.

"Seen any moose yet?" he asked.

"Not yet," I said. "Plenty of moose dung, and tracks."

"You might see one here," he said, as beams from the Toyota's headlights flashed along the edge of the woods bordering the road. "There's an old Bullwinkle lives up here who I've seen for a couple years now. Not for long, maybe. I know a fellow's won a hunting permit for moose season who's been keeping an eye on him."

He turned off the road and let me out at the trailhead of a blue-blazed path that led two miles from the road toward a notch in the ridge of the Mahoosucs. The light of dawn had begun to filter into the foggy sky as I left the Toyota behind, and I sensed mountains looming ahead, but at first I still had to use my headlamp to pick out the trail. By the time I reached the white blazes, though, morning light suffused the foggy forest around me, and the trail was clear. Straight ahead it led downhill into Mahoosuc Notch, a notorious milelong fissure between the mountains, sheer on both sides and filled with an obstacle course of tumbled boulders that caused it to be called the most difficult mile on the entire Appalachian Trail. I'd be back in a day to tackle it.

To my right the trail ran south, back toward New Hampshire, climbing steeply up Fulling Mill Mountain and the twenty-three miles back south to Gorham. I put my head down and started up the steep 800-foot ascent toward the South Peak.

About halfway up, I took a step and planted my left foot in a narrow cranny between two calf-high rocks, pushing off with my right foot to stride over them. The loose, wet soil there formed a thin sheet over underlying stone, and it suddenly gave way, just as I brought my weight to bear on the ball of the right foot, which slid out from under me. I tried to catch myself with my hiking poles but it was too late, and in one awful moment I realized I was going over sideways, to my right, my left leg pinned between the two rocks. The lever of my weight against the rocks would snap it between knee and ankle. At the last instant, just as the weight came upon it, the sole of the left boot lost traction and my foot came up a little from the cranny, allowing me to bend at the knee and go over backward, rather than sideways. The foot came free and I fell on my butt, half rolling about five feet down the steep slope until I could twist around and stop myself.

I sat there for a couple of minutes, facing downhill toward the notch, the misty woods dripping around me, and replayed the moment in my mind. If my foot had stuck, rather than come out, the leg would have snapped—a compound fracture, maybe. That would have been it—the end of the pilgrimage, the end of the thruhike with 276 miles still to go.

I felt sick at my stomach and retched to one side of the trail.

Mahoosuc Notch, the next morning, had been even worse. It wouldn't have been so bad without the pack, but with over fifty pounds throwing my balance off, and my legs still weak and exhausted from the previous long day of slackpacking, I was in no condition for bouldering.

Imagine a steep, rocky defile, about a mile long, claustrophobic as hell and overhung by bushes and trees leaning crazily out from sheer rocky sides. The sun only shines in that narrow notch for an hour or so a day, and under some of the rocks lie ice and snow that have lasted unmelted all summer long. More snow will soon cover it as winter sets in. Imagine great house-sized blocks of chill granite, sweating and damp in the foggy air, that over the centuries have tumbled down from the steep sides until they clog the way along the bottom of the notch. The painted blazes lead over, under, and around them—fun on a warm, dry day; miserable on a wet, rainy day when the rocks become slick as creek stones. This is no place to fall and hurt yourself with no one around to go for help. Now imagine trying to negotiate these huge boulders with a heavy pack, and boots so worn that they won't grip.

It took me nearly three hours to scramble down that mile, and my knees were bloody by the time I finished. Add to the ordeal a precipitous 1,500-foot climb up Mahoosuc Arm afterward, and that short day had left me completely drained.

And now, as I drowse away the afternoon in my sleeping bag a day later, and the trees whip around the shelter near Baldpate, I find myself wondering whether I'll even be able to hike out in the morning. How many days will I lay up in this shelter? What if the front brings in a heavy blanket of snow? What if Baldpate becomes covered in ice? What if I break a leg, or an arm?

It isn't that I don't want to keep going. But right now I can't get my body to move, and I'm sure not going anywhere without it.

45

NO TRUE WILDERNESS REMAINS in Maine—at least not the sort Thoreau talked about when he ventured up the Penobscot River to climb Katahdin in 1846, not the howling Wholly Other so dear to the nineteenth-century Romantic imagination. Even by his day, though, loggers had found their way into the Maine hinterlands and stripped out many of the most valuable white pines, the tall, shapely trees that served as masts for ships and beams for houses. Within twenty years of his expedition, an average of a billion board feet of lumber was being harvested from the Maine woods to build the beehive cities of the East Coast and the ships that plied the waters of Walt Whitman's beloved New York Harbor.

We have come back to the woods, as the old century runs out. Now cities and suburbs and the global village have walled us in even as E-mail, good roads, fast cars, and cheap airfares have diminished the great open spaces. But the mountains are still there. Their very inconvenience and inaccessibility once prompted us to pass them by for the spaces that we've now filled up. Consequently, no one ever effectively fenced off and claimed those high prospects, for you couldn't live there conveniently: no water, thin soil, bad weather, wary creatures and wild. When we went to the mountaintops, we went to see for a little while more clearly, and farther, or for a vision, to bring back some revelation. We didn't go to stay.

"The tops of mountains are among the unfinished parts of the globe," Thoreau wrote, as he prepared to tell the story of his journey to

Katahdin. "It is a slight insult to the gods to climb and pry into their secrets, and try their effect on our humanity. Only daring and insolent men, perchance, go there. Simple races, as savages, do not climb mountains—their tops are sacred and mysterious tracts never visited by them. Pomola [the mountain's spirit] is always angry with those who climb to the summit of Ktaadn."

These days there are plenty of daring and insolent men and women, but few of them bother much with the northern Appalachian Mountains that Thoreau knew. His "Ktaadn" is just a middling high mountain at one end of a low, eroded range of old hills that the frontier left behind long ago. Eastern mountains don't offer much to the extreme sports lovers, the thin-air junkies and rock climbers, the alpinists who pay tens of thousands of dollars to join expeditions to Nepal and China. They were mastered back in Thoreau's day, and now offer a challenge only to the day hikers and tourists, the weekend backpackers looking for a taste of wilderness, the ramblers seeking a stiff climb with a fine prospect at the top.

Of course the top is what we think of when we talk about mountains: the romantics have taught us well. It is crowded these days, though, even for the thin-air expeditions; oxygen tanks and garbage dumps and the frozen bodies of climbers litter the slopes of Everest. Climbers must take a number before attempting Mount Rainier. And in the old mountains of the East, roads lead to the summits of the tallest. Ascend there and you're likely to find a tour bus or a ski lift, or both. Their trails are well marked, minutely described in guidebooks. The daring and insolent look elsewhere.

Thus the eastern mountains have opened to the rest of us, their inconvenience having made possible their preservation as parks or recreation areas, a kind of unintended museum to the dream Thoreau dreamed. Each year millions of ordinary people go up for an hour, or the afternoon, or the day, or even for a week in the wilderness, and come down flushed and sore and grinning broadly. So it isn't Everest. Something of the essence remains—the transaction with gravity, and limits, and time—the progress through the trees to a prospect, to possibility and room for imagining. For that moment, at least, as we climb those wooded hills, we leave a part of ourselves behind. We make it to the top, admire the view, and consider the air-blue horizon so impossibly far away. And then we descend, maybe a little sad that it's over, feeling maybe a little better about ourselves. We head back to our cars and the drive home.

For of course we come back down. We do have to come down, after all. Don't we?

Today the whole vast forest of western Maine is threaded throughout by a network of gravel and asphalt logging roads, over which the eighteen or so timber and paper companies that own or manage the land send crews in to harvest selected sections. As I was hiking through, the *Maine Sunday Telegram* sent a reporter out retracing Thoreau's travels in the Maine woods. He called the area "a woodlot for papermakers and a playground for thousands of canoeists, campers, hunters, and fishermen." Once I left the national forest, I often heard intermittently the hum of heavy logging machinery from pulpwood operations. And though the nearest town or settlement was miles away, again and again I'd cross logging roads—some so new they were not yet marked on the year-old trail maps I carried.

A.T. hikers call the hundred-mile stretch leading to Baxter State Park the "Hundred-Mile Wilderness." A more accurate term might simply be the Hundred Miles. Judging from my maps, the trail never ventured more than two or three miles from some kind of logging road there. What made it formidable was the absence of dwellings. Unless you happened across a lumber truck, or hunters and fishermen, you probably wouldn't see anyone in the Hundred Miles except hikers. No stores awaited at road crossings, no state highways offered yellow-blazers a quick out after a bad day, and, though cell phones sometimes worked, there were no land lines and no amenities besides trail shelters.

It was wild in the sense that moose, and deer, and bear, and lynx could be found there, but only because we suffered it to be so. Rather than the fact of wilderness, Maine offered its illusion, its promise, its memory.

And maybe that was enough.

46

White Blaze—Day 181
Sunday, September 28, 1997 • *West Peak, Bigelow Mountain* • *Maine*
Bigelow Range • *1,979* miles hiked • *181* miles to go
Clear • *Low 33, high 64*
Elevation 4,145 feet

AFTER MY ROUGH NIGHT on Baldpate, and another day stumbling down through the Maine woods, the bathroom scale and mirror at the Pine Ellis Bed and Breakfast in Andover had pointed out the obvious: I don't need a doctor, I need food. At two hundred pounds, down seventy-five from Springer Mountain, over a fourth of my body weight has burned away; now I weigh less than I did as a gangly college freshman, twenty years before. All the fat is gone from my legs, my chest, my belly, my jowls, my neck, the undersides of my arms, and my butt. Even my wedding band dangles loosely between knuckles.

All spring and summer, as I've built up my speed and endurance and taught the blood to flow efficiently once again after all the years behind a desk, I've burned more calories than I've taken in. Coming out of the Whites and pushing into the Mahoosucs I simply hit a wall: no margin of body fat remains on which to draw, and my metabolism starts to consume its own strength, its own muscle. Despite big breakfasts of oatmeal and raisins or Pop-Tarts and dried fruit, despite vitamins every night, despite lunchtime sandwiches dripping with peanut butter and dried fruit, despite four or five Snickers bars a day, despite carbo-loaded dinners of rice, noodles, beans, and canned tuna or chicken, doused generously with margarine, despite all the donuts, I'm gradually starving to death.

The remedy is simple: eat even more; stop pushing so hard.

I decide to try slackpacking awhile, hiking low-mile days at a relaxed pace with a light pack, and coming back at the end of the day to stay at bed-and-breakfasts in the small towns of Andover and Oquossoc, where I can get rides. Counting my short days in Mahoosuc Notch and crossing Baldpate, my passage of southern Maine has begun with days of five, seven, eight, ten, thirteen, and thirteen miles—the last three slackpacking, with big breakfasts each morning and restaurant dinners in the evening when I get to town. Soon I feel ready to put a pack on again.

Even slackpacking has its hazards. It rains every day, leaving me with the impression that the boreal forests of the northern Mahoosucs and southern Longfellow Mountains have little to commend them besides rocks, mud, steep climbs, blind fog-shrouded treeline crests, and frequent piles of moose dung. At the end of one day I find myself soaking wet and stranded along Maine Highway 17, as another front moves through and temperatures plunge toward the thirties, trying to hitchhike the eleven miles to Oquossoc's Horsefeathers Inn as sunset nears. After over an hour and a half in the sharp northwest wind from over Mooselookmeguntic Lake I begin shivering uncontrollably. Finally a car going in the other direction, *away* from Oquossoc, stops and rolls down a window to see if I'm okay. It's Jerry and Esther Richard, a retired couple driving to their home in Rumford, another twenty-six miles down the road; they have a soft spot in their hearts for thruhikers—their son had been one—and when they find out how long I've been waiting for a ride, they turn around, drive twenty-two miles out of their way, and bring me back to the town they've just left.

The next day, my last without a pack on, the weather begins clearing and I cross a low section between the Saddleback and Bemis Ranges where the hardwood overstory has changed into a dizzying whirl of red and yellow and orange and green, and each gust of wind looses a cloudburst of shifting colors around me. As I climb one low hill I hear something rustling leaves ahead of me. A bull moose swings around a bend of the trail. He's been ambling in my direction, but he comes up short when he sees me; he occupies the entire trail, leaves reeling all around him, and probably weighs a good six to eight hundred pounds. It's rutting season, during which the bulls get aggressive. Now's the time to find a tree to climb.

I once read that "Moose" was the last word from the lips of the dying Henry David Thoreau. "Hello, moose," I say, unable to think of anything better. It's apparently a satisfactory acknowledgment. He nods, raises his big rack, spins and twinkles off in the direction he's come from, leaving deep prints in the soft pathway. The tracks lead on along the trail for maybe a quarter of a mile before it apparently occurs to the moose to abandon the footpath and watch from the woods as I slog past. I see two more bulls that day, moving deliberately through the trees, oblivious to the clatter of my hiking poles and tramp of my boots.

THREE DAYS LATER I stop for lunch at Safford Notch campsite, nestled in a boulder field halfway down the other side of Bigelow Mountain. A shelf of cloud is moving in, the treetops begin swaying in the wind, and countless yellow leaves flutter down through slanting sunlight to the understory. Three other thruhikers are at the campsite: Stoutheart, Numb, and Not Yet. They passed me the day I slackpacked south from Mahoosuc Notch, and I assumed that they were well ahead by now, but apparently they took time off in the town of Stratton.

They're a loud, lively trio—particularly Numb and Not Yet. Numb has came to the trail right out of college, a tall, lanky guy with jet-black hair and a bushy pirate beard; he has a mischievous, teasing sense of humor, the object of which is generally Not Yet, with whom he is sharing a tent and gear. She's a short, physical, sunny-faced young woman with brown hair who started the trail in Virginia after her sophomore year of college ended; her big, infectious whoop of a laugh often rings out through the woods as she and Numb tease and wrestle each other. Stoutheart is the outsider of the trio, the observer and commentator, with a dry, ironic wit; unlike the others he's worked for a few years before quitting a computer job to do the trail. He's a compact, sharp-featured young man with brown hair. We leave about the same time, but as I start my usual pack-heavy struggle up the first stiff uphill they swing past me and out of sight up Little Bigelow Mountain.

As I start down a narrow spine of rocks on the far side, a small brown dog approaches from the opposite direction, sees me, stops short, and looks back toward its owner, who is approaching through the woods below. He isn't dressed in usual hiking gear but wears a flannel shirt, sneakers, and a day pack; there's something familiar about him.

"Mark?" I say.

He looks up, a little confused, and grimaces self-consciously. "Who's asking? I don't have my glasses on."

I almost use my trail name, but say: "Your old basketball buddy, Robert."

"Ruby," he says, his old joking nickname for me. "Ruby! Hey, I'd have never recognized you!"

What are the chances? One of the two people I knew in Maine (the other being his wife), and he is out hiking the Appalachian Trail the same day as me, on the same stretch of trail, in the opposite direction. We'd shared the same office for a year, spent five years together in graduate school, and he'd been a guest at my wedding. We clap each other on the back and marvel at the coincidence. He convinces the dog to let me pet it, and we spent fifteen minutes catching up, talking about old friends, talking about his work, his wife's, talking about my plans for getting home and Cathy's plans to meet me, the sort of things you might say running into an old acquaintance in an airport between flights. My "flight" isn't leaving for a while, of course—I have a tent and can camp right there, as I did with Kilgore Trout—but Mark has a daypack, a day job, and needs to get off the mountain by dark. I tell him that I'll be in the town of Monson in a few days, and I'd probably be staying in Millinocket after I summit. Call if you need any help, he says, and gives me his number. He lives an hour or two away.

"Hey Ruby, been great seeing you," he says. "Wait till I tell the woman. It's been wild."

About an hour later, as evening is coming on, I reach Little Bigelow Lean-to. Stoutheart and company have already arrived and apparently decided not to push farther. I hear the hoot of Not Yet's laughter echo through the trees as I clamber over the rocky stream crossing and up to the shelter.

47

THE GUIDEBOOKS SAY that on a clear day you can see Katahdin from the summit of Saddleback Mountain, over a hundred air miles to the south. It was clear the day I crossed Saddleback, but I must have been looking in the wrong direction. I didn't get my first look at Katahdin until three days later, from the west peak of Bigelow Mountain.

About fifty people, mostly weekenders up for the changing leaves, stood with me at the summit that morning, which offered an above-treeline view of Maine's lake country, brilliantly carpeted with red and orange and yellow hardwoods across the valleys, the dark green of boreal forest climbing the hillsides in every direction, and the blue rim of mountains all around. South of me I could see the ridges and ranges I'd climbed during the last week—Saddleback, Sugarloaf, Crocker, Old Speck, the Mahoosucs—and to the hazy north I could see a number of distant mountains, one of which marked the end of my walk. I had to resort to asking a weekender who was pointing out features of the landscape to his wife.

"Katahdin? Oh, no, you're looking too far west. That way." He pointed over Flagstaff Lake, which stretched sky blue beneath us, toward a distant line of filmy blue mountains over the shoulder of another closer mountain. One of them looked slightly taller than the others, like a canine tooth rising above the incisors on a jawbone.

Funny how Katahdin comes to seem so big. True, it poses the single most sustained climb of the A.T., a steep, spectacular ascent of nearly 5,000 feet from swampy lowlands to well above treeline, but it's hardly the highest mountain a thruhiker sees. Clingmans Dome, Roan Mountain, Mount Washington, even Standing Indian and Mount Rogers are all taller. When we start our hikes in Georgia, though we know it waits at the other end, it's an arbitrary end. There's no law decreeing that the walk north has to stop at Katahdin. Every year there's talk of extending the Appalachian Trail from Springer southward into the mountains of Alabama and northward beyond Katahdin into Canada's Gaspé Peninsula. What does it matter? People are building the trails anyway, just calling them by names other than the Appalachian Trail. What difference where one begins or ends?

For southbounders, Katahdin is the beginning—an initial slap-in-the-face challenge to get them ready for the harsh Maine mountains and the Whites: the worst first. Imagine finishing at Springer Mountain, with its placid west-looking view, and the plaque bolted into the rock. Or put yourself in the shoes of Kilgore Trout, for whom Katahdin had been the halfway point, and who would be finishing up southbound around the picnic pavilions of Pen-Mar Park, in Pennsylvania. Both offer the satisfaction of a project completed. Any of these variations require you to walk the same miles, climb the same mountains, visit the same places, stay at the same shelters. What I'd done had been no harder. No particular virtue attended a south-to-north thruhike. Katahdin was just a mountain, among many mountains.

And yet . . .

As we move north, away from sea level at the Hudson, Katahdin looms larger and larger. It's as if, having done our penance in the south, having purified ourselves in the fire and heat of the mid-Atlantic, having tasted the physical dangers of the Whites, the final hike toward Katahdin promises a kind of redemption. And as we move farther into the backwoods of Maine, as we cross the last interstates, pass the last roadside delis, leave behind the last ATM machines, and enter a great spreading woodland where many people still make a living cutting down trees, everything begins to come together—a spring and summer's bug-swarmed nights, a fall of falls. We've walked this crooked trail to mend the crazing of our lives; we reek of sweat and smoke, wear Gore-Tex shells to turn the storm away, take on new names, our talk all aches, and boots, and food; and yet we yearn to strip the armor from our hearts, to wash ourselves in mountain rain and air until, like the wild columbine and black cohosh, we can be merely what we are, until out of the stone-strewn ground we bloom again, until the weathered sign on Baxter Peak points along the path to where we've been.

48

White Blaze—Day 187
Saturday, October 4, 1997 • State Route 15, Monson • Maine
The Hundred Miles • 2,045 miles hiked • 115 miles to go
Cloudy • Low 33, high 57
Elevation 1,210 feet

"KATAHDIN IS CLOSED." That's the word in Monson as I buy groceries for my last week of hiking: the Hundred Miles. Two nights ago snow flurries rattled on my tent fly as I camped on an esker along the

Piscataquis River, but on Katahdin the system left a treacherous sheathing of snow and ice that prompted the park rangers to close the trail to hikers. Ten days remain in the season, and we've yet to see Indian summer. It may reopen, so there's no sense waiting here, I figure. A car ferries me to the trail crossing north of town.

The sign marking the start of the Hundred Miles is meant to put people off:

> CAUTION: THERE ARE NO PLACES TO OBTAIN SUPPLIES OR HELP UNTIL YOU REACH ABOL BRIDGE—90 MILES NORTH. YOU SHOULD NOT ATTEMPT THIS SECTION UNLESS YOU CARRY A MINIMUM OF TEN DAYS' SUPPLIES. DO NOT UNDERESTIMATE THE DIFFICULTY OF THIS SECTION. GOOD HIKING!

Actually, according to the current maps, it's just under one hundred miles to the store at Abol Bridge, and another fifteen through Baxter State Park to the summit of Katahdin. I've put eight days' supply of food in my pack; if I can't hike a hundred miles in eight days by now, I am one sorry northbounder.

Everything is arranged, finally. Cathy will fly to Boston on the ninth, and we'll fly home together on the fifteenth. As I have it figured, I'll summit on the eleventh.

Before I've gone two miles I hear steps behind me: Stoutheart, Numb, and Not Yet. They've been slackpacking, and have stayed in Monson for two nights, but their arrangements haven't worked out well: they've spent so much time waiting for rides and shuttling through the countryside that it has taken them two days to cover what I've walked in one. So they haven't had a full day off the trail. But no matter. All the weariness from two thousand miles of hiking has washed away from us, and suddenly, like that night at Hawk Mountain so long ago when it had all been new, we are embarking on a great adventure together. This is it! Woo-hoo! After six months of sauntering to the holy land, we've reached its outer precincts. Somewhere beyond the red-and-yellow canopy of trees looms Katahdin.

One hundred and fifteen miles to go. We stop for lunch along Big Wilson Stream, a wide rolling creek tumbling down from the divide between the Kennebec and Penobscot Basins, and the first major ford of the hike. Other thruhikers show up before we cross—Lost Soul, Beer Gurl and her partner Bill from San Diego. After lunch we all strip off our boots, put on our Tevas, and one by one start across the rocky, moss-slick ford, through chill, breath-catching water that rushes from ankle-high to knee-high to crotch-high, until its chill incessant surge pushes us off balance, making us stagger hilariously across hidden boulders and holes, threatening to sweep us off our feet and dunk us.

Late that afternoon it starts raining as we ford Long Pond Stream, which isn't as wide. Afterward, as I'm climbing a muddy slope to a crowded campsite above the ford, my boot slips out from under me when I step on a wet root, and I go down hard, the heavy pack on my back slamming my face into the mud. One of my hiking poles snaps off near its tip—the third to break on the trip. I bloody a knee and a hand, neither seriously. A front moves in that night, and I go to sleep to the sound of rain on the shelter roof and the rush of white water in the gorge below.

One hundred miles to go. A rainy, fog-shrouded day as we climb a notoriously difficult stretch, the high, ragged ridge from Barren Mountain to Chairback Mountain. Stoutheart and I stop for lunch at Cloud Pond Lean-to, a few hundred muddy, rooty yards off the trail. The pond is invisible in the fog, with only the sound of its water lapping along the rocky shore to give it away. I can hear something splashing on the far side. A moose, perhaps. I shout into the fog, but whatever it is takes no notice.

That evening, after slipping and clambering with heavy packs across the bogs and ledges of the ridge, we arrive at Chairback Gap Lean-to to find it full of thruhikers and southbound section hikers. Beer Gurl and Bill have been fighting over whether to stop, and Bill has moved on with the tent, leaving Beer Gurl glowering from her sleeping bag in the shelter. It rains most of the night.

Eighty-nine miles to go. A road crossing, and another big stream to ford—the West Branch of the Pleasant River. The sun is obscured by a high shelf of overcast, but the rain and fog of the day before are gone as we descend from Chairback. In the distance stands 3,654-foot White Cap Mountain, the last real climb before Katahdin. In front of us lies the river and a logging road. Day hikers with permits sometimes drive in to park and hike a scenic gorge nearby. Once again, as if by magic, my old friend Trip, whom I've not seen since New York, appears at the roadside, having yellow-blazed in with some day hikers. He wanders over from the parking area to greet everybody, genial as ever, and hits on Not Yet as we prepare to ford the river, then remains behind on the bank, somber and meditative without his guitar, as we splash across. Yellow-blazing out of there to Katahdin may be tough.

From the river the trail runs through a Nature Conservancy preserve of mature white pines, a species mostly gone from the Maine woods because it made such desirable timber. Stoutheart, Numb, and Not Yet split off here to tour the gorge, but I push on up the lower slopes of White Cap Mountain. I hear gunshots across the valley: Maine's week-long moose season opened the day we left Monson. Perhaps that's why moose have been scarce along the trail all week.

By late afternoon the overcast has cleared off and wind sings across the crest of Gulf Hagas Hill, halfway up White Cap, as I work my way toward a campsite in a sag between two minor crests. Looking through the trees over the mountain's west shoulder I can see the expanse of the Penobscot Basin opening out below me, dotted with wide blue lakes between me and the big mountain on the far side. And then, with a jolt, I realize I'm looking at Katahdin.

Seventy-seven miles to go. The next morning dawns clear, the horizon a little hazy but the sky cloudless, and as I work my way through the krummholz and scree around the east side of White Cap's summit, I finally get a good look at what I glimpsed the previous afternoon. Spreading out across the far side of the Penobscot Basin lies the whole Katahdin monadnock, a serrated mountain rising northwest-to-southeast to a high crest, the bone-gray, rockslide-scarred face of Baxter Peak. No snow tops it now. Katahdin is open again. In between, lowlands roll lake to lake, hillsides rust-red or yellow or orange, with wide green patches of spruce and fir in the dells and hollows. Contrast—maybe that explains it: the brilliant lowlands spreading around the blue-gray massif, its ancient granite top scraped and glacier-harrowed. I have never seen a view like it in my life. And for a few minutes that morning I can't leave; I can only look. Six months suddenly have a shape and name; the completion of something—a pilgrimage, maybe. But to what end?

Numb, Stoutheart, and Not Yet catch me on the far side of White Cap, and together we dash down the gentling hillside, talking about what we've seen, hurrying to get there. Suddenly the roots and rocks and mud of the first three day are gone, and the trail turns solid, level, and straight. The last faded reds and burnt yellows of fall wheel down around us, covering the forest floor in a dizzying quilt of sunlit color as we stride through—eighteen miles whirl by, and we shelter at Cooper Brook.

Fifty-nine miles to go. Here blue lakes spread wide over the Penobscot Basin: Upper and lower Jo-Mary Lakes, Pemadumcook Lake. These are the open waters Thoreau described traversing, waters that the wind could whip up and that would swamp a riverman's laden bateau. We lunch on a gravel beach of Lower Jo-Mary Lake, stretching out behind rocks, out of the cool wind so that the sun beats down and makes the sweat run. Then away again, charging through the low woods, four in file, nineteen miles to the beach on the south end of Nahmakanta Lake, a long narrow glacial slash surrounded by 1,400-foot mountains. Several backpackers have camped in the area already, away from the shore. Section hiking? we ask. No, they say. Just bushwhacking around in the wild. Our ride's picking us up tomorrow. Your ride? we ask. They smile knowingly. What time are you planning to get up? they ask.

Forty miles to go. And the next morning, as the sun peeks over the surrounding mountains, we hear their ride approach, a single-engine floatplane coming in low from the south. It waggles at us and then moves far out over the lake, where it banks steeply, its white wings catching the sun against the shadowed hillside, and glides down to the surface. It skims in, then races toward us, hydroplaning across the lake like a speedboat until it's within several hundred yards of shore, at which point the pilot throttles down and it settles onto the floats and motors slowly closer at hull speed. The bushwhackers wade out with their packs to the pilot, who comes down on a pontoon and stows the gear carefully to balance weight; then the campers climb aboard the plane. It revs up again, pivots, and moves out to deeper water. Once away from shore the pilot throttles up, plowing down the lake away from us until the water lets go and they slowly rise toward the far horizon, bank, swing behind a mountain, and are gone.

That day we hike nineteen miles to the southeast end of Rainbow Lake, where we camp among some boulders and listen to loons cry out on the water after sunset.

Twenty-one miles to go. The brightest reds and yellows are behind us now; it's Indian summer for certain. Mid-October sun dazzles down on us as we descend the last miles to the Penobscot River, and the end of the Hundred Miles. Hurd Brook Lean-to, four miles from the river and the last shelter outside of Baxter State Park, has a reputation as a place where thruhikers stop to jot down concluding messages in the register, but when I stop by to read it, the register is missing. We push on to the river. A white-tailed deer bolts across the trail, the first I've seen in Maine. Before we see the road, or the river, we hear the sound of traffic. We are through the Hundred Miles.

Katahdin comes into view again as we cross Abol Bridge: impossibly close now, its top cotton-covered with spun clouds. Across the river stands a camp store, and we greedily load up on snacks. They won't take credit cards there, and don't have an ATM—why have I expected one? I've only ten dollars in my pocket, and use up seven on packaged cupcakes for the next day's climb. Well, I won't need any money between here and Millinocket tomorrow. As we leave, a pickup truck passes on the road towing a flatbed trailer, laid out upon which is the body of an immense bull moose.

From the bridge, the trail leads into the park, then along the Penobscot for a couple of miles before turning up Nesowadnehunk Stream, which we follow uphill again. We are climbing Katahdin now, if only its skirts. We check in at the ranger station and I remember, to my chagrin, that they charge a camping fee: six dollars. Numb rolls his eyes and spots me the three I'm short. The thruhiker shelter at Daicy Pond Campground fills up quickly that night, as several others arrive from behind us, or from Millinocket, where they've been taking time off. Stoutheart paces around the campsite nervously. I just know I'm not going to get any sleep, he says.

That night the sky comes alive with the aurora borealis.

49

IN MY MIND I HAVE CALLED IT a pilgrimage, and have thought of the thruhikers on the trail with me as pilgrims, though I know most of them would laugh at the idea. No, it just sounded like fun, they'd say—just something I've always wanted to do, just a goal I've set for myself, just something to do because it can be done. But why, really? Why have we quit our jobs, left our wives, our husbands, our children, left school, interrupted perfectly good retirements, put off promising careers? Why come to the woods for half a year of rodents and rain and pain?

Perhaps because this particular walk in the woods is, as the century turns, about the last pilgrimage left that one can take without being overwhelmed by irony. Each year Americans go to Disneyland by the millions, or take the Universal Studios tour, or visit Graceland, or Opryland, or look at Dorothy's ruby slippers at the Smithsonian, or take the O.J. tour in Brentwood. Some even call such trips pilgrimages, but with a cynical half smile so no one will think they mean it, as if the very idea of believing is something to scoff at. After all, what's left to come home to? The American Dream? The one true faith? Please. If we haven't found what we're looking for in the great religions, or in the method of science, or in drink and drugs, or in the well-earned comfort of a new BMW, where can we go? Where can we find healing, blessing, hope for the future, a way to belong in the world?

Few visitors to Disneyland expect their lives to be changed by what they find there, and at the end of the week, after they've been beguiled, they climb back into their cars and drive home. It's about all most of us have come to expect in the age of information and entertainment: a brief diversion. Had we felt that way about the trail, we'd have left at Fontana Dam, or in Damascus, once the novelty wore off. But no, we've stayed, we've made the pilgrimage, and now the end lies before us.

We came out here in the woods looking for something. We've found Katahdin: real, granite solid, solitary, and beautiful—so beautiful it can break your heart. No hype has manufactured it, no spin doctoring applied, no marketing necessary. There it stands, a rock at the end of the long walk, soaring like the Emerald City in The Wizard of Oz, but real: a mountain, not an empty narrative or a calculated illusion, a matte painting in a special-effects studio.

Perhaps, all along, we have been dreaming of wilderness, of that most primeval of stories. If you go to the wilderness, if you climb to the mountaintop, if you sail away to the forest savage, surely an answer will present itself. At a time when so many other of the old stories seem hollow, still something quickens in the blood when we hear this one. It's the national story we were taught while growing up, after all—the Pilgrim fathers, the great push west, Lewis and Clark, Daniel Boone, Brigham Young.

I've come to believe the essence of that story over these two thousand miles—even though my waking intellect tells me that it is a myth concocted for the benefit of those with money and guns enough, with many of its chapters dark and horrible. But my heart is telling me to believe. And now Katahdin too is telling me to believe. So I will. Surely in the wild—even in this remnant we have left ourselves as the old century winds down—surely here we can reinvent ourselves somehow, found anew, start afresh, begin again.

Tomorrow I will have reached the end of that beginning.

And then what?

IN KEEPING WITH THE RULE OF Diminishing Vistas, the trail up Katahdin on October 11 is less than solitary. With the weather fair, and views likely, several hundred people have come to dare Pomola this morning. An estimated 50,000 people try Katahdin each year, which averages out to 450 for each day it is open during the summer and fall. Most Saturdays it's hurry-up-and-wait, with children and older adults picking their way precariously from rock to rock and strong young hikers steaming in frustration behind them, or shortcutting the trail over rocky sections to pass slow traffic. The only thing in our favor is a forecast for cold weather on top—windchill down near zero, which discourages a number of would-be daring, insolent Pomola baiters.

Here too are other thruhikers: Mr. Clean, Lost Soul, Brooster, Cape Town Jenny, and Mike Without Laura. Mr. Clean starts well before dawn, intent on being far up the mountain before the sun shows up and the crowds start ascending. The rest of us leave after breakfast, arriving at the foot of the mountain near midmorning, by which time most of the day hikers have already started up. At Katahdin Stream Campground, we stop to deposit the heavy items from our backpacks at the ranger station: we too will be day hikers today, on this last five-mile climb; all we need is lunch and some warm clothes for the top. I wait for Numb, Stoutheart, and Not Yet. We've done the Hundred Miles together, we can do Katahdin together.

What is it like? Like Springer, only longer; like Bly Gap, but not so muddy; like Clingmans Dome, only steeper; like the Lehigh Valley, only greener; like Franconia Ridge, but without the sleet; like Mahoosuc Notch, only vertical; like . . . like them all, like every mountain, every boulder field, every gorge I have climbed all spring, and all summer, and all fall—only more so. And it is different from them all. More beautiful, steeper, longer, more varied, a better view, more crowded on the way up, more exciting to climb. Up we go, from the hardwoods, to the boreal forest, to the subalpine krummholz, to the rocks above treeline. Up we go, through a steep boulder field that requires scrambling, where steel handholds have been pounded into the rock at particularly difficult pitches. Up we go, to the Table Lands, an open, nearly level expanse of scree and alpine vegetation, a moonscape of rocks slanting up to a high ridge, and then Baxter Peak, the summit of Katahdin. Up we go, Numb giggling and teasing, Stoutheart ironic and amazed, Not Yet hooting with laughter, me sweating and falling behind, my knee bloody from a slip on one of the boulders, the cold wind stinging my face. Up we go, past Thoreau Spring, slick with ice now, here where Thoreau never climbed. Up the talus, up the rock pathways marked off in a futile attempt to keep hikers from trampling alpine vegetation, up the last slopes until we can see a crowd of people clustered around a signboard. The last white blaze. Mile 2,160. Northern terminus of the Appalachian Trail.

Ahead of me the others rush up to the summit and touch the sign, in an enduring thruhiker ritual. They hand cameras to bystanders and snap their summit shots, arms raised in triumph. We did it! We made it! There's quite a crowd. Photographers from *Backpacker* are hurrying around for a feature on Katahdin: they're fascinated by my bloody knee and intercept me before I reach the sign to take a few pictures of it and make me sign a photo release. Mr. Clean is there, in a Gore-Tex "bivy sack" to stay warm.

"I'm staying up here tonight," he says, passing a small flask around. Both actions are illegal. "And then I'm hiking south—until I'm up to my waist in snow."

Eventually things calm down a little. I start getting cold in the zero-degree windchill and put on my long underwear and my rain pants and extra fleece and mittens and a polypro mask, until I look like some strange blue-and-purple knight errant with hiking-pole lances and nylon armor. No one is near the sign now, so I walk up and touch it. One of the photographers offers to take my picture, and I strike a dumb pose—too reserved, too self-conscious. But happy. It's over. I look east, out to where the lowlands give way to islands, and the islands give way to ocean. I look south, back in the direction I've come from, and I can see all the way back to the Bigelows, tiny on the horizon. The trail leads back that way. Mr. Clean says he's going. Why not stay out another six months?

You could stay up here forever, I suppose. People do. They come off the trail, they work for a while and make enough money to thruhike again. They do it over and over again, north and south, middle to outside, flip and flop. Some have made the pilgrimage five or ten times. And then they walk the other great trails: the Pacific Crest, the Continental Divide, the east-west paths still on the drawing boards of the Benton MacKayes of the world, who would link us all, foot by foot, until all the world moves at a walker's pace.

Yes, you could stay up here, make it an unending pilgrimage, with no Katahdin at the end, and nowhere else to go, just the endless, glacial geologic time of mountains, where the horizon forever opens out over the world at the bottom of the hill.

You, maybe. Not me.

Today I am expected.

Epilogue: Facing South

For every walk is a sort of crusade, preached by some Peter the Hermit in us, to go forth and reconquer this Holy Land from the hands of the Infidels."
—Henry David Thoreau, "Walking"

SEVEN MONTHS LATER, the old dog knows I'm headed off again. As I bumble around the house, reassembling my gear, she noses the rumpled hiking clothes, follows me around with her snout to my calves, and yawns nervously every time I sit down to consider my checklist.

"Okay," I say after I've loaded the pack into the car's trunk. "You can go this time."

She jumps happily into the back seat and stretches out to snooze as I back out of the driveway and once more thread my way through the empty midmorning streets of our subdivision on my way to the interstate highway. All the little commuters have parked their bikes outside the elementary school, and as I drive past I can hear them playing at recess behind the main building.

By now, from letters, E-mail, and phone calls, it's become clear that many of those who walked with me plan to meet again at Trail Days in Damascus, about four hours away. Cathy isn't aboard. We've worked hard at our marriage over the winter, and I have started looking for a new job. She's not quite ready to believe me when I tell her that the thruhike is behind me. We need the money, but somehow it has been harder than I expected to put the tie back on and burnish the résumé anew. When the first of April arrived again, I could not help remembering that cold, windy day, a year earlier above Amicalola Falls. I've invited her to come up to Damascus for Trail Days, but she's never liked tenting, the whole ordeal still rankles a little, and, well, she really wants to go to the beach with friends, as we'd done last year when I came off the trail during Trail Days. So it's just me and the dog.

Damascus means so much to thruhikers that it's easy to forget how small it really is. There's exactly one traffic light, and that's at a dangerous intersection to the west rather than downtown. Coming in by car on a normal day, you might be able to pass through on U.S. 58 in about two minutes, even if you obeyed the posted speed limits. Just don't try it during Appalachian Trail Days.

Banners welcome motorists to the annual celebration, and all the town merchants set up window displays or stands in front of their stores. The town park flowers with pavilions, booths, and concession stands. Town residents set out yard-sale tables in front of their houses. All the bed-and-breakfasts display NO VACANCY signs. The Methodist Church has thrown its sanctuary doors open, advertising hikers' slide and video presentations inside and a fund-raising pancake breakfast in the basement; its hostel, the Place, is packed with thruhikers, and tents fill its yard. Along the river near the post office, behind tents and stands erected for the weekend by hiking gear manufacturers, a tent city springs up—hundreds and hundreds of tents of all colors and shapes—tiny bivy sacks, large spreading tarps, dome tents, small backpacking tents, and various makeshift shelters from sun and rain.

And hikers. The town crawls with them—as if a strange cult has invaded, a cult that never bathes, and whose devotional garments, instead of flowing saffron robes or black Nikes, consist of polypropylene shirts, nylon shorts, gaiters, Tevas, and bandannas. Thruhikers from this year's pilgrimage, just beginning to shed the soft sheath of body fat for the knotty leanness of the trail, stream in from north and south of town: bewildered solitaries gawking at the crowds, rowdy "trail families" looking for free food and drink, injured and sick and convalescent thruhikers here for one last taste of trail life before they leave for good. Here too are A.T. legends like ten-time thruhiker Warren Doyle, long-time trail aficionados, members of trail-maintaining clubs, repeat thruhikers, as well as hostel owners, disciples of Never-Never Land handing out directions for finding it, members of computer hiking lists, and even a few stunned tourists stumbling upon the scene by accident.

Most of all, though, here are familiar faces—the faces of my pilgrimage year, all on the trail again, if only for a weekend. Bigfoot, RockDancer, Mossman and Tonic, Broken Arrow, Dancing Bear and Icebox, Southpaw, Ox, Kadiddle, Numb, 180°, Dingle and Hat Trick, Hiker Ned and Sweet Pee, Globetrotter, Shaman, Space Wrangler, Luna and Six-String Hillbilly, Mass, the Connecticut Kid and Hungry Tortoise, One Ramp, Rambleon, Trip, Time to Fly, the Hiking Viking, Fire Marshal, Gold Thumb, Solo, No Stove, Texas Tapeworm, Solophile. Here too are some of those who didn't make it: the Princess and the Pea, Domino, Good to Go, the Doobie Brothers, Loon, Sleepyfeet and Bunnyhead. And dozens of others who finished early, or late, or southbounders I never met—names I knew from trail registers and photos in the book in Harpers Ferry, or who knew me from following the ongoing "Ballad of the Rhymin' Worm," all 190 stanzas of insiderish doggerel.

"Worm!" Bigfoot rumbles when I walk up, and he rises grinning from the circle of other familiar faces amid the sea of tents to clap a great wing around me. He climbed Katahdin in late October, one of the last northbounders to finish, after the mountain was closed and snow-covered, cloaked in cloud and bitter cold. He's just begun work as paid crew on a racing sailboat around Boston.

Here is RockDancer, who summited about a week after me, after a long final month through New Hampshire and Maine. He went off the trail briefly, one last time, in the White Mountains, learning from an

AMC hut's caretaker that his father had died. They had not been close for many years, but the funeral had brought some healing and forgiveness. Like me he's still out of a job.

Dancing Bear and Icebox summited two days before me. Now, the partnership over, Dancing Bear has started work as cook for an AMC hut in New Hampshire. It isn't on the A.T., but sixty miles of mountain trails lead right to his door, he says. Icebox is back in school.

Mossman and Tonic summited together six days after me; they parted company with Broken Arrow back at Mahoosuc Notch, wanting to finish as a couple rather than a threesome. He's returned to his landscaping job in Florida, and Tonic has moved in with him—a big change for her, after years in the Colorado mountains.

Kilgore Trout doesn't show. We've talked a couple times by phone. He finished his hike in November, in Waynesboro, Pennsylvania, the place from which he'd sent the postcard when he left the trail in July. It was something of an anticlimax, he said. He just emerged at the roadside trailhead where he'd ended his northbound walk, stuck his thumb out, and hitched a ride to town. Then he'd gone home to New Hampshire. In April he'd gotten married again, becoming in the process the stepfather of a teenage girl.

"Some days," he told me, "I wake up in the morning and in my half fog of sleep I'm either in my tent, or at the Kincorra hostel in Tennessee. And then . . . and then I'm not. Sometimes I wake up just dreaming I'm still walking."

We'd talked about hiking in to Trail Days together from north of Mount Rogers and agreed that he would drive down from New Hampshire the week before, and I'd meet him at the trailhead. But finally neither of us could afford the time.

By now, you see, life off the trail has gripped all of us, to greater and lesser extents, and no longer are our days governed by sun and cloud, measured by the distance between beginning and end. Even Mr. Clean, who had immediately hiked south from Katahdin again, has reportedly taken a job at a ski resort near Andover, Maine. Here at Trail Days we keep our backpacks close at hand, we sleep in tents, we dress once again in polypropylene and Gore-Tex—in many cases the same clothes and gear that saw us through our long walk. But they're costumes now, not uniforms. Cotton would be more comfortable and practical around town: we'd have smelled better, and after Trail Days we could simply throw it in the dryer. We wear hiking clothes so we won't look out of place, the way you might dress to attend a party. We're writers, or computer programmers, or prison guards, or cooks, or students, or job hunters now, here for the weekend to reminisce and watch the new pilgrims walk through.

Friday evening some of us sit around in a circle, talking, and watching as the current crop of thruhikers line up for a free barbecued-chicken dinner, banging their pans impatiently. Smoke from the charcoal braziers drifts across the vast, buzzing riverside tent city. Several hikers break out hand drums and maracas, which fill the open field with an insistent beat. The old dog sniffs around at the end of her leash, bewildered by the crowds, the strange smells, and the trail dogs here with their pilgrim parents. At one point Tagalong, Mass's ingratiating companion, rushes out snarling and righteous to chase the old dog away from tent and food bowl. Mass apologizes. I think of the turd in the playroom of the Zion Episcopal Church in Manchester Center. Now several campers begin shooting off fireworks, which spooks the old dog, making her bark and quiver and press up against me in my tent. I fall asleep to the sound of beating drums, the whoops of celebration, the murmur and laughter of conversation.

Next day is the thruhiker parade, a Trail Days tradition, where past and present thruhikers join together in a raucous half-mile stroll through the town streets. We gather in front of Dot's Tavern, west of town, in a grand, electric gathering. A marching band musters in one parking lot, several Model T and Model A Fords cough and idle in another, county deputies tool around in ATVs with signs on them reading, THIS EQUIPMENT PURCHASED WITH MONEY SEIZED FROM DRUG RAIDS. Rumor is that the FBI's in town looking for information about a suspect wanted in a bombing, thought to have made his getaway along the Appalachian Trail during the winter. A fire engine stands ready to bring up the rear of the parade. In one corner, four or five male thruhikers have donned dresses and face paint. One of them is Loon, wearing a frilly turquoise nightgown, his head shaved bald. He's northbound again this year, and has made it to Damascus without injury. Several people have rigged up banners, like a college reunion parade. Class of 1996. Class of 1997. Most of the familiar faces gather behind the Class of 1997 banner, so I move toward it. Then a kid in a polypro shirt elbows his way into our part of the crowd.

"Hey," he says. "Where are the hikers gathering?" We look at each other, confused. Is he blind?

"Oh, you mean this year's thruhikers," someone says, the distinction slowly dawning.

He nods.

"You guys go in front, I think."

Then, with a bump and a bang, the parade starts, and a whoop goes up from all assembled. The old dog paces along next to me, nervous about getting stepped on. We shuffle forward and water balloons begin arcing back and forth, splattering on the blacktop. Any supposed order to the groupings of thruhikers breaks down quickly, as everyone crowds to the front. Townspeople and tourists gather along the way to watch and cheer, along with former thruhikers taking pictures and throwing water balloons. Many of us have brought our own water cannons and buckets and pay the balloon bombers back in kind. On through town we march, in fits and starts behind the cars and the band—one last saunter with our fellow pilgrims. The procession turns left in front of the post office, away from the main street, to the old railroad bridge over the river. Off speed the cars and fire trucks and ATVs to meet us on the far side, near the town park with its pavilions and booths and concession stands. Over the bridge we walk, two or three abreast, quiet and a bit subdued now, as the voice of the river grows around us and the grand procession crosses over.

We leave the trail and disperse into the world that buzzes ahead of us with its voices and loudspeakers and souvenir T-shirts and funnel cakes and homemade ole-fashioned lemonade and Trail Days gear specials and commercially led thruhike programs and mountain souvenirs and Philly cheese steaks. Pretty soon the old dog and I have walked through the crowd, so we sit down on the grass in front of the grandstand and listen as the proud citizens of Damascus, Virginia, hold a memorial presentation for a local coordinator of Appalachian Trail Days. On and on they drone.

I look at my watch. The annual hiker talent show begins in fifteen minutes, and more events are planned for tonight and tomorrow morning. But as I gaze around at the crowd in the park, it comes to me that I don't belong here anymore. Time to fly. Time to finish. Time to leave the Rhymin' Worm behind. Time to start something new.

"Come on, old girl," I say to the dog, "let's go home."

When we get back to the car, I refill the water dish in the back seat and the old dog drinks gratefully. It's a hot May afternoon. I shut the door, turn on the ignition, and back out. We pick our way through the parked cars near the tent city to a sun-dappled side street, and then to U.S. 58. From there we turn east, driving into the high country near Mount Rogers.

Five miles out of town, as the way begins to climb, we approach a place where the Appalachian Trail crosses. A young woman in drab polypropylene, with a backpack, metal hiking poles, and knee-high gaiters, emerges from the trees near the white blaze and waits for the car to go by. She is small and bony, her head shaved bald. She must have left Damascus this morning, overwhelmed by crowds, perhaps, or maybe just trying to keep on schedule. I wave as we go by but she doesn't notice. In my rearview mirror I watch as she looks carefully both ways, then steps forward strongly, crosses the road in a few strides, and, without hesitating, vanishes into the woods.